ROCKET RACCOON AND GROOT

CIVIL WAR II

ROCKET AND GROOT ARE **BEST FRIENDS** ALL THE TIME.
THEY ARE **GUARDIANS OF THE GALAXY** MOST OF THE TIME.
THEY ARE **HEROES**...LET'S SAY...AT LEAST HALF OF THE TIME. MAYBE MORE. THAT'S JUST A CONSERVATIVE ESTIMATE.

ROCKET AND GROOT LAUGH IN THE FACE OF DANGER. THEY LAUGH IN THE FACE OF WAR, VOLCANOES, FOOTBALL, DOPPELGANGERS AND COUP D'ÉTATS. WHAT WON'T THEY LAUGH IN THE FACE OF? OR, OF WHAT'S FACE WON'T THEY LAUGH IN? WAIT, IS "IN" A PREPOSITION? ... IN THE FACE OF WHAT WON'T THEY LAUGH? THE POINT IS, SOMETIMES YOU HAVE TO GET SERIOUS.

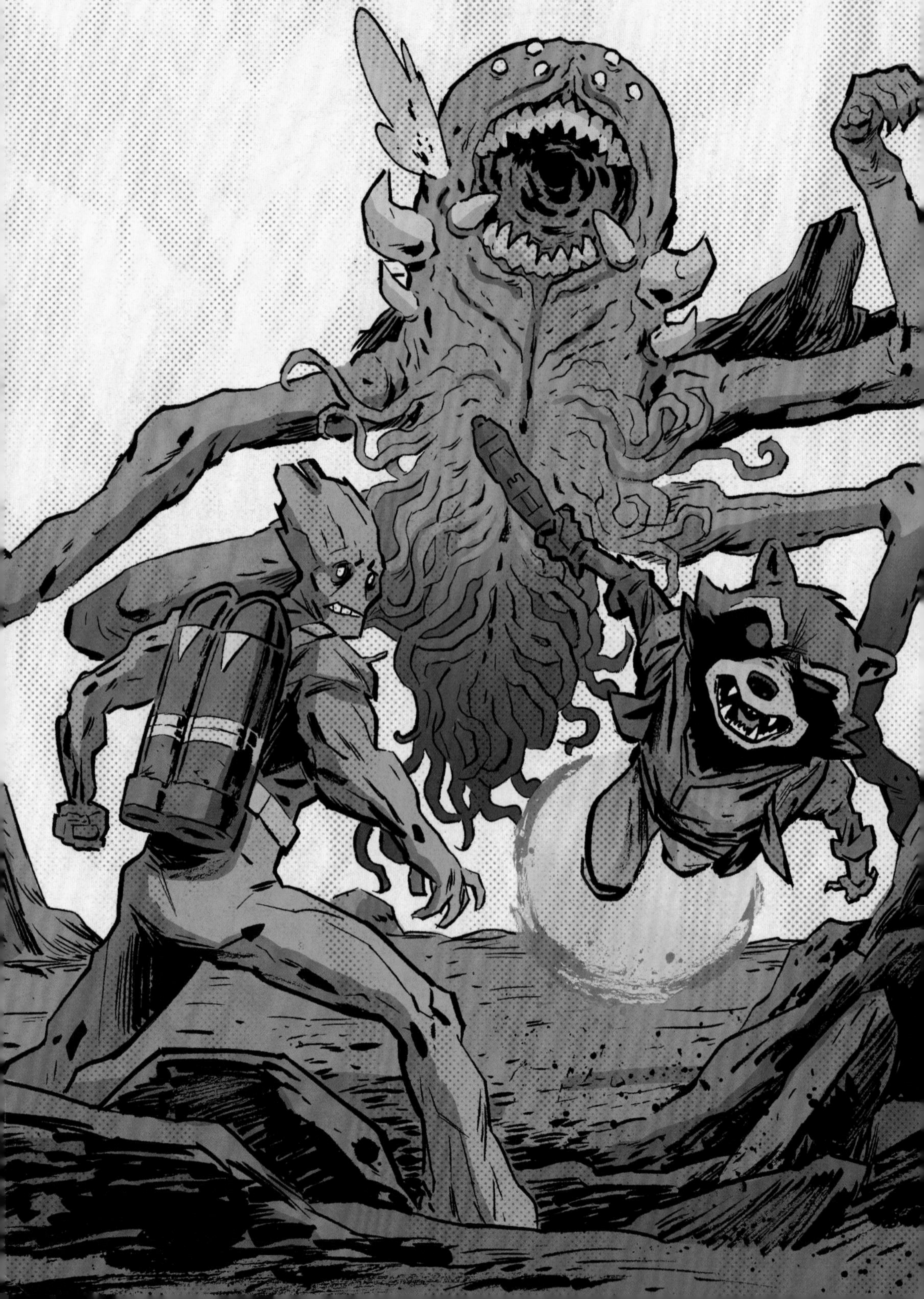

ROCKET RACCOON AND GROOT

CIVIL WAR II

NICK KOCHER
WRITER

MICHAEL WALSH
PENCILER

MICHAEL WALSH & JOSH HIXSON
INKERS

CRIS PETER (#7) & MICHAEL GARLAND (#8-10)
COLOR ARTISTS

JEFF ECKLEBERRY
LETTERER

DAVID LOPEZ
COVER ART

KATHLEEN WISNESKI
ASSISTANT EDITOR

JAKE THOMAS
EDITOR

GROOT CREATED BY STAN LEE, LARRY LIEBER & JACK KIRBY
ROCKET RACCOON CREATED BY BILL MANTLO & KEITH GIFFEN

COLLECTION EDITOR: JENNIFER GRÜNWALD
ASSOCIATE MANAGING EDITOR: KATERI WOODY
ASSOCIATE EDITOR: SARAH BRUNSTAD
EDITOR, SPECIAL PROJECTS: MARK D. BEAZLEY

VP PRODUCTION & SPECIAL PROJECTS: JEFF YOUNGQUIST
SVP PRINT, SALES & MARKETING: DAVID GABRIEL

EDITOR IN CHIEF: AXEL ALONSO
CHIEF CREATIVE OFFICER: JOE QUESADA
PUBLISHER: DAN BUCKLEY
EXECUTIVE PRODUCER: ALAN FINE

KET RACCOON & GROOT VOL. 2: CIVIL WAR II. Contains material originally published in magazine form as ROCKET RACCOON & GROOT #7-10 and INCREDIBLE HULK #271. First printing 2016. ISBN# 978-0-7851-9974-8. Published by VEL WORLDWIDE, INC., a subsidiary of MARVEL ENTERTAINMENT, LLC. OFFICE OF PUBLICATION: 135 West 50th Street, New York, NY 10020. Copyright © 2016 MARVEL No similarity between any of the names, characters, persons, and/ stitutions in this magazine with those of any living or dead person or institution is intended, and any such similarity which may exist is purely coincidental. **Printed in Canada.** ALAN FINE, President, Marvel Entertainment; DAN BUCKLEY, dent, TV, Publishing & Brand Management; JOE QUESADA, Chief Creative Officer; TOM BREVOORT, SVP of Publishing; DAVID BOGART, SVP of Business Affairs & Operations, Publishing & Partnership; C.B. CEBULSKI, VP of Brand Management velopment, Asia; DAVID GABRIEL, SVP of Sales & Marketing, Publishing; JEFF YOUNGQUIST, VP of Production & Special Projects; DAN CARR, Executive Director of Publishing Technology; ALEX MORALES, Director of Publishing Operations; AN CRESPI, Production Manager; STAN LEE, Chairman Emeritus. For information regarding advertising in Marvel Comics or on Marvel.com, please contact Vit DeBellis, Integrated Sales Manager, at vdebellis@marvel.com. For Marvel cription inquiries, please call 888-511-5480. **Manufactured between 9/16/2016 and 10/24/2016 by SOLISCO PRINTERS, SCOTT, QC, CANADA.**

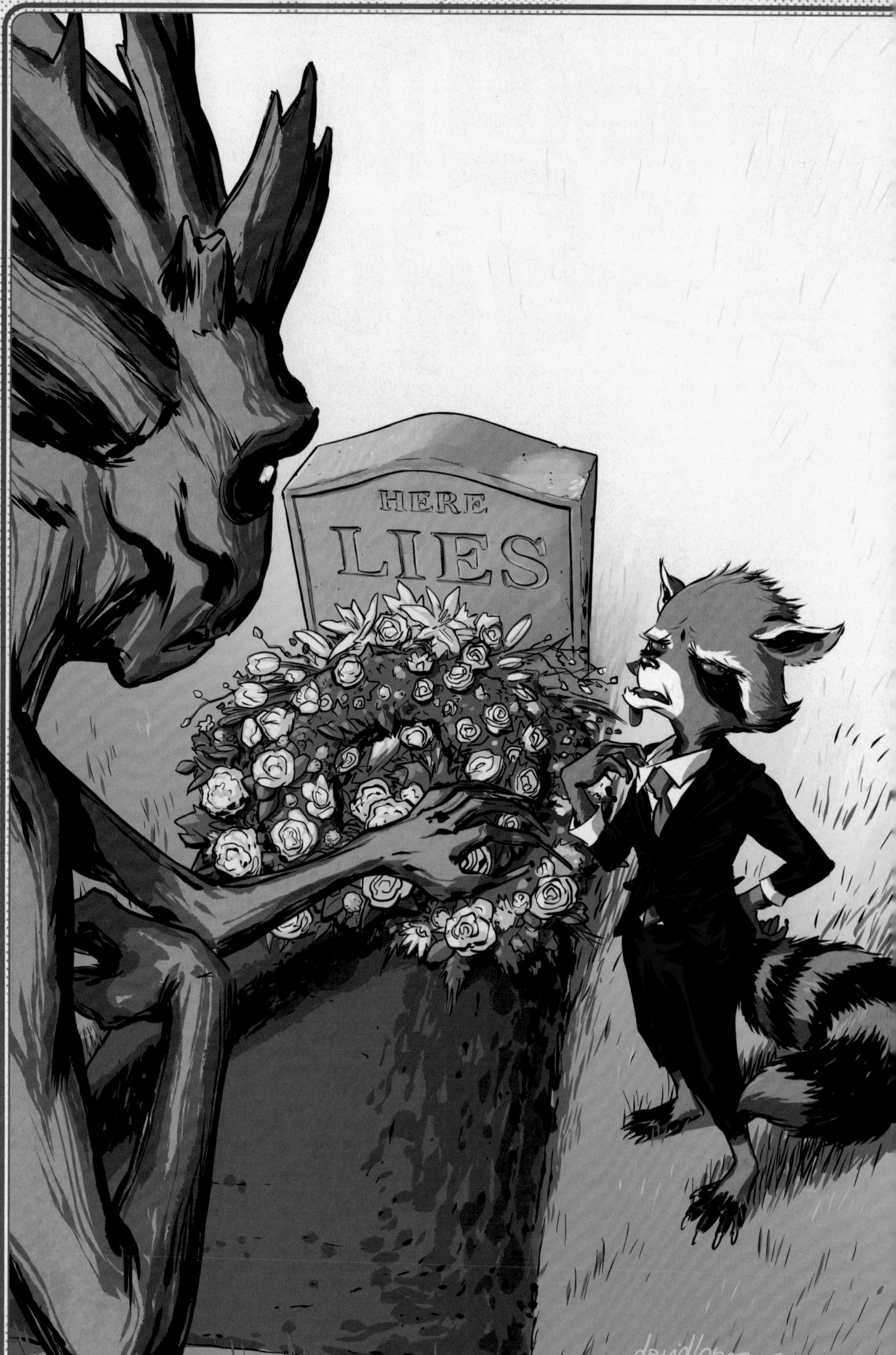
HERE
LIES
davidlopez

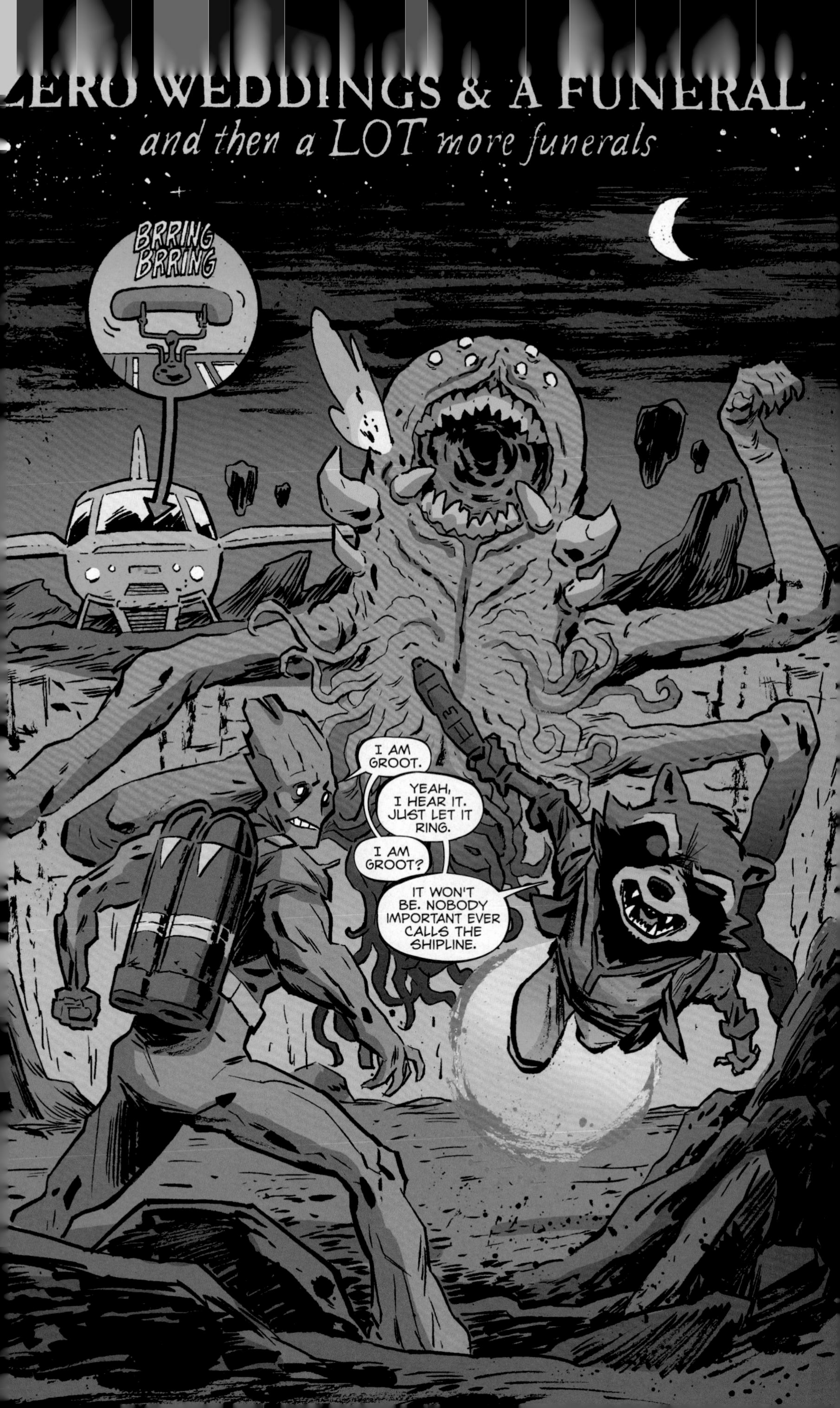
ZERO WEDDINGS & A FUNERAL
and then a LOT more funerals
BRRING BRRING
I AM GROOT.
YEAH, I HEAR IT. JUST LET IT RING.
I AM GROOT?
IT WON'T BE. NOBODY IMPORTANT EVER CALLS THE SHIPLINE.

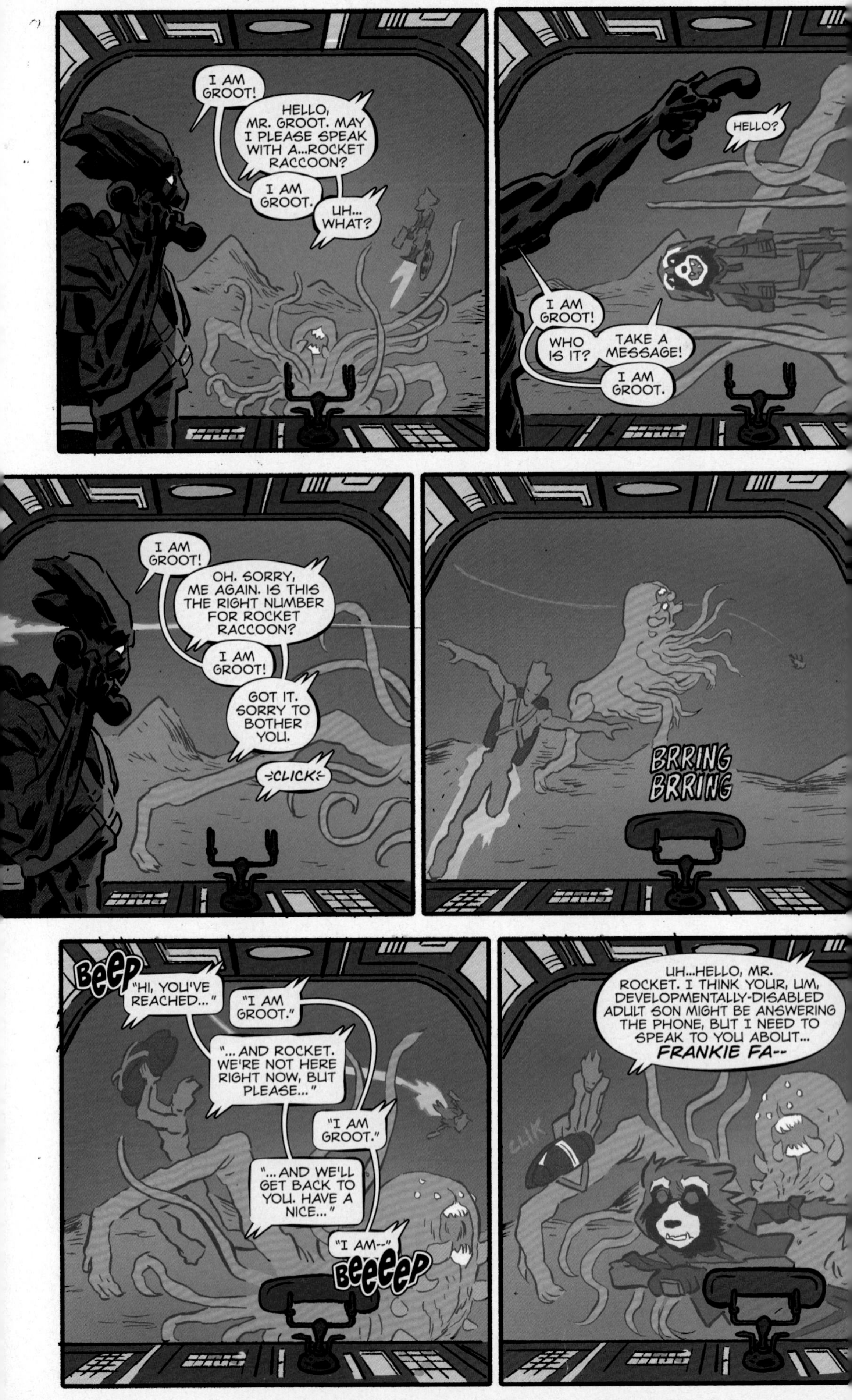
I AM GROOT!
HELLO, MR. GROOT. MAY I PLEASE SPEAK WITH A...ROCKET RACCOON?
I AM GROOT.
UH... WHAT?
HELLO?
I AM GROOT!
WHO IS IT?
TAKE A MESSAGE!
I AM GROOT.
I AM GROOT!
OH. SORRY, ME AGAIN. IS THIS THE RIGHT NUMBER FOR ROCKET RACCOON?
I AM GROOT!
GOT IT. SORRY TO BOTHER YOU.
CLICK
BRRING BRRING
BEEP
"HI, YOU'VE REACHED..."
"I AM GROOT."
"...AND ROCKET. WE'RE NOT HERE RIGHT NOW, BUT PLEASE..."
"I AM GROOT."
"...AND WE'LL GET BACK TO YOU. HAVE A NICE..."
"I AM--"
BEEEEEP
UH...HELLO, MR. ROCKET. I THINK YOUR, UM, DEVELOPMENTALLY-DISABLED ADULT SON MIGHT BE ANSWERING THE PHONE, BUT I NEED TO SPEAK TO YOU ABOUT... FRANKIE FA--
CLIK

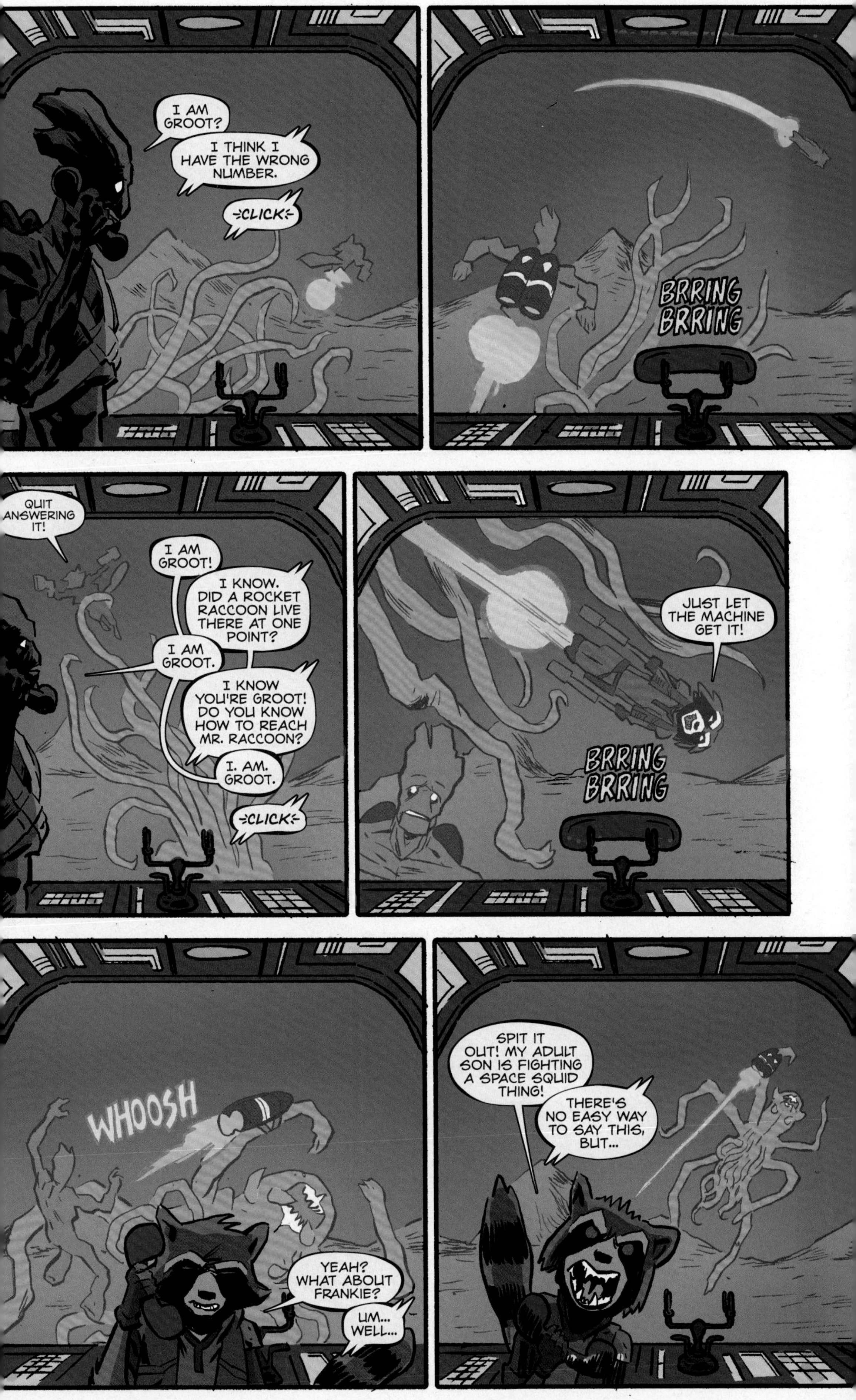
I AM GROOT?
I THINK I HAVE THE WRONG NUMBER.
CLICK
BRRING BRRING
QUIT ANSWERING IT!
I AM GROOT!
I KNOW. DID A ROCKET RACCOON LIVE THERE AT ONE POINT?
I AM GROOT.
I KNOW YOU'RE GROOT! DO YOU KNOW HOW TO REACH MR. RACCOON?
I. AM. GROOT.
CLICK
JUST LET THE MACHINE GET IT!
BRRING BRRING
WHOOSH
YEAH? WHAT ABOUT FRANKIE?
UM... WELL...
SPIT IT OUT! MY ADULT SON IS FIGHTING A SPACE SQUID THING!
THERE'S NO EASY WAY TO SAY THIS, BUT...

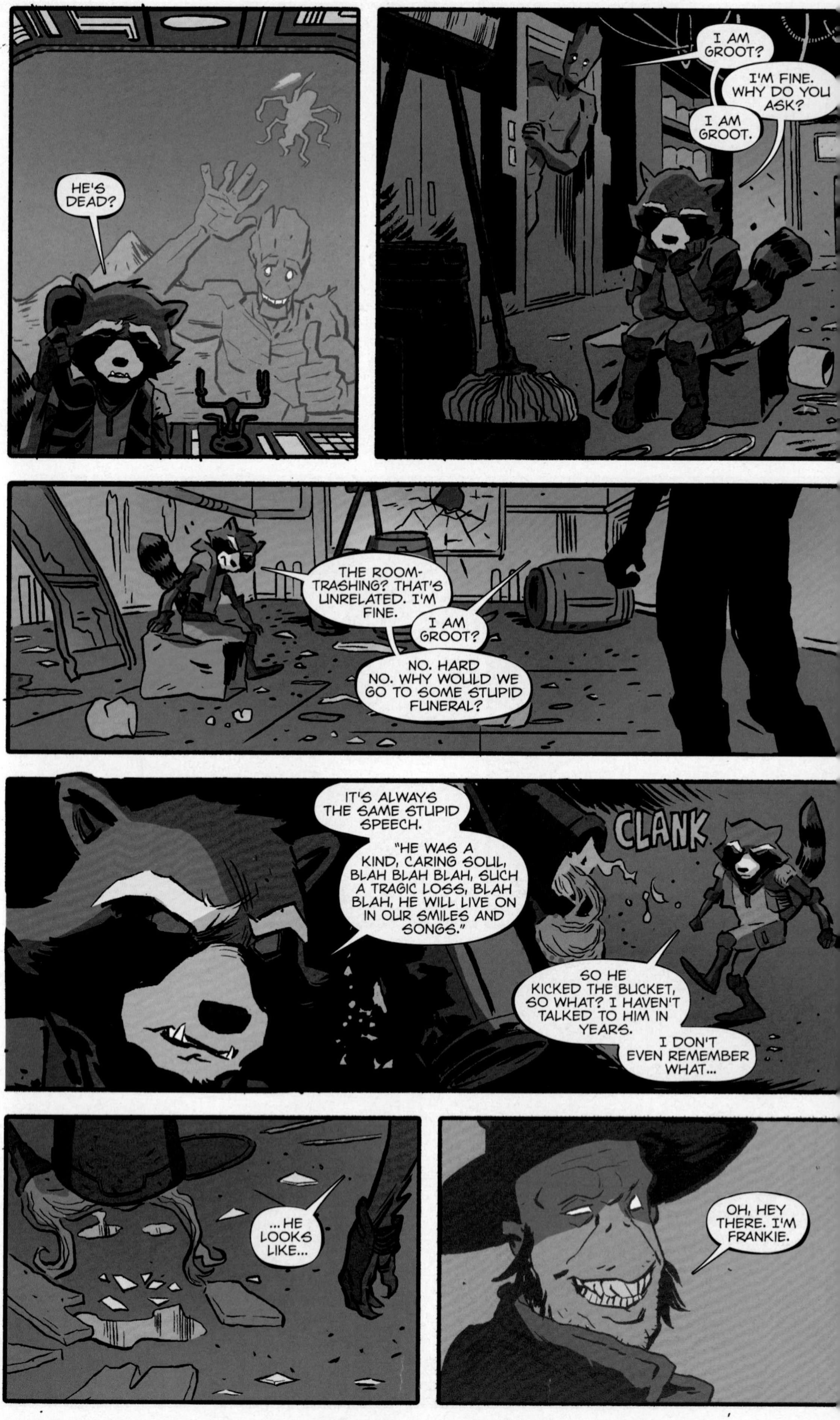
HE'S DEAD?
I AM GROOT?
I'M FINE. WHY DO YOU ASK?
I AM GROOT.
THE ROOM-TRASHING? THAT'S UNRELATED. I'M FINE.
I AM GROOT?
NO. HARD NO. WHY WOULD WE GO TO SOME STUPID FUNERAL?
IT'S ALWAYS THE SAME STUPID SPEECH.
"HE WAS A KIND, CARING SOUL, BLAH BLAH BLAH, SUCH A TRAGIC LOSS, BLAH BLAH, HE WILL LIVE ON IN OUR SMILES AND SONGS."
CLANK
SO HE KICKED THE BUCKET, SO WHAT? I HAVEN'T TALKED TO HIM IN YEARS.
I DON'T EVEN REMEMBER WHAT...
...HE LOOKS LIKE...
OH, HEY THERE. I'M FRANKIE.

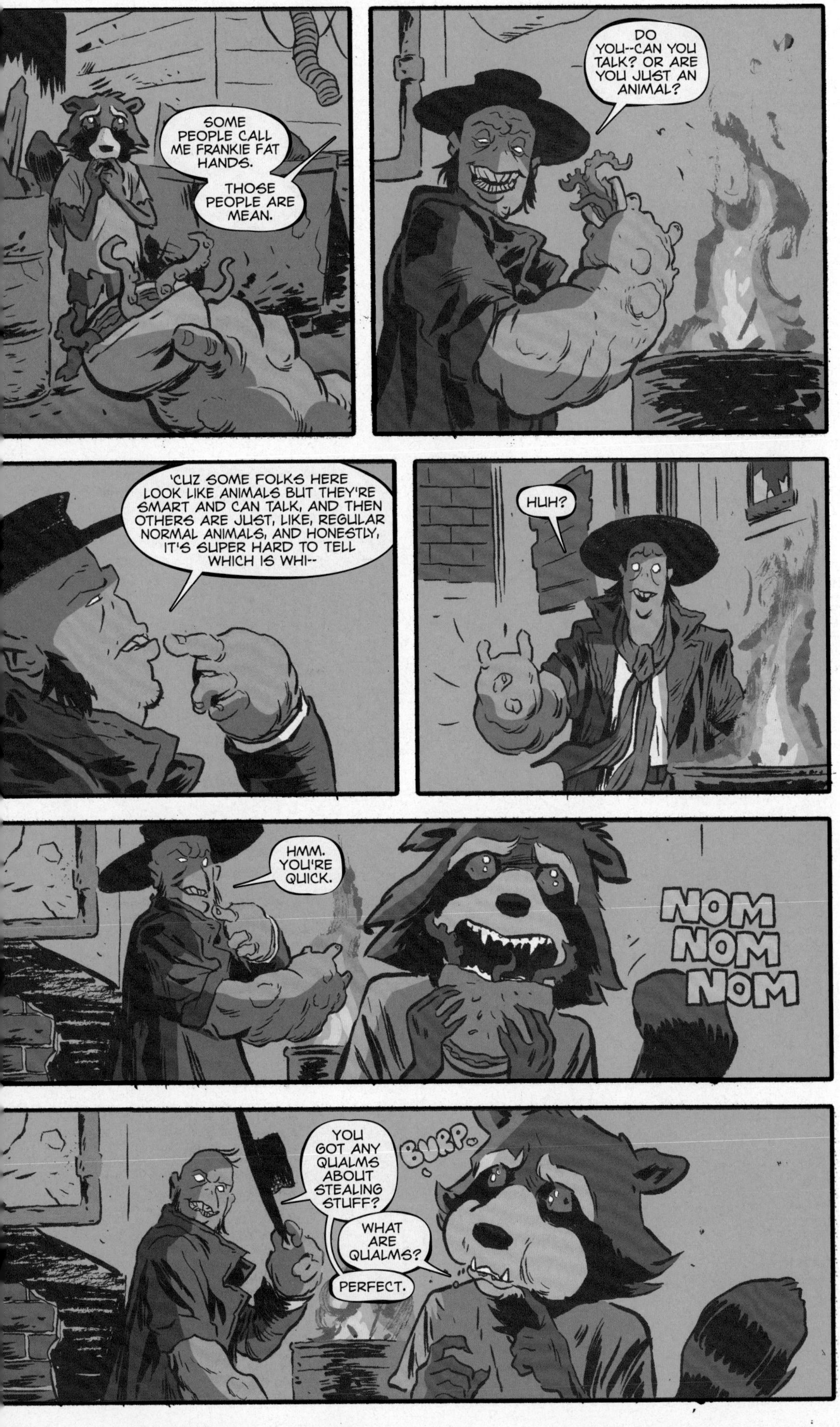
SOME PEOPLE CALL ME FRANKIE FAT HANDS.
THOSE PEOPLE ARE MEAN.
DO YOU--CAN YOU TALK? OR ARE YOU JUST AN ANIMAL?
'CUZ SOME FOLKS HERE LOOK LIKE ANIMALS BUT THEY'RE SMART AND CAN TALK, AND THEN OTHERS ARE JUST, LIKE, REGULAR NORMAL ANIMALS, AND HONESTLY, IT'S SUPER HARD TO TELL WHICH IS WHI--
HUH?
HMM. YOU'RE QUICK.
NOM NOM NOM
YOU GOT ANY QUALMS ABOUT STEALING STUFF?
BURP.
WHAT ARE QUALMS?
PERFECT.

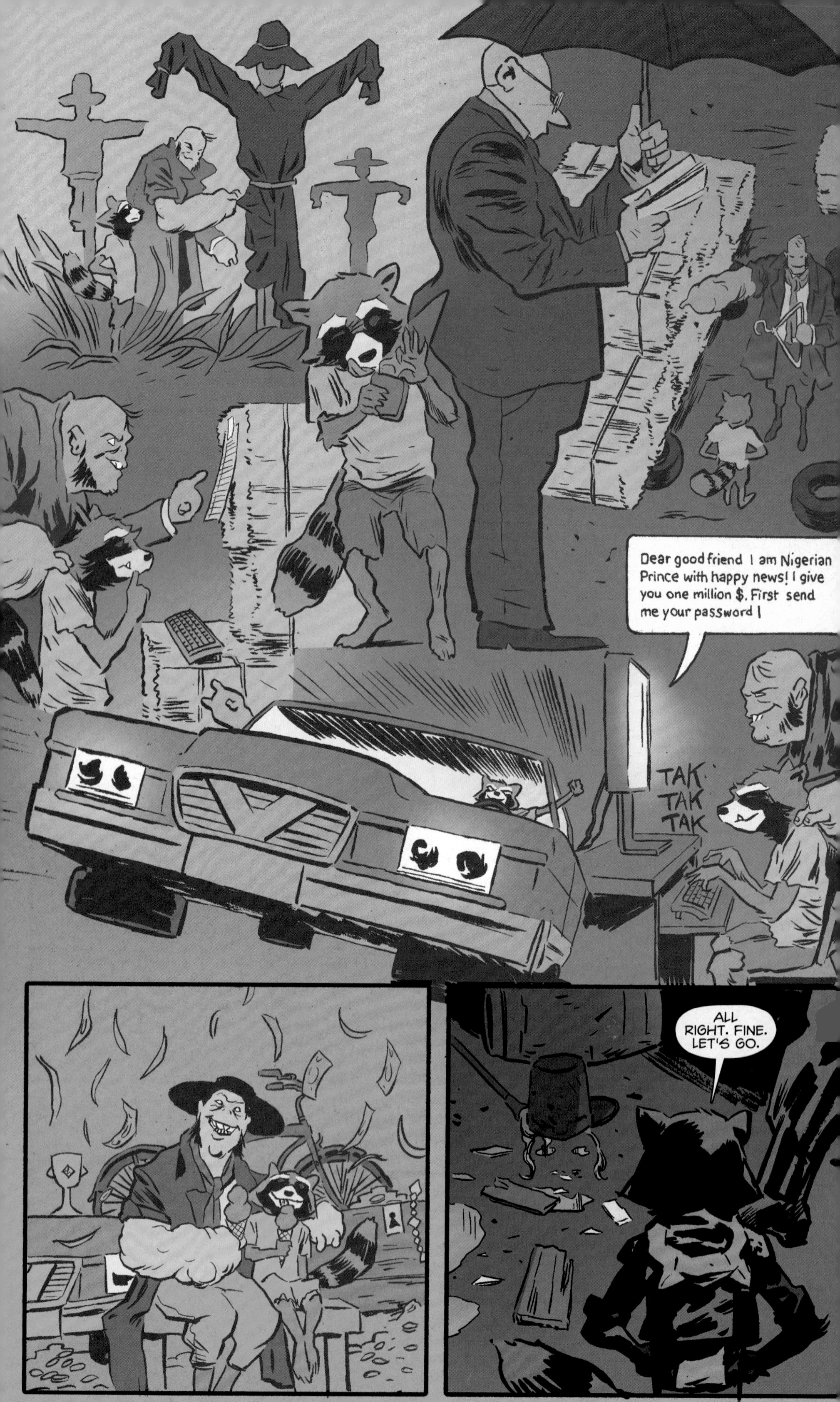
Dear good friend I am Nigerian Prince with happy news! I give you one million $. First send me your password!
TAK TAK TAK
ALL RIGHT. FINE. LET'S GO.

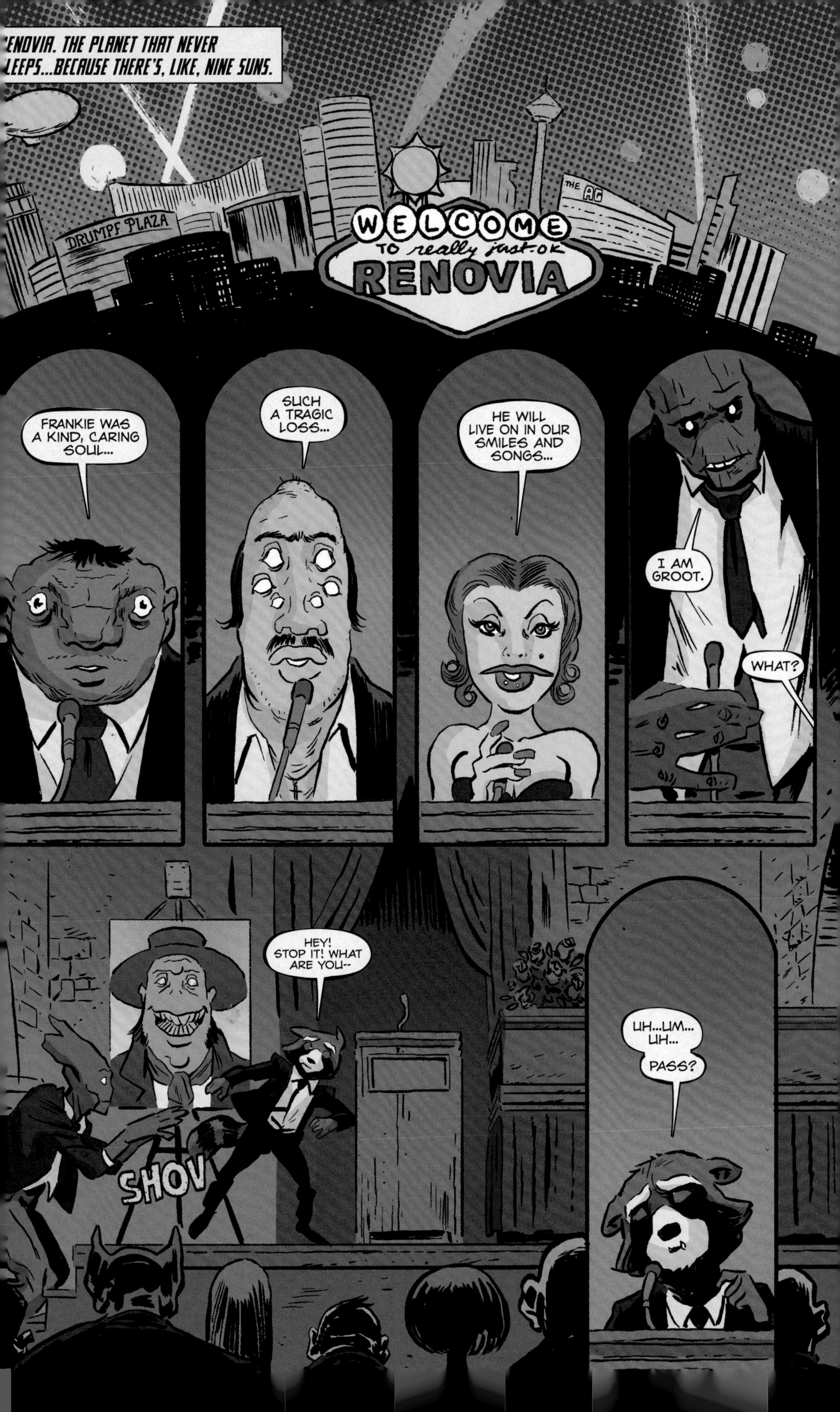
RENOVIA. THE PLANET THAT NEVER SLEEPS...BECAUSE THERE'S, LIKE, NINE SUNS.
DRUMPF PLAZA
THE AG
WELCOME TO really just-OK RENOVIA
FRANKIE WAS A KIND, CARING SOUL...
SUCH A TRAGIC LOSS...
HE WILL LIVE ON IN OUR SMILES AND SONGS...
I AM GROOT.
WHAT?
HEY! STOP IT! WHAT ARE YOU--
SHOV
UH...UM... UH...
PASS?

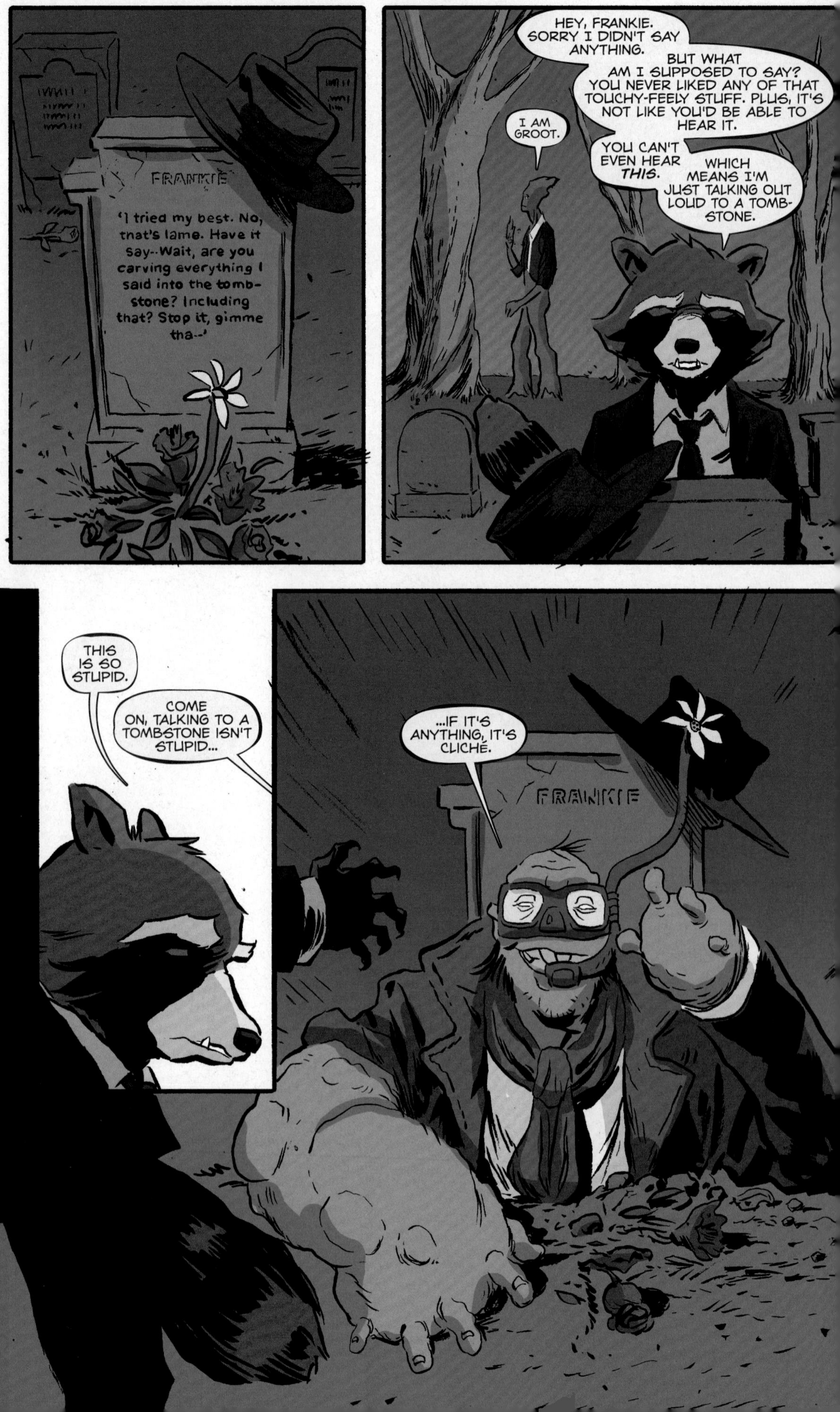
FRANKIE
'I tried my best. No, that's lame. Have it say--Wait, are you carving everything I said into the tombstone? Including that? Stop it, gimme tha--'
HEY, FRANKIE. SORRY I DIDN'T SAY ANYTHING.
BUT WHAT AM I SUPPOSED TO SAY? YOU NEVER LIKED ANY OF THAT TOUCHY-FEELY STUFF. PLUS, IT'S NOT LIKE YOU'D BE ABLE TO HEAR IT.
I AM GROOT.
YOU CAN'T EVEN HEAR *THIS*.
WHICH MEANS I'M JUST TALKING OUT LOUD TO A TOMBSTONE.
THIS IS SO STUPID.
COME ON, TALKING TO A TOMBSTONE ISN'T STUPID...
...IF IT'S ANYTHING, IT'S CLICHÉ.
FRANKIE

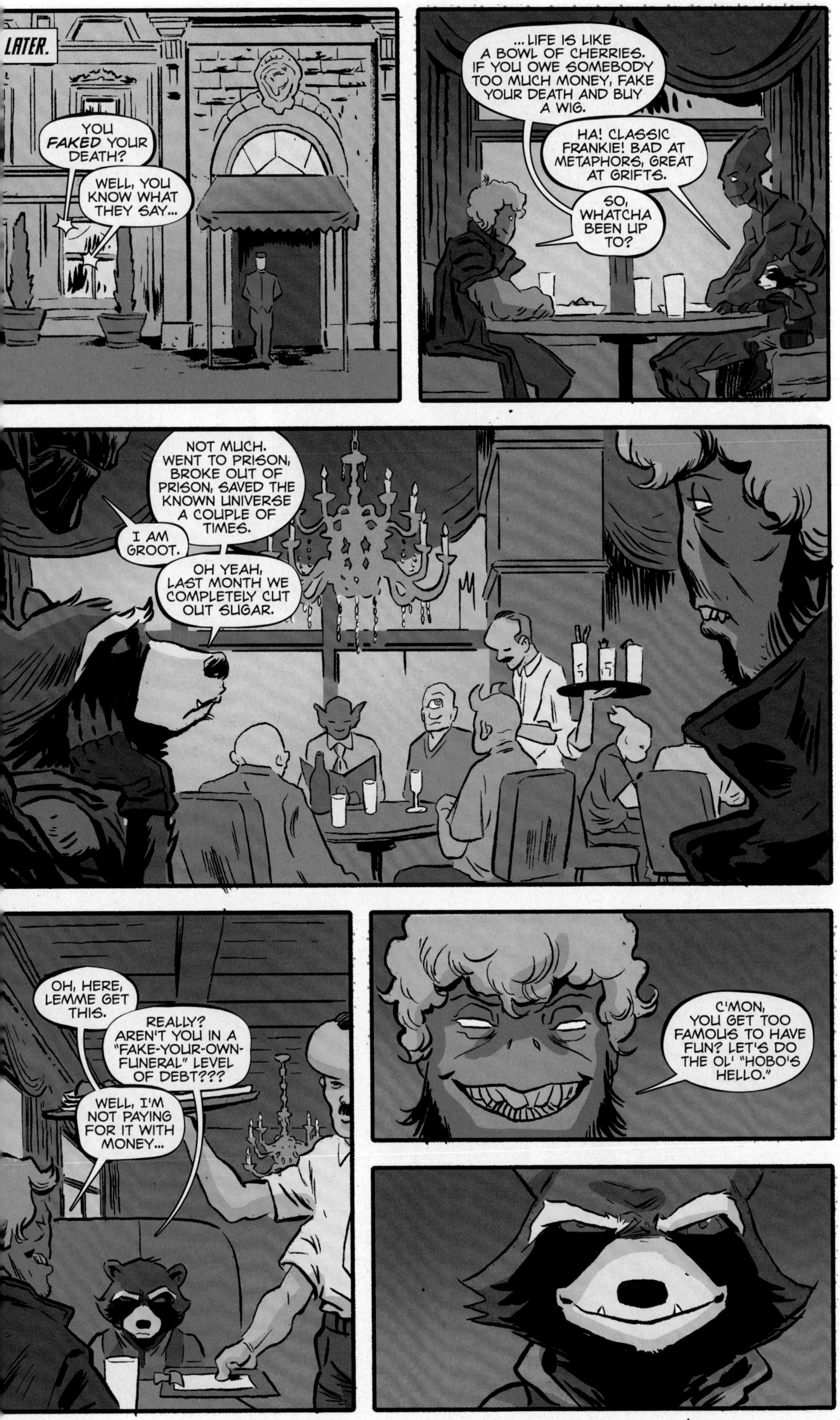
LATER.
YOU FAKED YOUR DEATH?
WELL, YOU KNOW WHAT THEY SAY...
...LIFE IS LIKE A BOWL OF CHERRIES. IF YOU OWE SOMEBODY TOO MUCH MONEY, FAKE YOUR DEATH AND BUY A WIG.
HA! CLASSIC FRANKIE! BAD AT METAPHORS, GREAT AT GRIFTS.
SO, WHATCHA BEEN UP TO?
NOT MUCH. WENT TO PRISON, BROKE OUT OF PRISON, SAVED THE KNOWN UNIVERSE A COUPLE OF TIMES.
I AM GROOT.
OH YEAH, LAST MONTH WE COMPLETELY CUT OUT SUGAR.
OH, HERE, LEMME GET THIS.
REALLY? AREN'T YOU IN A "FAKE-YOUR-OWN-FUNERAL" LEVEL OF DEBT???
WELL, I'M NOT PAYING FOR IT WITH MONEY...
C'MON, YOU GET TOO FAMOUS TO HAVE FUN? LET'S DO THE OL' "HOBO'S HELLO."

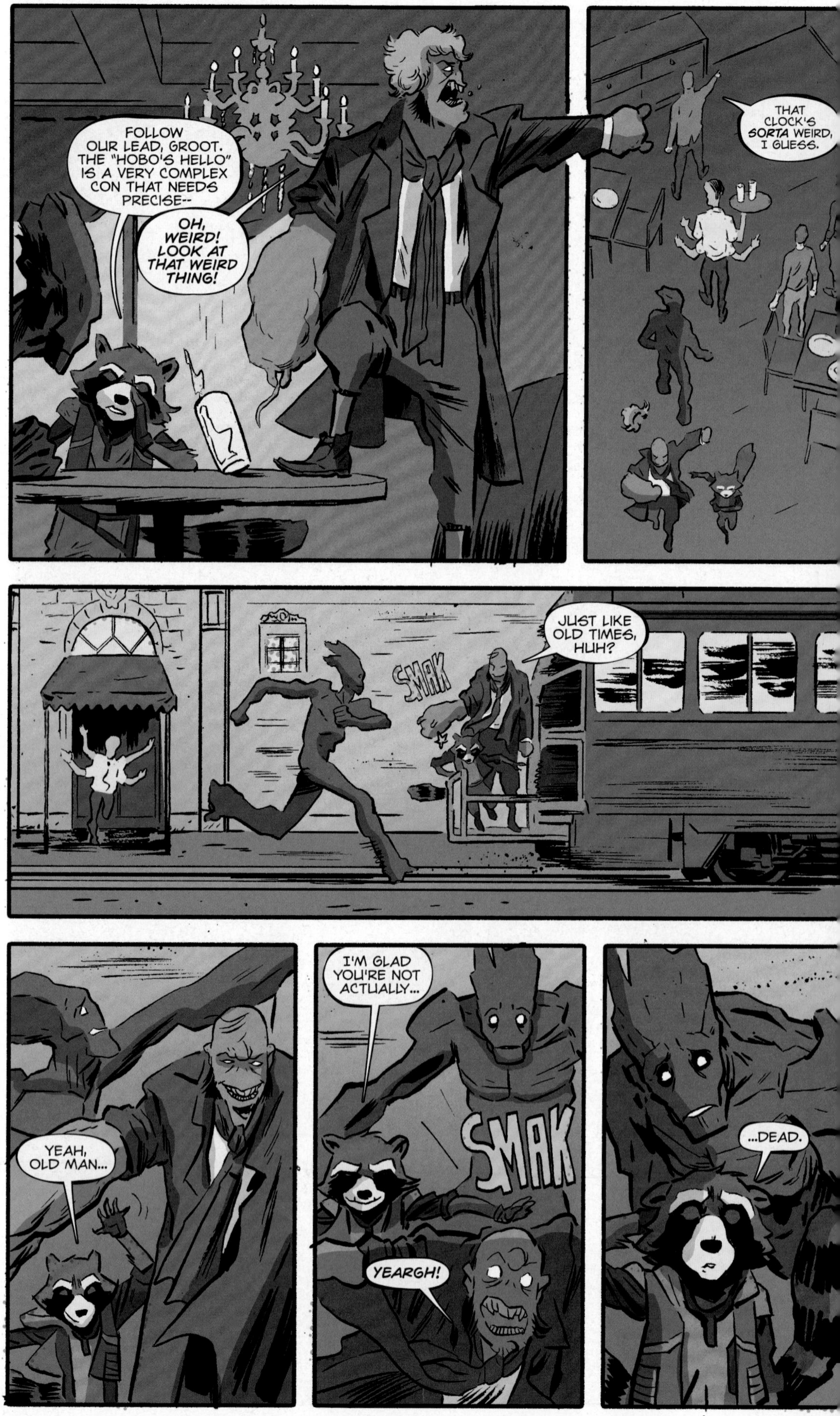
FOLLOW OUR LEAD, GROOT. THE "HOBO'S HELLO" IS A VERY COMPLEX CON THAT NEEDS PRECISE--
OH, WEIRD! LOOK AT THAT WEIRD THING!
THAT CLOCK'S SORTA WEIRD, I GUESS.
SMAK
JUST LIKE OLD TIMES, HUH?
YEAH, OLD MAN...
I'M GLAD YOU'RE NOT ACTUALLY...
SMAK
YEARGH!
...DEAD.

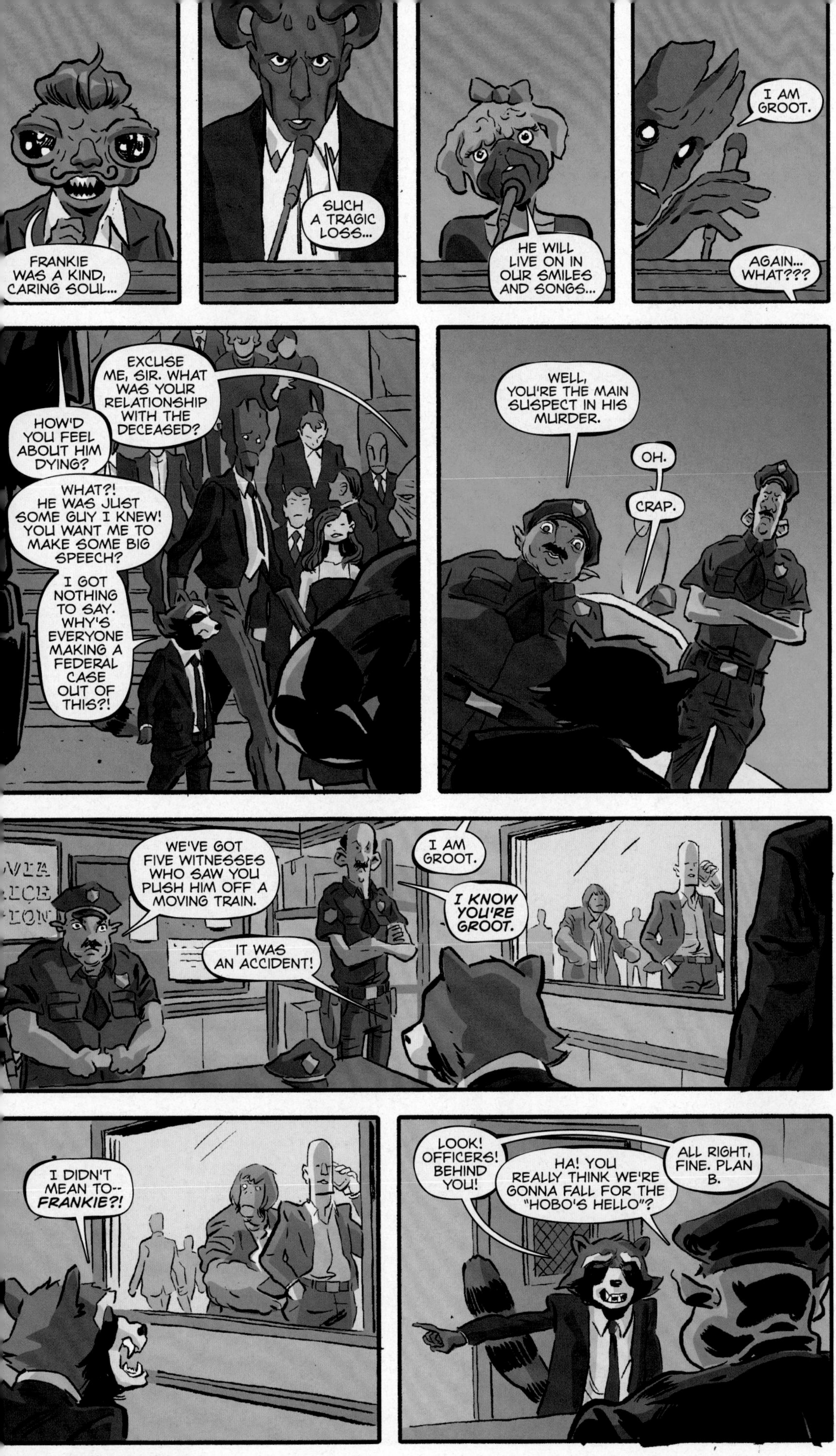
FRANKIE WAS A KIND, CARING SOUL...
SUCH A TRAGIC LOSS...
HE WILL LIVE ON IN OUR SMILES AND SONGS...
I AM GROOT.
AGAIN... WHAT???
HOW'D YOU FEEL ABOUT HIM DYING?
EXCUSE ME, SIR. WHAT WAS YOUR RELATIONSHIP WITH THE DECEASED?
WHAT?! HE WAS JUST SOME GUY I KNEW! YOU WANT ME TO MAKE SOME BIG SPEECH?
I GOT NOTHING TO SAY. WHY'S EVERYONE MAKING A FEDERAL CASE OUT OF THIS?!
WELL, YOU'RE THE MAIN SUSPECT IN HIS MURDER.
OH.
CRAP.
WE'VE GOT FIVE WITNESSES WHO SAW YOU PUSH HIM OFF A MOVING TRAIN.
IT WAS AN ACCIDENT!
I AM GROOT.
I KNOW YOU'RE GROOT.
I DIDN'T MEAN TO-- FRANKIE?!
LOOK! OFFICERS! BEHIND YOU!
HA! YOU REALLY THINK WE'RE GONNA FALL FOR THE "HOBO'S HELLO"?
ALL RIGHT, FINE. PLAN B.

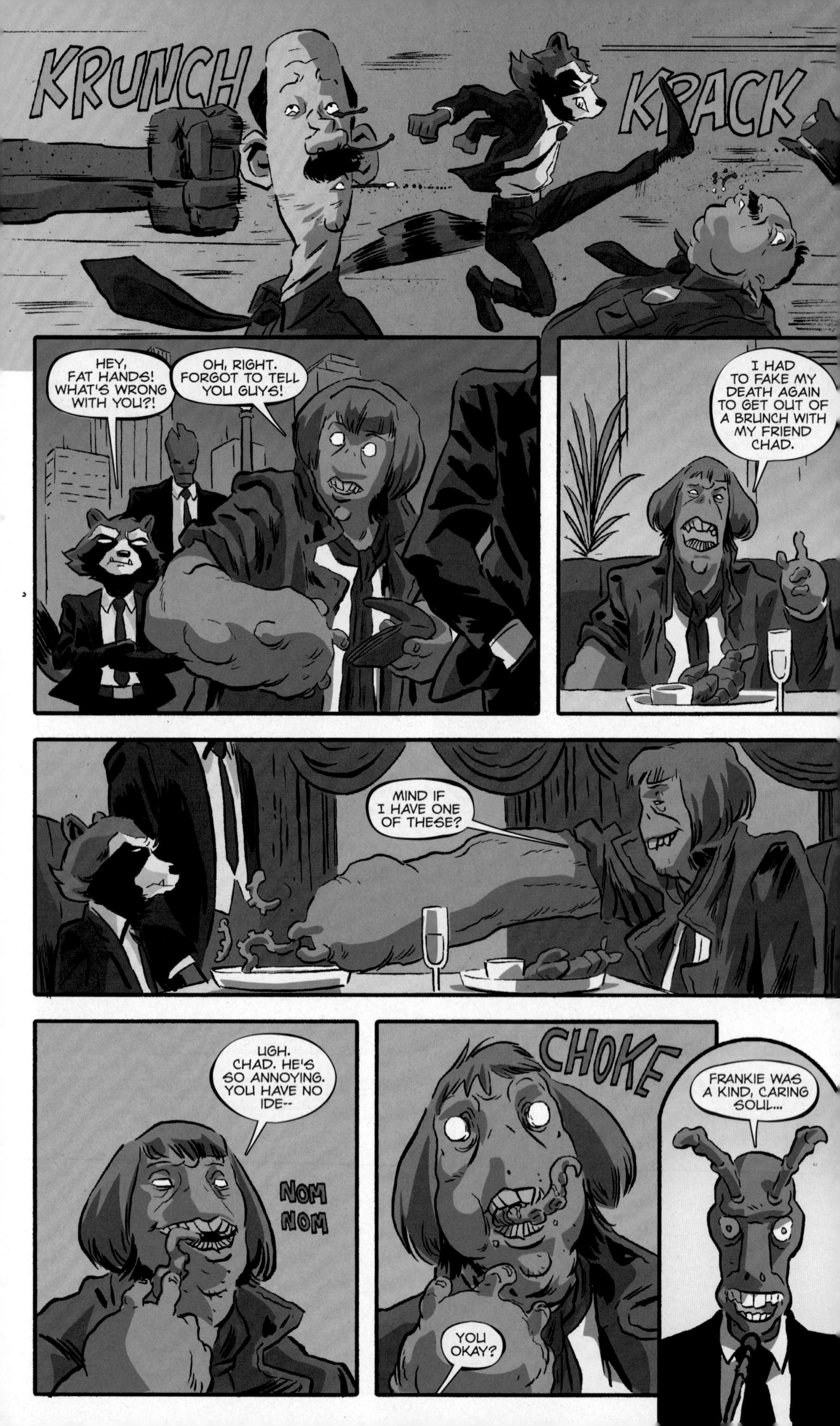
KRUNCH
KRACK
HEY, FAT HANDS! WHAT'S WRONG WITH YOU?!
OH, RIGHT. FORGOT TO TELL YOU GUYS!
I HAD TO FAKE MY DEATH AGAIN TO GET OUT OF A BRUNCH WITH MY FRIEND CHAD.
MIND IF I HAVE ONE OF THESE?
UGH. CHAD. HE'S SO ANNOYING. YOU HAVE NO IDE--
NOM NOM
CHOKE
YOU OKAY?
FRANKIE WAS A KIND, CARING SOUL...

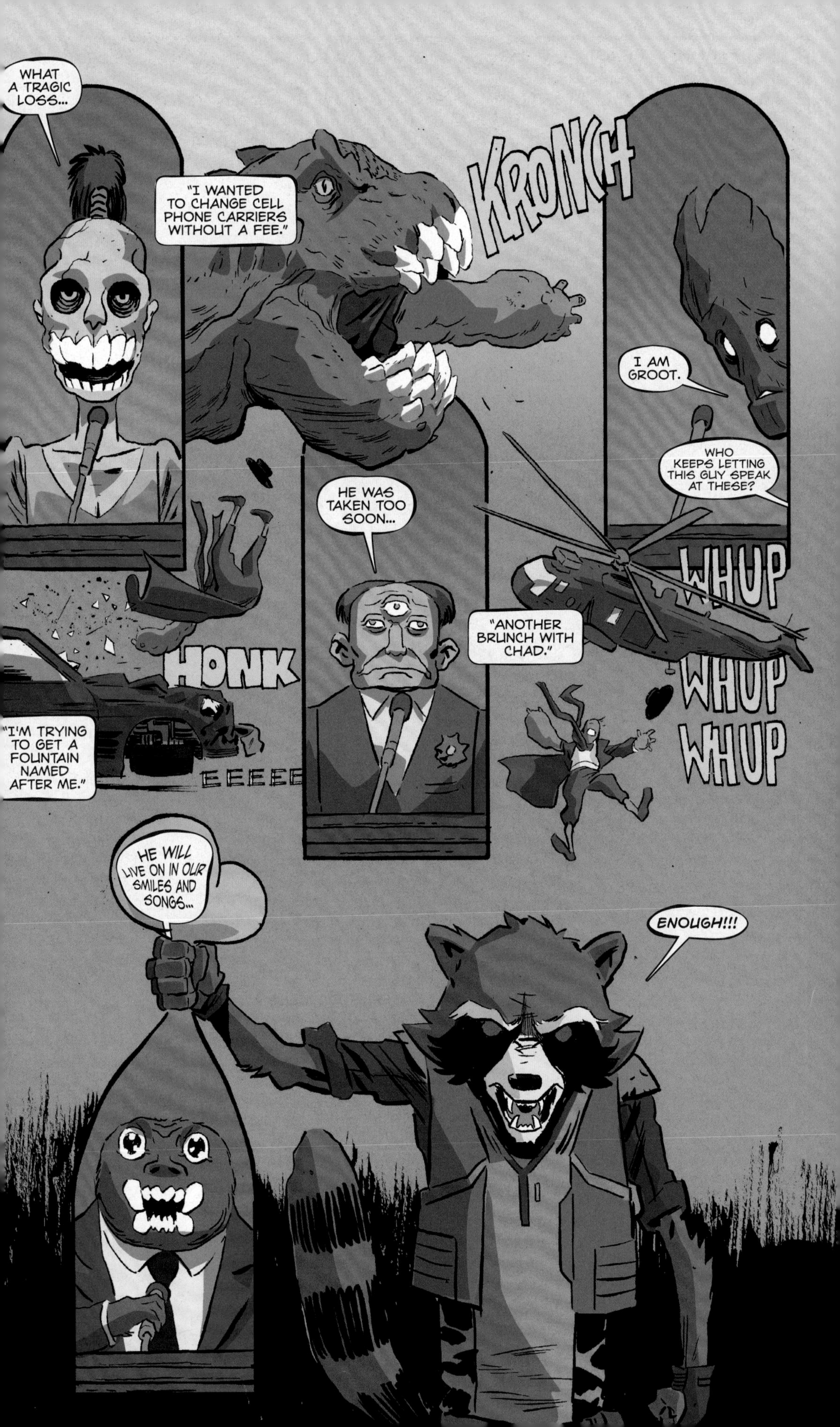
WHAT A TRAGIC LOSS...
"I WANTED TO CHANGE CELL PHONE CARRIERS WITHOUT A FEE."
KRONCH
I AM GROOT.
WHO KEEPS LETTING THIS GUY SPEAK AT THESE?
HE WAS TAKEN TOO SOON...
HONK
"I'M TRYING TO GET A FOUNTAIN NAMED AFTER ME."
EEEEE
"ANOTHER BRUNCH WITH CHAD."
WHUP
WHUP
WHUP
HE WILL LIVE ON IN OUR SMILES AND SONGS...
ENOUGH!!!

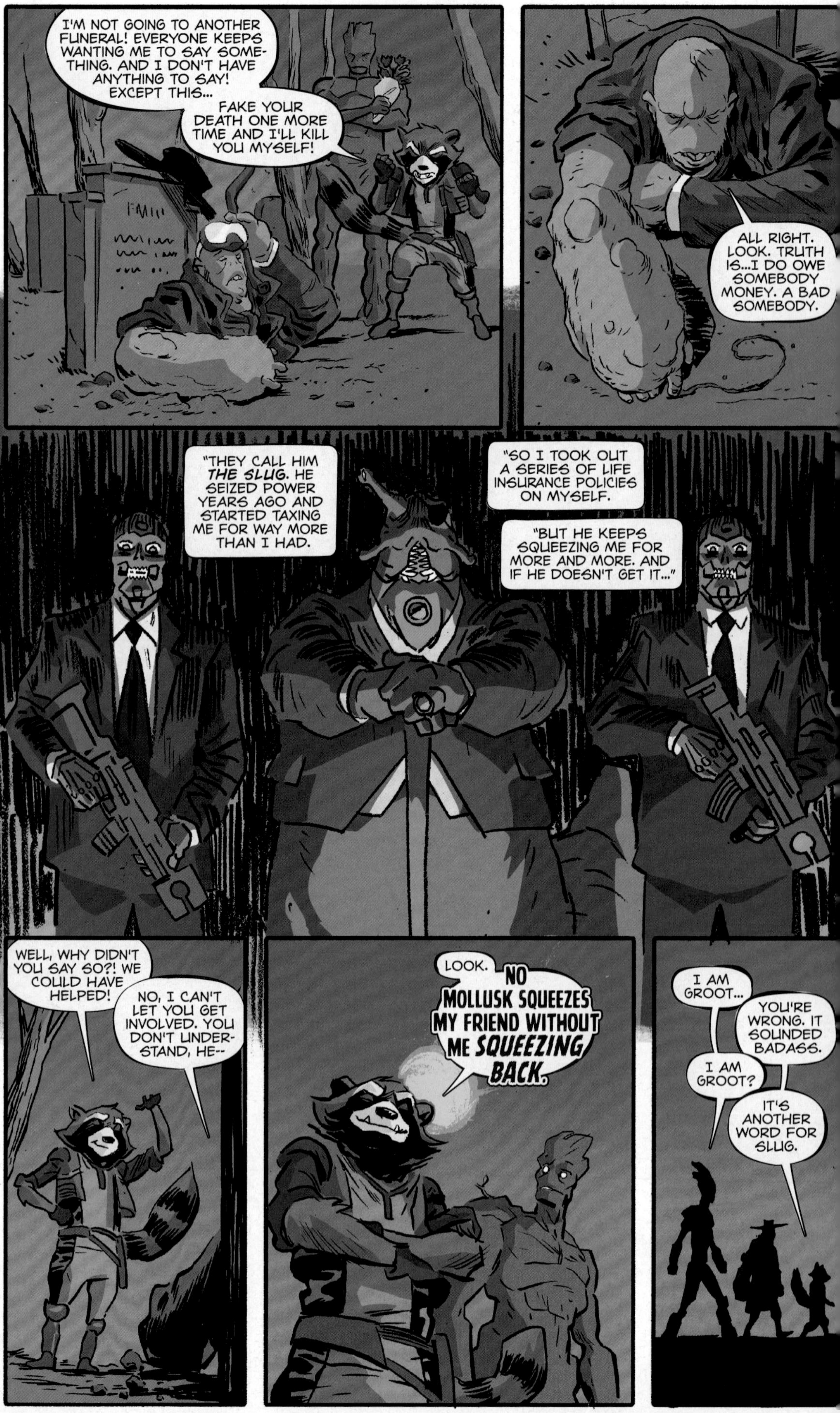

I'M NOT GOING TO ANOTHER FUNERAL! EVERYONE KEEPS WANTING ME TO SAY SOMETHING. AND I DON'T HAVE ANYTHING TO SAY! EXCEPT THIS...
FAKE YOUR DEATH ONE MORE TIME AND I'LL KILL YOU MYSELF!
ALL RIGHT. LOOK. TRUTH IS...I DO OWE SOMEBODY MONEY. A BAD SOMEBODY.
"THEY CALL HIM THE SLUG. HE SEIZED POWER YEARS AGO AND STARTED TAXING ME FOR WAY MORE THAN I HAD.
"SO I TOOK OUT A SERIES OF LIFE INSURANCE POLICIES ON MYSELF.
"BUT HE KEEPS SQUEEZING ME FOR MORE AND MORE. AND IF HE DOESN'T GET IT..."
WELL, WHY DIDN'T YOU SAY SO?! WE COULD HAVE HELPED!
NO, I CAN'T LET YOU GET INVOLVED. YOU DON'T UNDERSTAND, HE--
LOOK. NO MOLLUSK SQUEEZES MY FRIEND WITHOUT ME SQUEEZING BACK.
I AM GROOT...
YOU'RE WRONG. IT SOUNDED BADASS.
I AM GROOT?
IT'S ANOTHER WORD FOR SLUG.

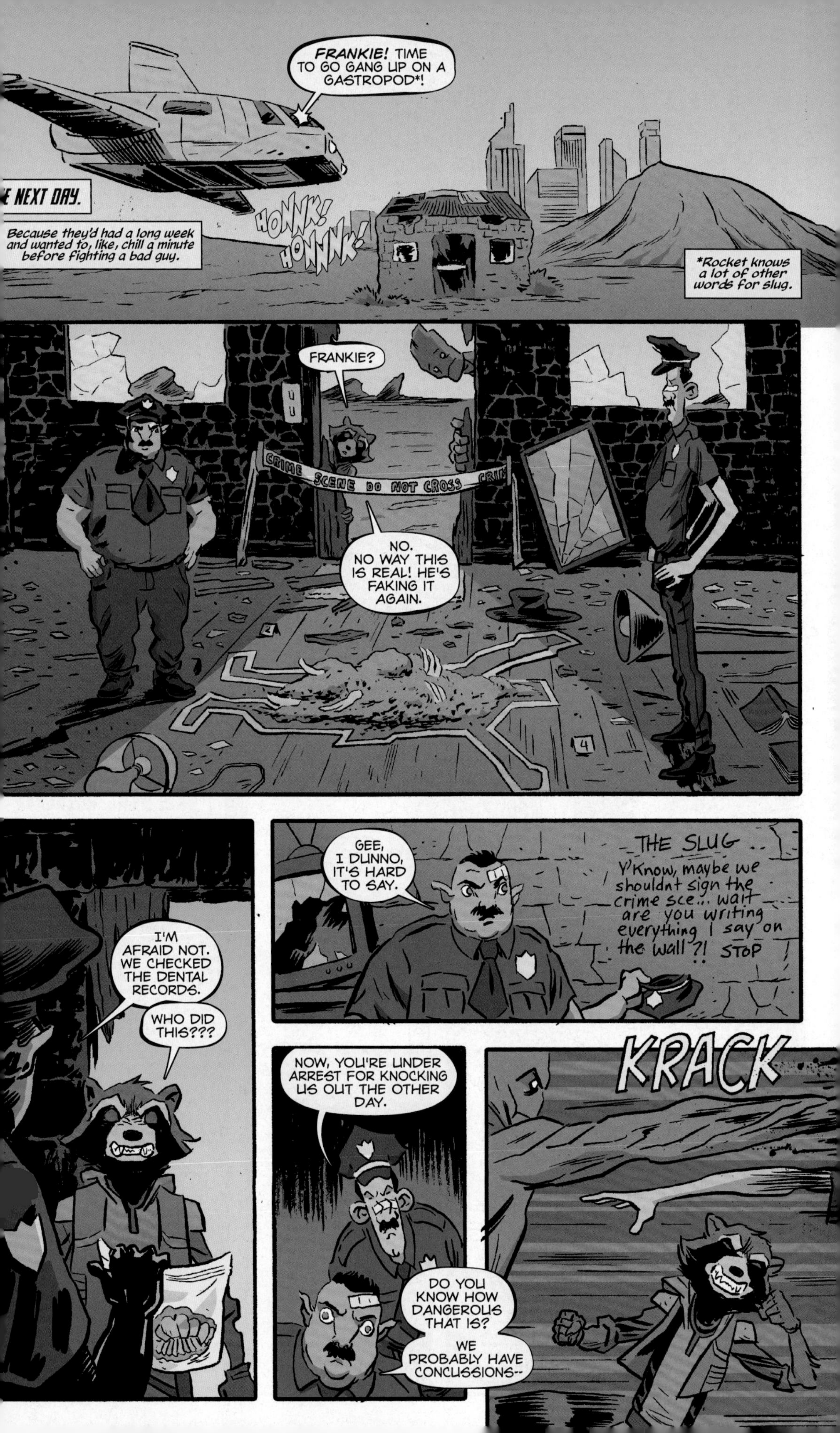
FRANKIE! TIME TO GO GANG UP ON A GASTROPOD*!
E NEXT DAY.
Because they'd had a long week and wanted to, like, chill a minute before fighting a bad guy.
HONNK! HONNNK!
*Rocket knows a lot of other words for slug.
FRANKIE?
CRIME SCENE DO NOT CROSS
NO. NO WAY THIS IS REAL! HE'S FAKING IT AGAIN.
I'M AFRAID NOT. WE CHECKED THE DENTAL RECORDS.
WHO DID THIS???
GEE, I DUNNO, IT'S HARD TO SAY.
THE SLUG
Y'Know, maybe we shouldnt sign the crime sce... wait are you writing everything I say on the wall ?! STOP
NOW, YOU'RE UNDER ARREST FOR KNOCKING US OUT THE OTHER DAY.
DO YOU KNOW HOW DANGEROUS THAT IS?
WE PROBABLY HAVE CONCUSSIONS--
KRACK

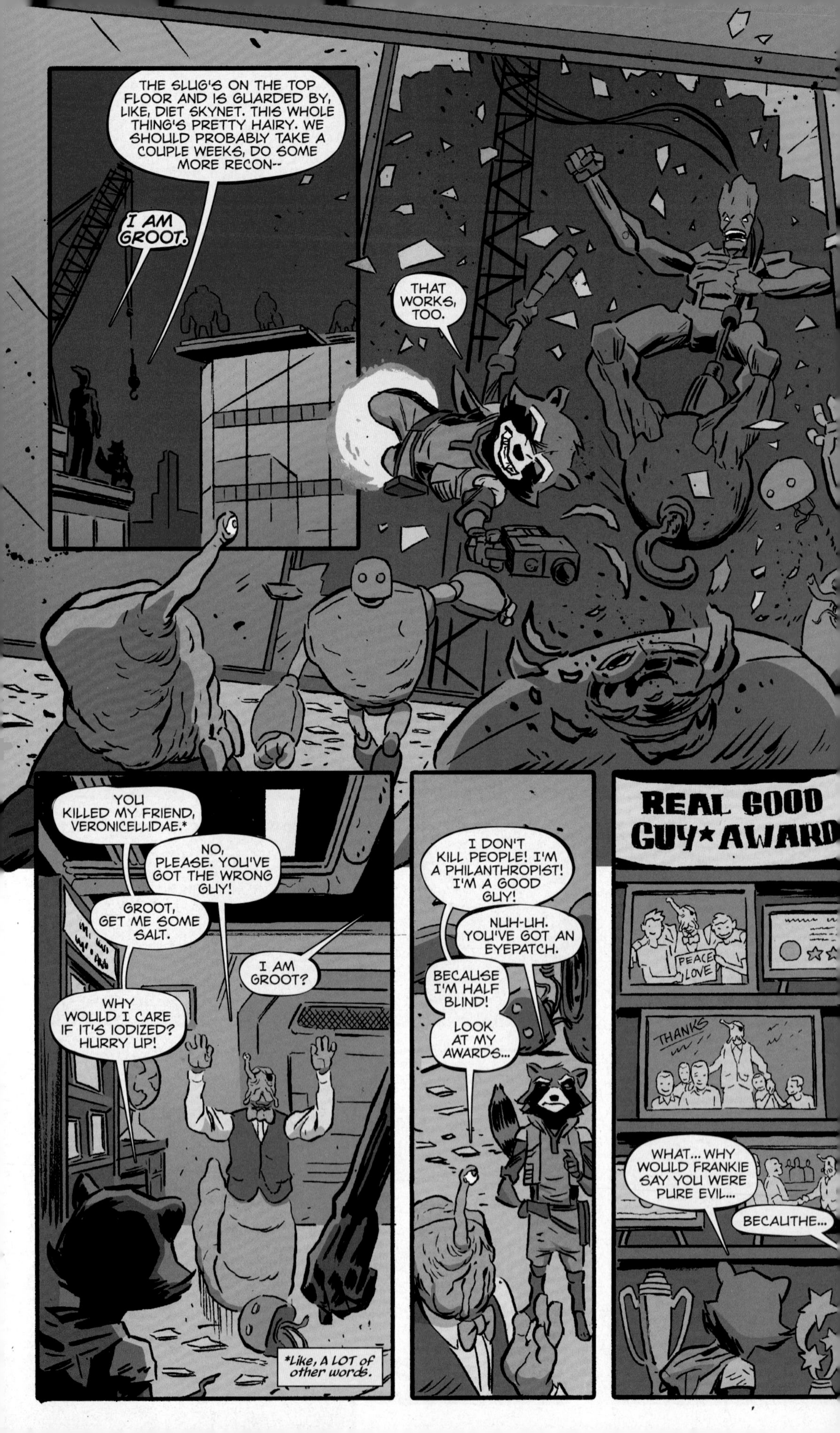
THE SLUG'S ON THE TOP FLOOR AND IS GUARDED BY, LIKE, DIET SKYNET. THIS WHOLE THING'S PRETTY HAIRY. WE SHOULD PROBABLY TAKE A COUPLE WEEKS, DO SOME MORE RECON--
I AM GROOT.
THAT WORKS, TOO.
YOU KILLED MY FRIEND, VERONICELLIDAE.*
NO, PLEASE. YOU'VE GOT THE WRONG GUY!
GROOT, GET ME SOME SALT.
I AM GROOT?
WHY WOULD I CARE IF IT'S IODIZED? HURRY UP!
*Like, A LOT of other words.
I DON'T KILL PEOPLE! I'M A PHILANTHROPIST! I'M A GOOD GUY!
NUH-UH. YOU'VE GOT AN EYEPATCH.
BECAUSE I'M HALF BLIND!
LOOK AT MY AWARDS...
REAL GOOD GUY★AWARD
PEACE LOVE
THANKS
WHAT... WHY WOULD FRANKIE SAY YOU WERE PURE EVIL...
BECAUTHE...

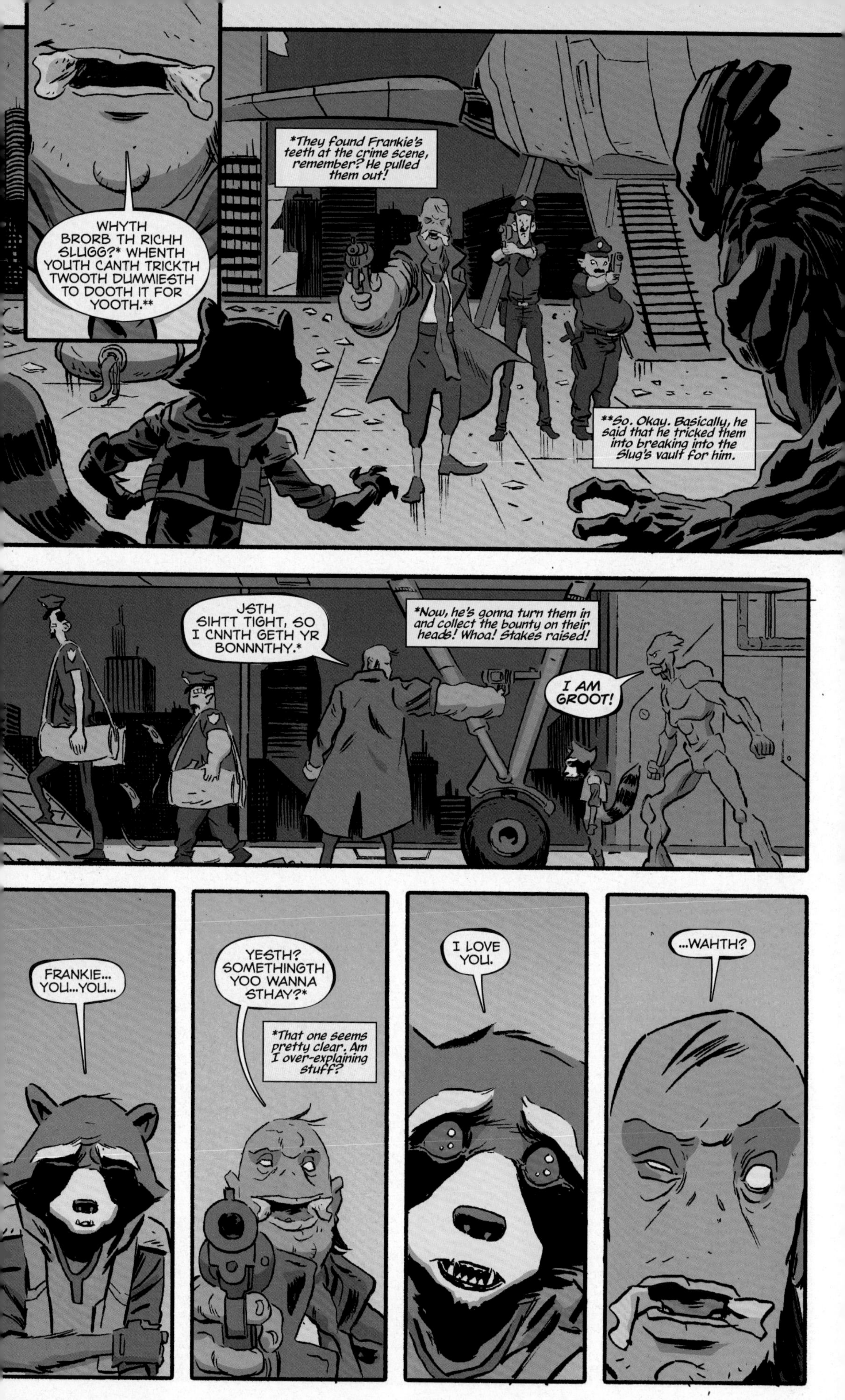

WHYTH BRORB TH RICHH SLUGG?* WHENTH YOUTH CANTH TRICKTH TWOOTH DUMMIESTH TO DOOTH IT FOR YOOTH.**
*They found Frankie's teeth at the crime scene, remember? He pulled them out!
**So. Okay. Basically, he said that he tricked them into breaking into the Slug's vault for him.
JSTH SIHTT TIGHT, SO I CNNTH GETH YR BONNNTHY.*
*Now, he's gonna turn them in and collect the bounty on their heads! Whoa! Stakes raised!
I AM GROOT!
FRANKIE... YOU...YOU...
YESTH? SOMETHINGTH YOO WANNA STHAY?*
*That one seems pretty clear. Am I over-explaining stuff?
I LOVE YOU.
...WAHTH?

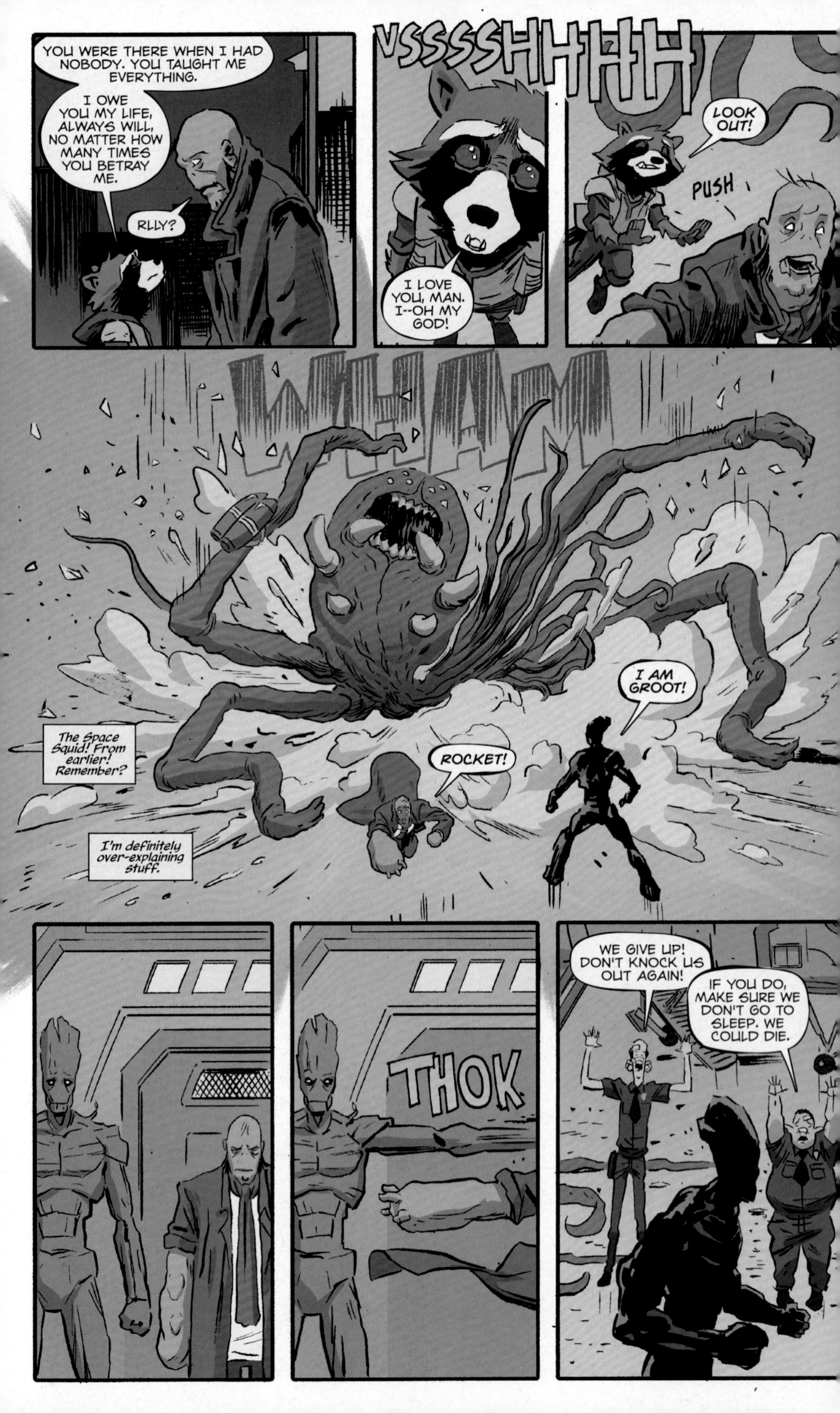
YOU WERE THERE WHEN I HAD NOBODY. YOU TAUGHT ME EVERYTHING.
I OWE YOU MY LIFE, ALWAYS WILL, NO MATTER HOW MANY TIMES YOU BETRAY ME.
RLLY?
VSSSSHHHH
I LOVE YOU, MAN. I--OH MY GOD!
LOOK OUT!
PUSH
WHAM
I AM GROOT!
The Space Squid! From earlier! Remember?
ROCKET!
I'm definitely over-explaining stuff.
THOK
WE GIVE UP! DON'T KNOCK US OUT AGAIN!
IF YOU DO, MAKE SURE WE DON'T GO TO SLEEP. WE COULD DIE.

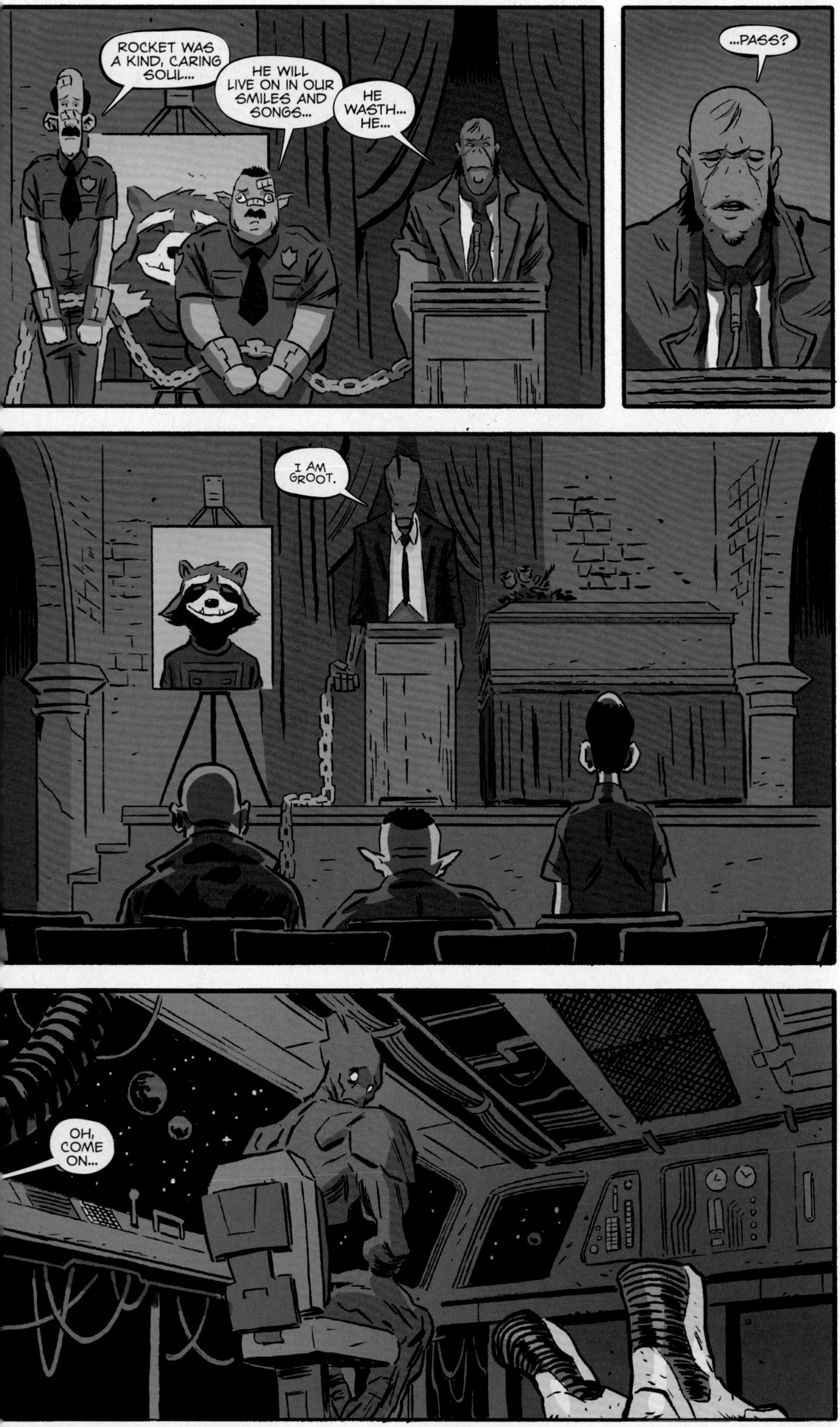
ROCKET WAS A KIND, CARING SOUL...
HE WILL LIVE ON IN OUR SMILES AND SONGS...
HE WASTH... HE...
...PASS?
I AM GROOT.
OH, COME ON...

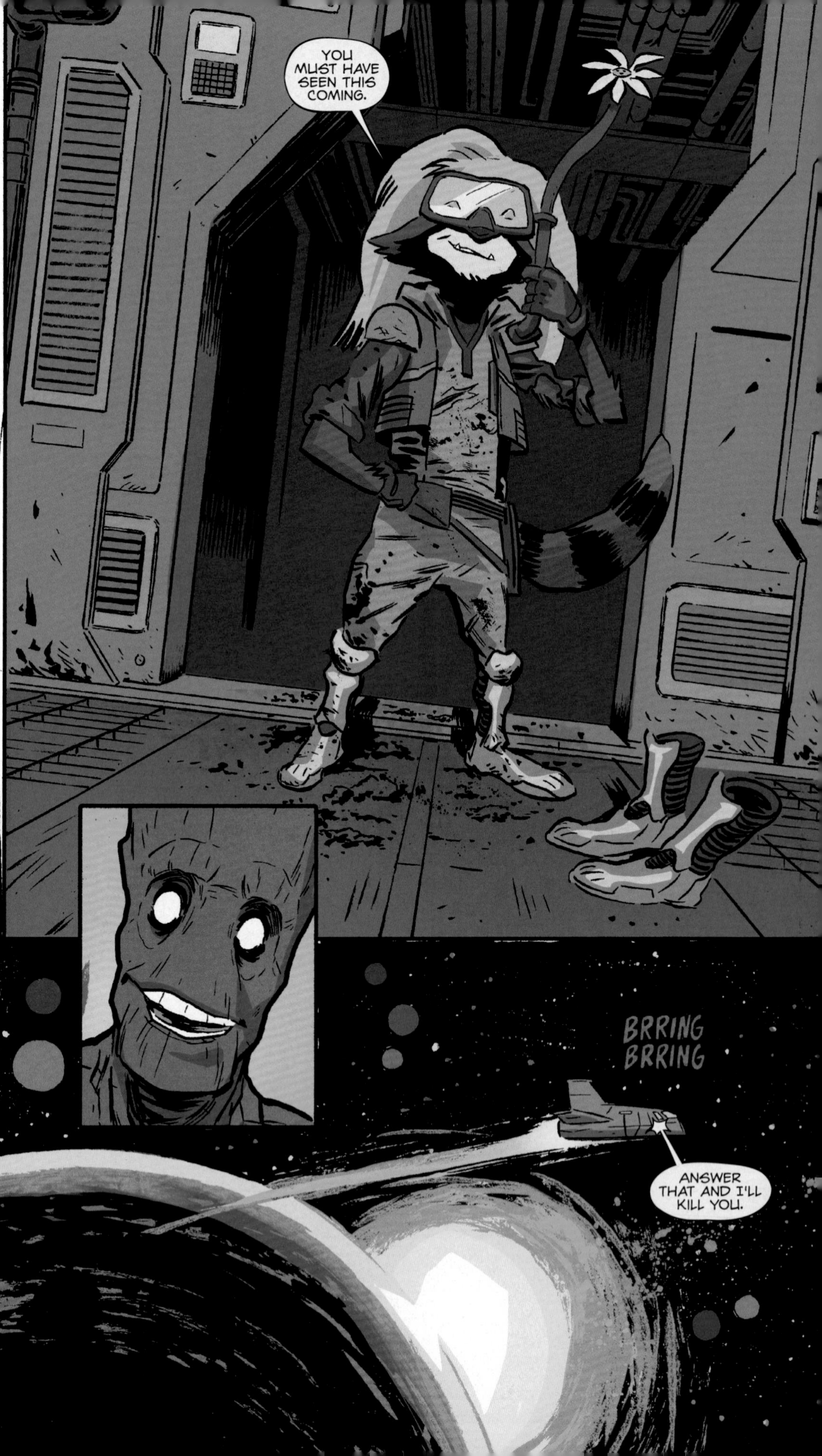
YOU MUST HAVE SEEN THIS COMING.
BRRING BRRING
ANSWER THAT AND I'LL KILL YOU.

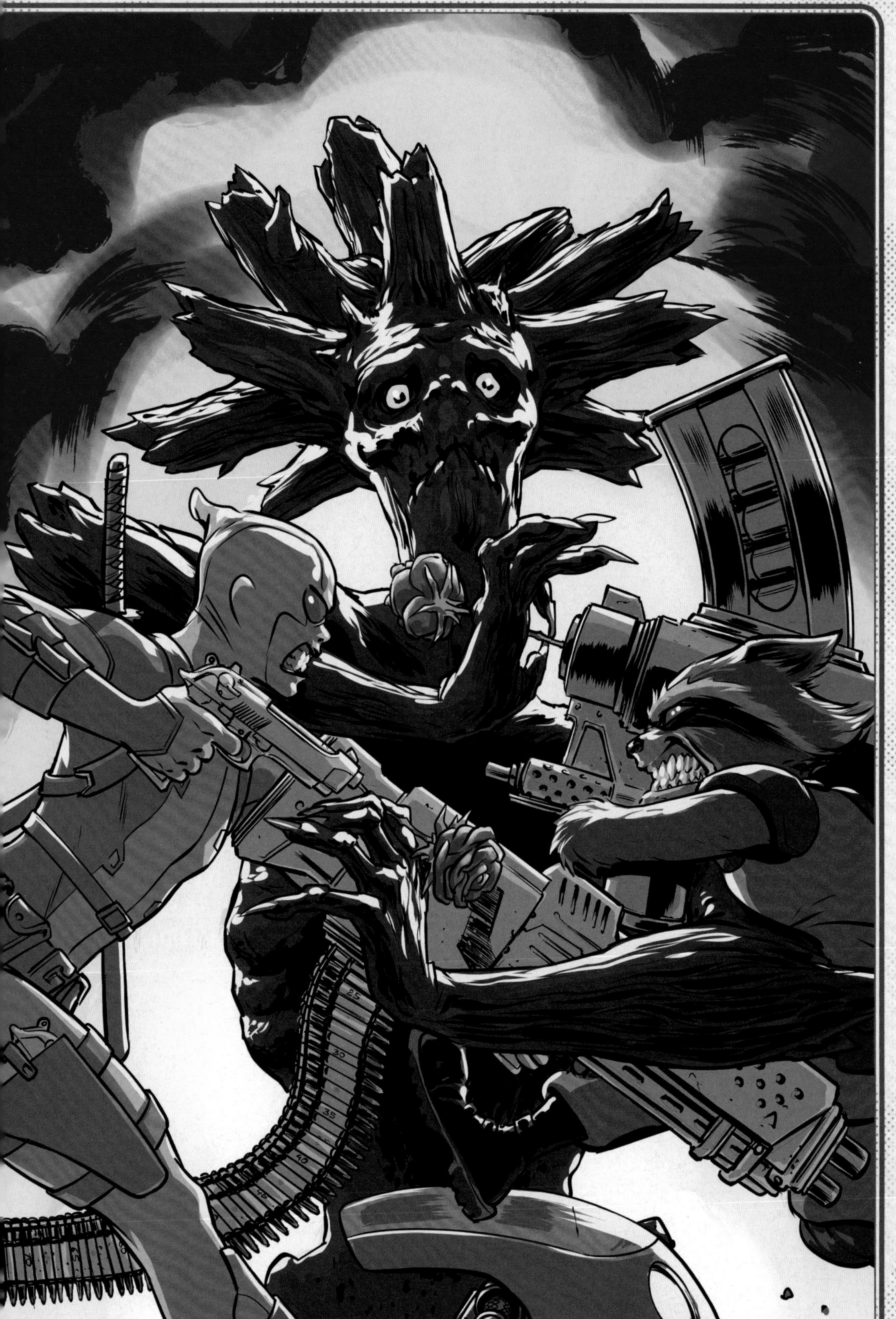
david lopez

EARTH'S HEROES PREVENTED A CATACLYSMIC EVENT
THANKS TO A NEW INHUMAN NAMED ULYSSES, WHO
SEEMS TO BE ABLE TO PREDICT THE FUTURE. NOW,
EARTH'S GREATEST CHAMPIONS ARE FORCED TO MAKE A
CHOICE: **PROTECT** THE FUTURE...OR **CHANGE** IT?

FORMER GUARDIANS OF THE GALAXY TEAMMATE AND
CURRENT COMMANDER OF ALPHA FLIGHT CAPTAIN
MARVEL WANTS TO **CHANGE** THE FUTURE TO **PROTECT**
THE STUFF IN IT. SHE'S ASKED ALL HER ALLIES TO HELP
RESPOND TO ULYSSES' PREDICTIONS, INCLUDING THE
GUARDIANS. ROCKET PILOTS THEIR SHIP, AND CAROL
COULDN'T JUST ASK HIM AND GROOT TO WAIT OUTSIDE.

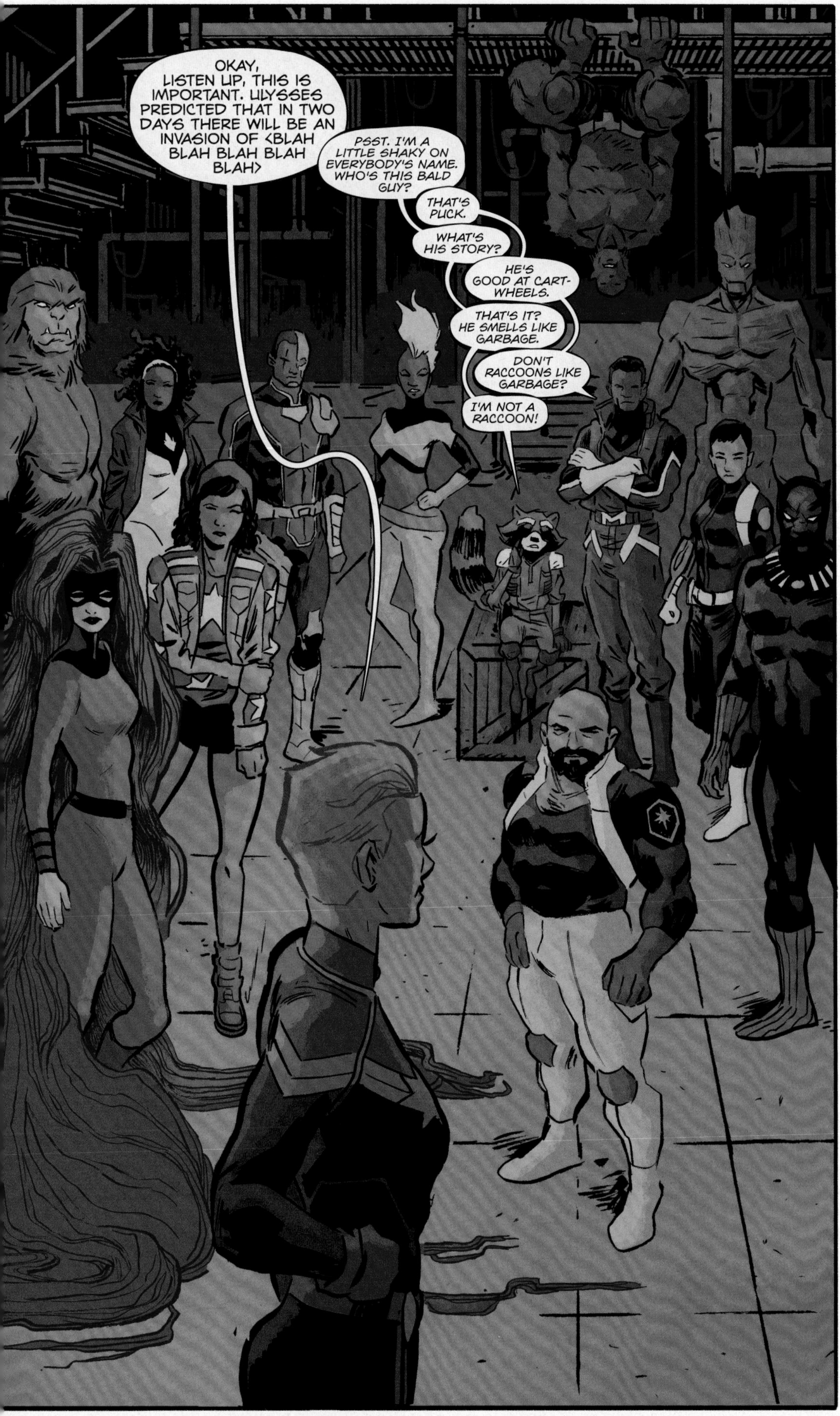
OKAY, LISTEN UP, THIS IS IMPORTANT. ULYSSES PREDICTED THAT IN TWO DAYS THERE WILL BE AN INVASION OF <BLAH BLAH BLAH BLAH BLAH>
PSST. I'M A LITTLE SHAKY ON EVERYBODY'S NAME. WHO'S THIS BALD GUY?
THAT'S PUCK.
WHAT'S HIS STORY?
HE'S GOOD AT CART-WHEELS.
THAT'S IT? HE SMELLS LIKE GARBAGE.
DON'T RACCOONS LIKE GARBAGE?
I'M NOT A RACCOON!

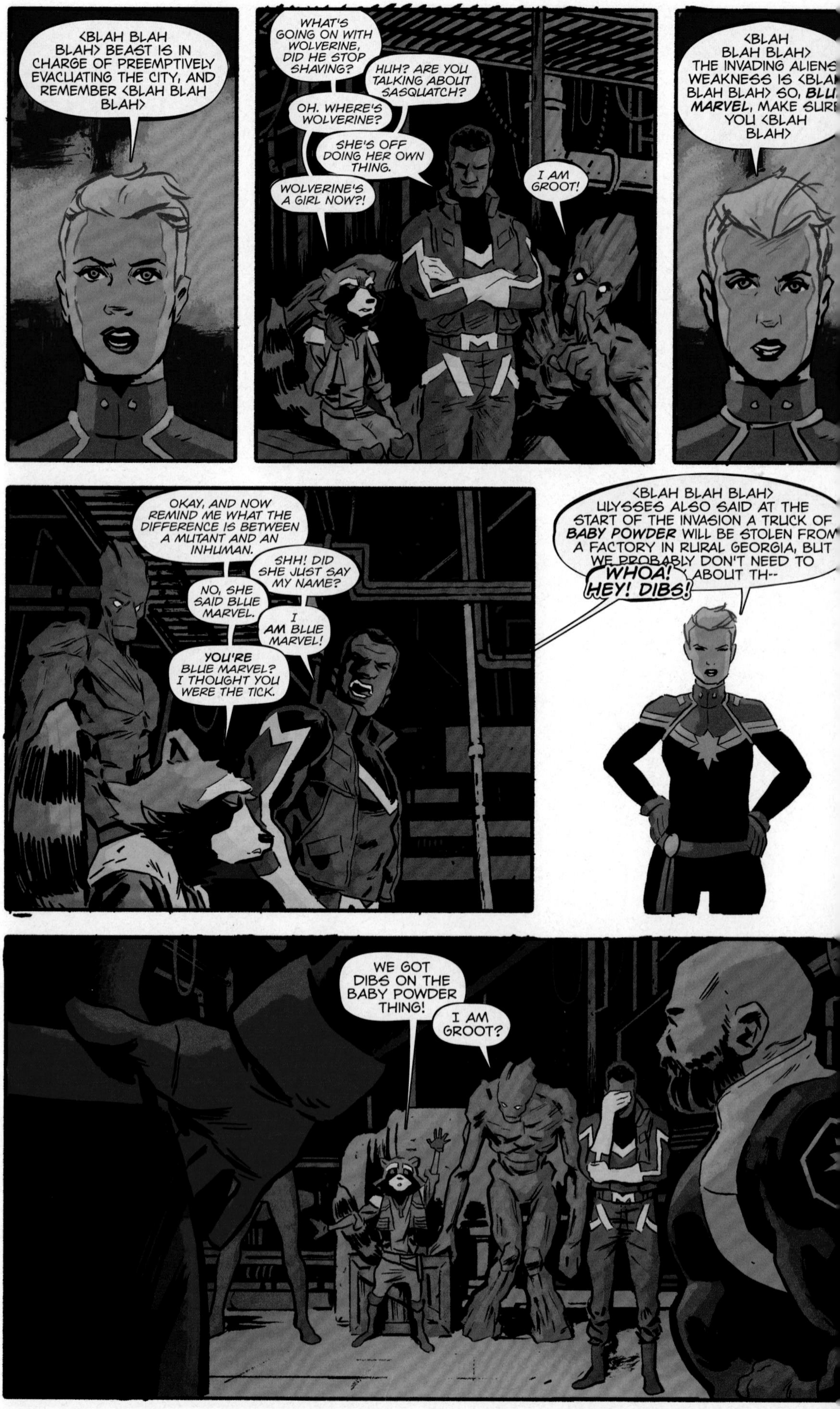
<BLAH BLAH BLAH> BEAST IS IN CHARGE OF PREEMPTIVELY EVACUATING THE CITY, AND REMEMBER <BLAH BLAH BLAH>
WHAT'S GOING ON WITH WOLVERINE, DID HE STOP SHAVING?
HUH? ARE YOU TALKING ABOUT SASQUATCH?
OH. WHERE'S WOLVERINE?
SHE'S OFF DOING HER OWN THING.
WOLVERINE'S A GIRL NOW?!
I AM GROOT!
<BLAH BLAH BLAH> THE INVADING ALIENS WEAKNESS IS <BLA BLAH BLAH> SO, **BLU MARVEL**, MAKE SURE YOU <BLAH BLAH>
OKAY, AND NOW REMIND ME WHAT THE DIFFERENCE IS BETWEEN A MUTANT AND AN INHUMAN.
SHH! DID SHE JUST SAY MY NAME?
NO, SHE SAID BLUE MARVEL.
I **AM** BLUE MARVEL!
YOU'RE BLUE MARVEL? I THOUGHT YOU WERE THE TICK.
<BLAH BLAH BLAH> ULYSSES ALSO SAID AT THE START OF THE INVASION A TRUCK OF **BABY POWDER** WILL BE STOLEN FROM A FACTORY IN RURAL GEORGIA, BUT WE PROBABLY DON'T NEED TO ABOUT TH--
WHOA! HEY! DIBS!
WE GOT DIBS ON THE BABY POWDER THING!
I AM GROOT?

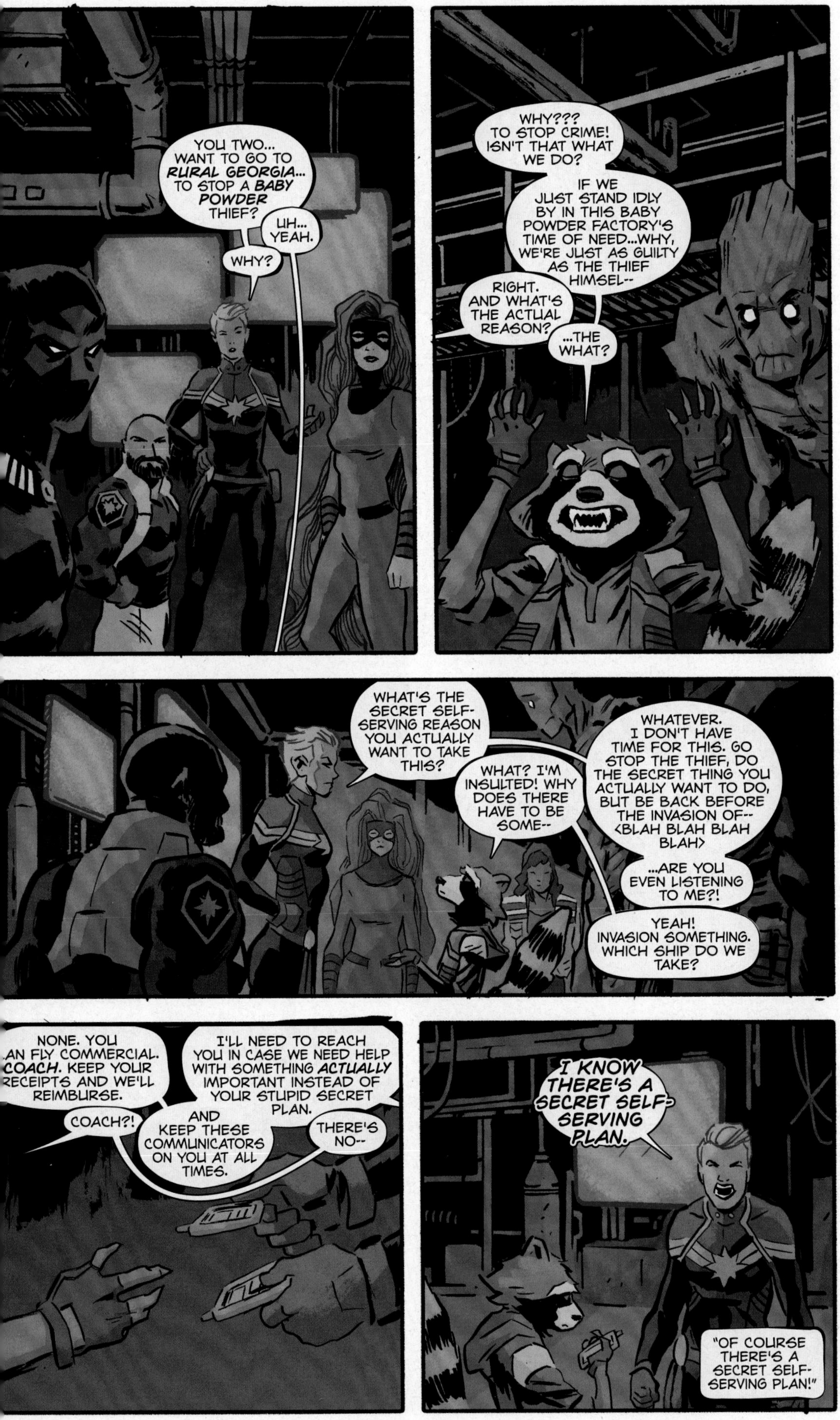
YOU TWO... WANT TO GO TO RURAL GEORGIA... TO STOP A BABY POWDER THIEF?
UH... YEAH.
WHY?
WHY??? TO STOP CRIME! ISN'T THAT WHAT WE DO?
IF WE JUST STAND IDLY BY IN THIS BABY POWDER FACTORY'S TIME OF NEED...WHY, WE'RE JUST AS GUILTY AS THE THIEF HIMSEL--
RIGHT. AND WHAT'S THE ACTUAL REASON?
...THE WHAT?
WHAT'S THE SECRET SELF-SERVING REASON YOU ACTUALLY WANT TO TAKE THIS?
WHAT? I'M INSULTED! WHY DOES THERE HAVE TO BE SOME--
WHATEVER. I DON'T HAVE TIME FOR THIS. GO STOP THE THIEF, DO THE SECRET THING YOU ACTUALLY WANT TO DO, BUT BE BACK BEFORE THE INVASION OF-- <BLAH BLAH BLAH BLAH>
...ARE YOU EVEN LISTENING TO ME?!
YEAH! INVASION SOMETHING. WHICH SHIP DO WE TAKE?
NONE. YOU CAN FLY COMMERCIAL. COACH. KEEP YOUR RECEIPTS AND WE'LL REIMBURSE.
COACH?!
I'LL NEED TO REACH YOU IN CASE WE NEED HELP WITH SOMETHING ACTUALLY IMPORTANT INSTEAD OF YOUR STUPID SECRET PLAN.
AND KEEP THESE COMMUNICATORS ON YOU AT ALL TIMES.
THERE'S NO--
I KNOW THERE'S A SECRET SELF-SERVING PLAN.
"OF COURSE THERE'S A SECRET SELF-SERVING PLAN!"

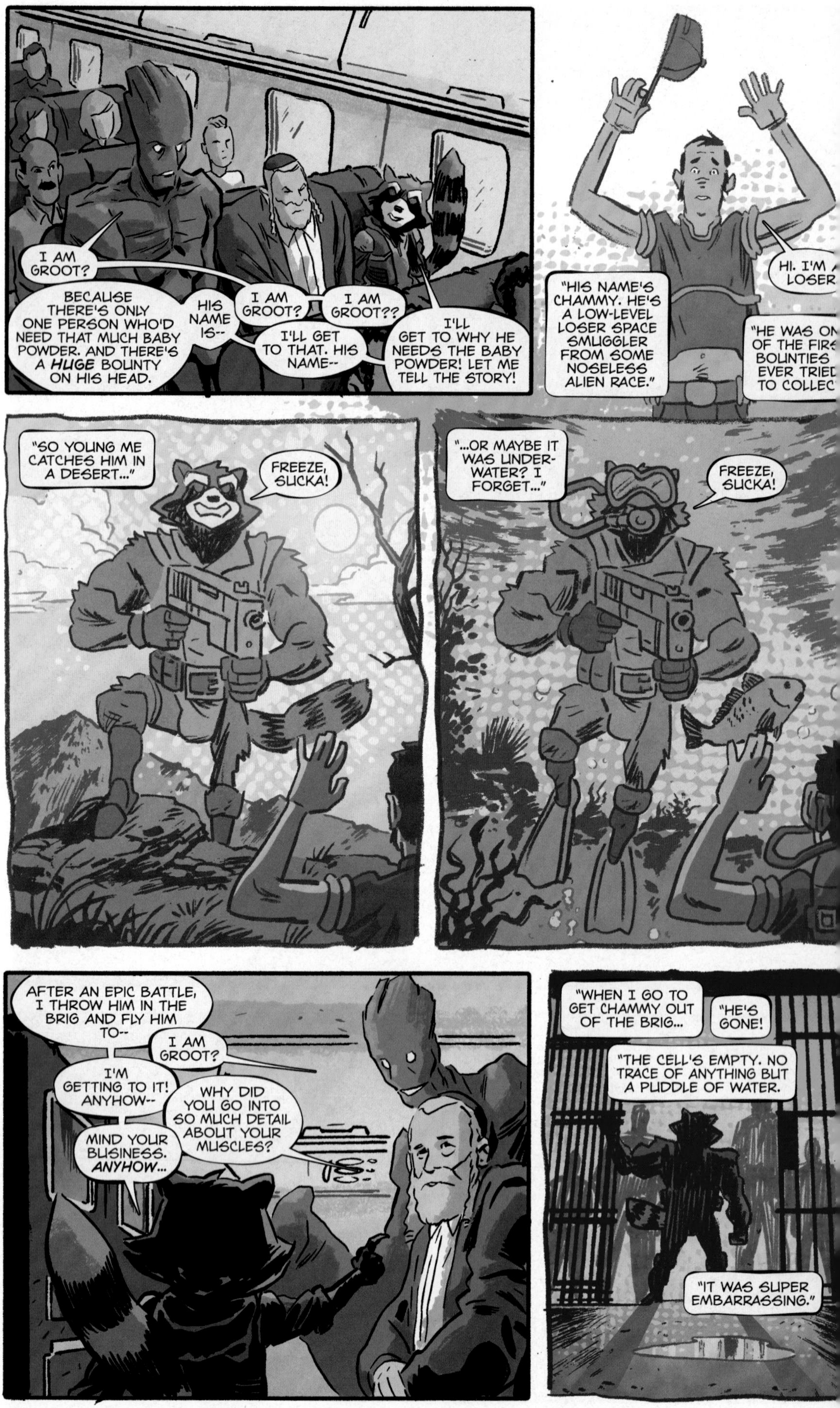
I AM GROOT?
BECAUSE THERE'S ONLY ONE PERSON WHO'D NEED THAT MUCH BABY POWDER. AND THERE'S A *HUGE* BOUNTY ON HIS HEAD.
HIS NAME IS--
I AM GROOT?
I AM GROOT??
I'LL GET TO THAT. HIS NAME--
I'LL GET TO WHY HE NEEDS THE BABY POWDER! LET ME TELL THE STORY!
"HIS NAME'S CHAMMY. HE'S A LOW-LEVEL LOSER SPACE SMUGGLER FROM SOME NOSELESS ALIEN RACE."
HI. I'M A LOSER
"HE WAS ON OF THE FIRS BOUNTIES EVER TRIED TO COLLEC
"SO YOUNG ME CATCHES HIM IN A DESERT..."
FREEZE, SUCKA!
"...OR MAYBE IT WAS UNDER-WATER? I FORGET..."
FREEZE, SUCKA!
AFTER AN EPIC BATTLE, I THROW HIM IN THE BRIG AND FLY HIM TO--
I AM GROOT?
I'M GETTING TO IT! ANYHOW--
WHY DID YOU GO INTO SO MUCH DETAIL ABOUT YOUR MUSCLES?
MIND YOUR BUSINESS. *ANYHOW*...
"WHEN I GO TO GET CHAMMY OUT OF THE BRIG...
"HE'S GONE!
"THE CELL'S EMPTY. NO TRACE OF ANYTHING BUT A PUDDLE OF WATER.
"IT WAS SUPER EMBARRASSING."

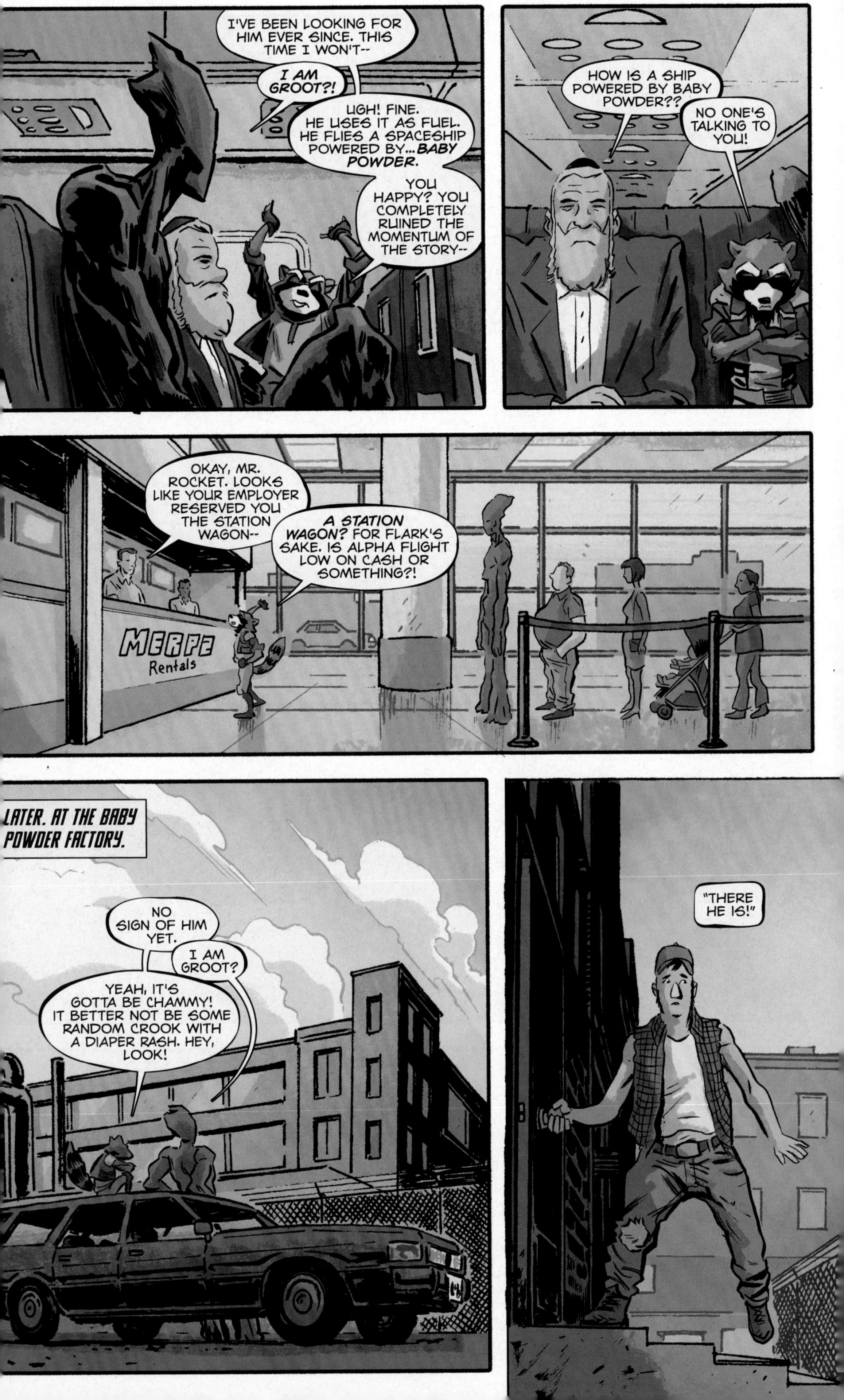

I'VE BEEN LOOKING FOR HIM EVER SINCE. THIS TIME I WON'T--
I AM GROOT?!
UGH! FINE. HE USES IT AS FUEL. HE FLIES A SPACESHIP POWERED BY... BABY POWDER.
YOU HAPPY? YOU COMPLETELY RUINED THE MOMENTUM OF THE STORY--
HOW IS A SHIP POWERED BY BABY POWDER??
NO ONE'S TALKING TO YOU!
OKAY, MR. ROCKET. LOOKS LIKE YOUR EMPLOYER RESERVED YOU THE STATION WAGON--
A STATION WAGON? FOR FLARK'S SAKE. IS ALPHA FLIGHT LOW ON CASH OR SOMETHING?!
MERPZ
Rentals
LATER. AT THE BABY POWDER FACTORY.
NO SIGN OF HIM YET.
I AM GROOT?
YEAH, IT'S GOTTA BE CHAMMY! IT BETTER NOT BE SOME RANDOM CROOK WITH A DIAPER RASH. HEY, LOOK!
"THERE HE IS!"

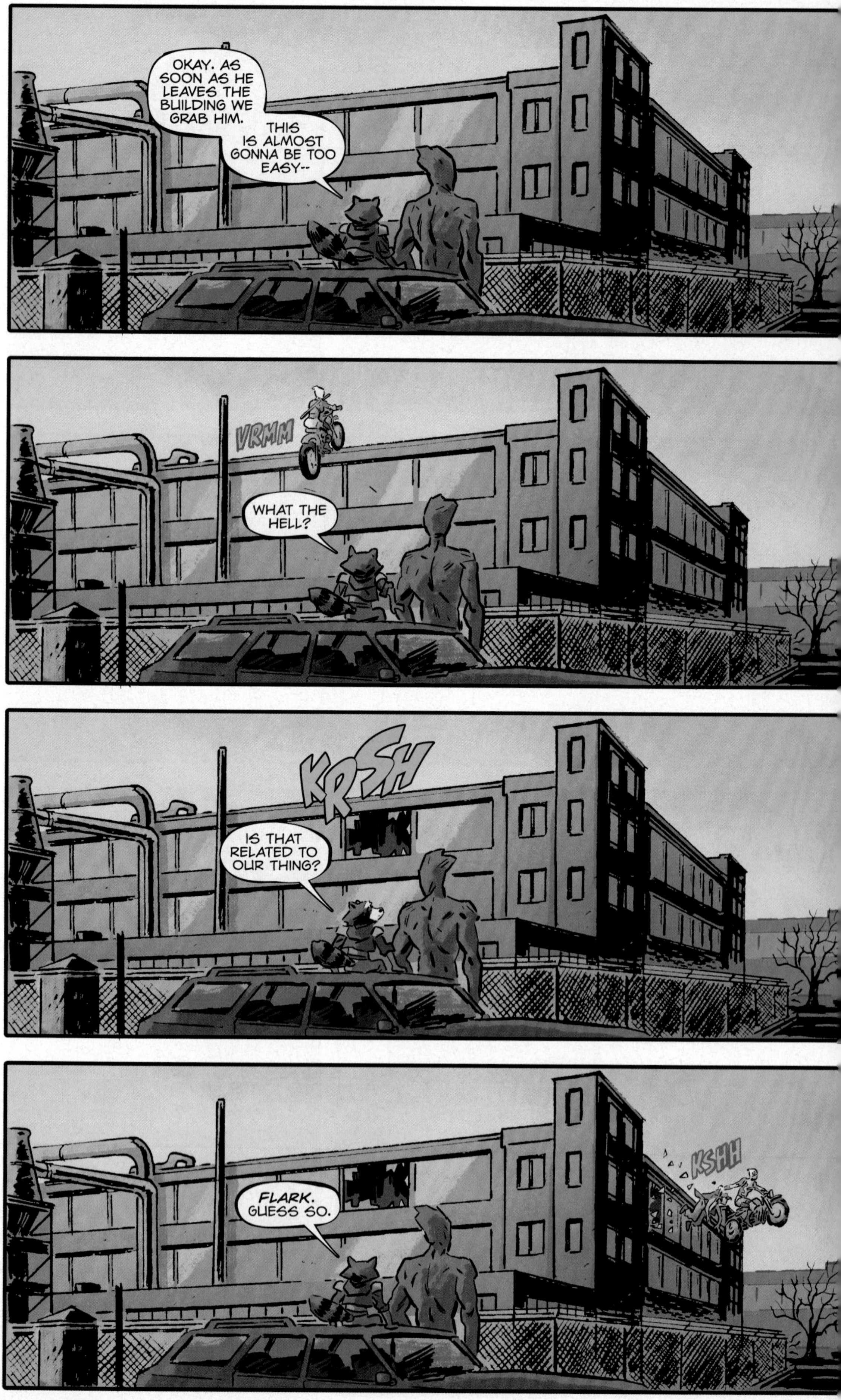
OKAY. AS SOON AS HE LEAVES THE BUILDING WE GRAB HIM.
THIS IS ALMOST GONNA BE TOO EASY--
VRMM
WHAT THE HELL?
KRSH
IS THAT RELATED TO OUR THING?
KSHH
FLARK. GUESS SO.

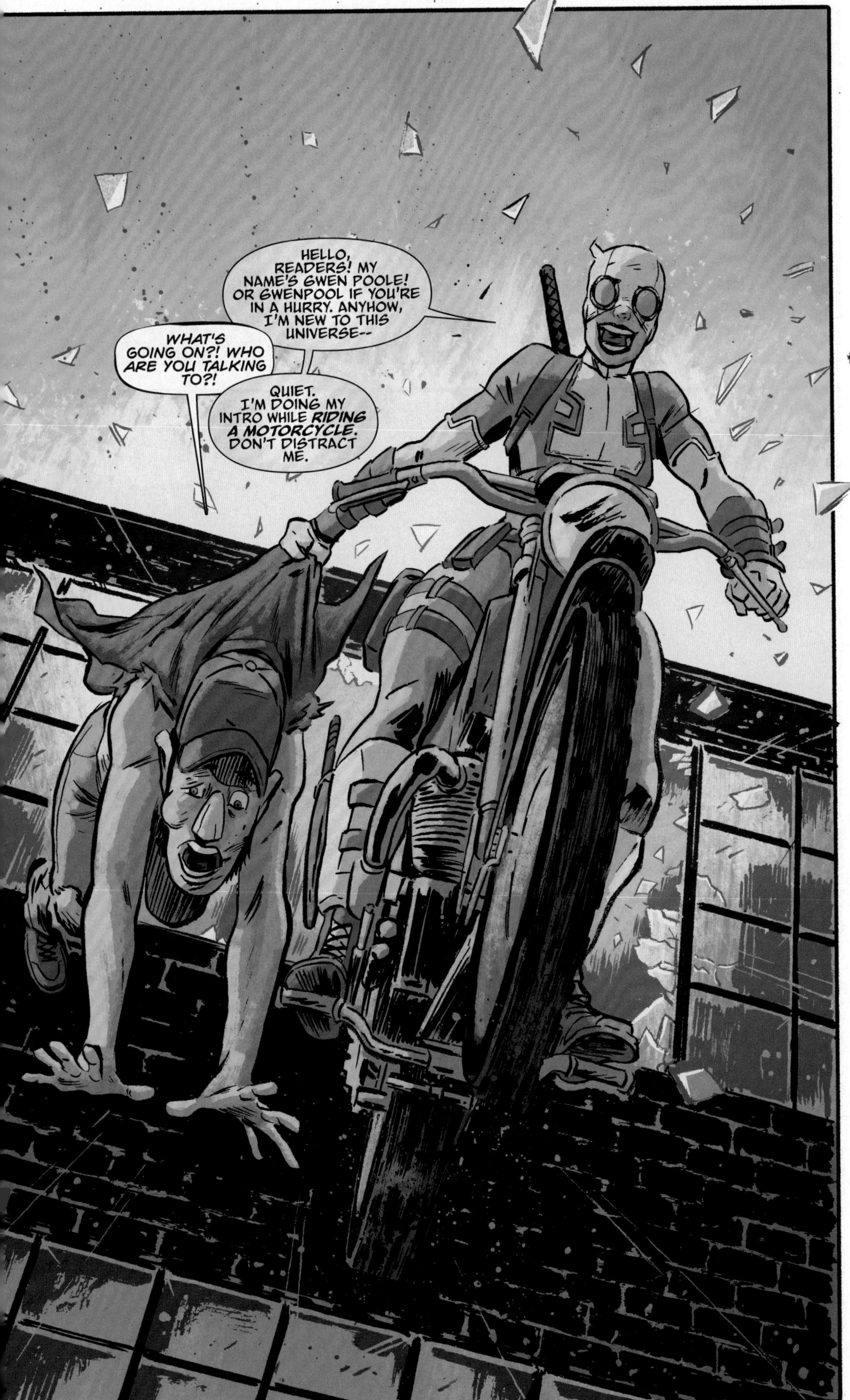
HELLO, READERS! MY NAME'S GWEN POOLE! OR GWENPOOL IF YOU'RE IN A HURRY. ANYHOW, I'M NEW TO THIS UNIVERSE--
WHAT'S GOING ON?! WHO ARE YOU TALKING TO?!
QUIET. I'M DOING MY INTRO WHILE *RIDING A MOTORCYCLE*. DON'T DISTRACT ME.

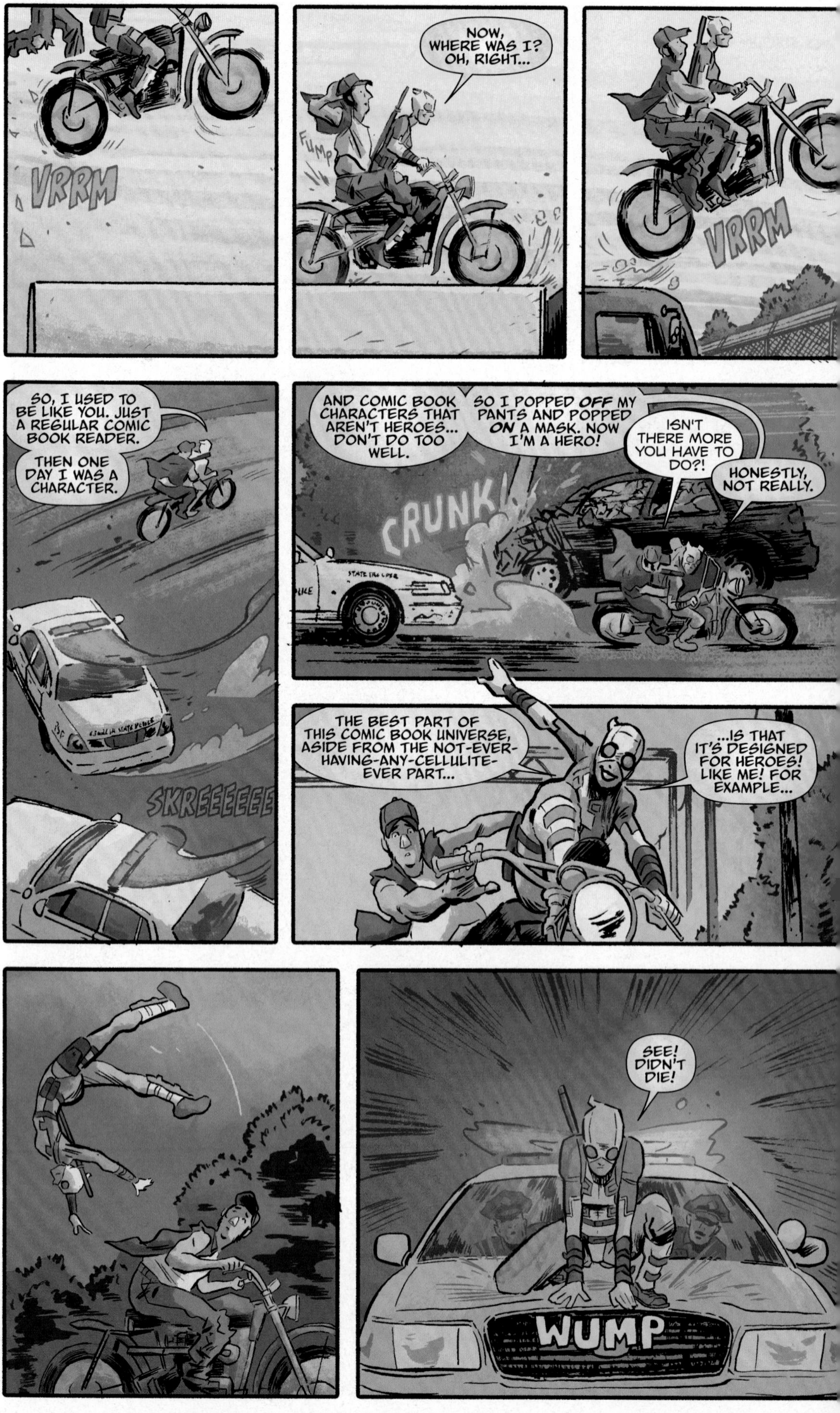
VRRM
NOW, WHERE WAS I? OH, RIGHT...
FUMP
VRRM
SO, I USED TO BE LIKE YOU. JUST A REGULAR COMIC BOOK READER.
THEN ONE DAY I WAS A CHARACTER.
SKREEEEEEE
AND COMIC BOOK CHARACTERS THAT AREN'T HEROES... DON'T DO TOO WELL.
SO I POPPED OFF MY PANTS AND POPPED ON A MASK. NOW I'M A HERO!
ISN'T THERE MORE YOU HAVE TO DO?!
HONESTLY, NOT REALLY.
CRUNK
THE BEST PART OF THIS COMIC BOOK UNIVERSE, ASIDE FROM THE NOT-EVER-HAVING-ANY-CELLULITE-EVER PART...
...IS THAT IT'S DESIGNED FOR HEROES! LIKE ME! FOR EXAMPLE...
SEE! DIDN'T DIE!
WUMP

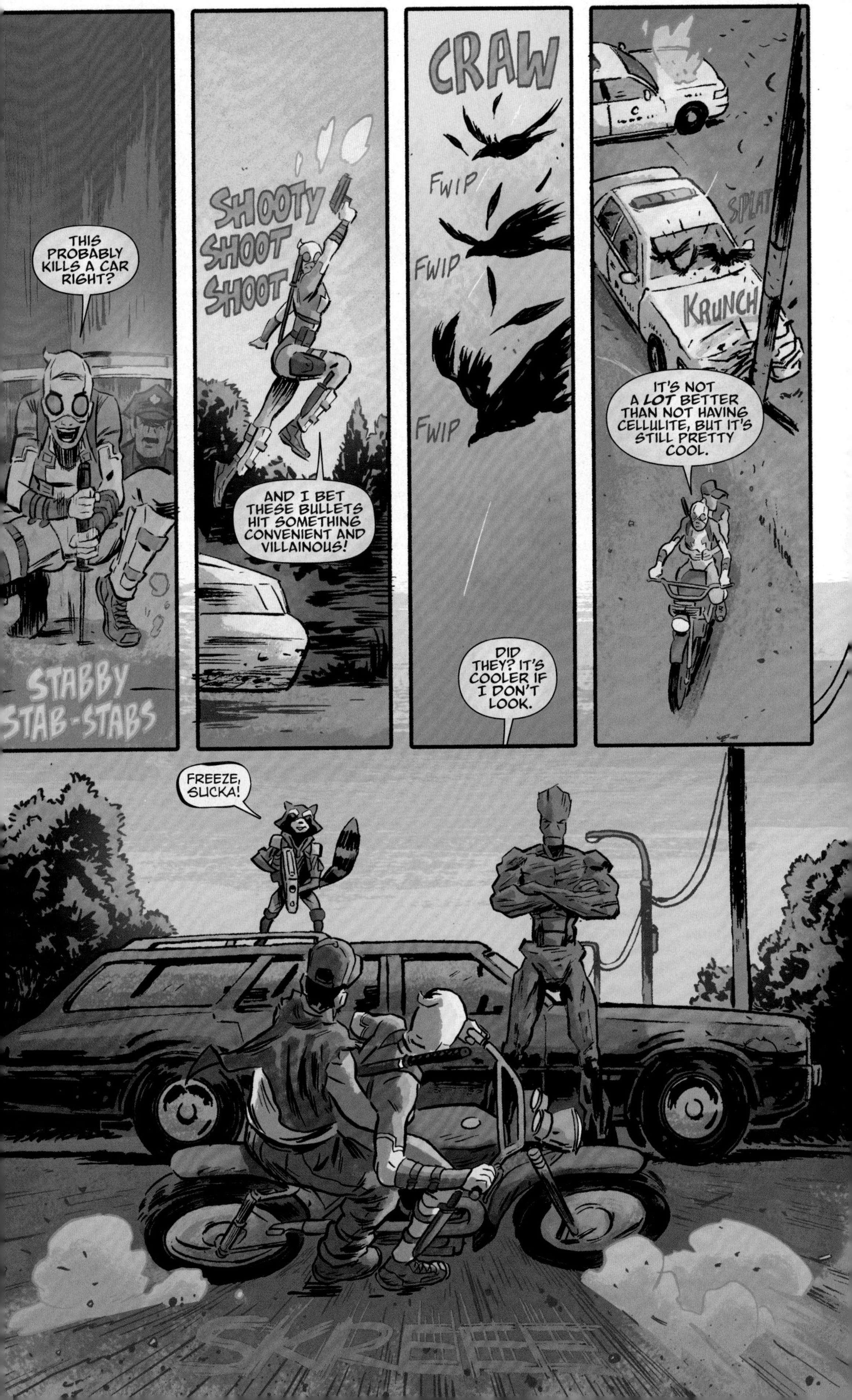

THIS PROBABLY KILLS A CAR RIGHT?
STABBY STAB-STABS
SHOOTY SHOOT SHOOT
AND I BET THESE BULLETS HIT SOMETHING CONVENIENT AND VILLAINOUS!
CRAW
FWIP
FWIP
FWIP
DID THEY? IT'S COOLER IF I DON'T LOOK.
SPLAT
KRUNCH
IT'S NOT A LOT BETTER THAN NOT HAVING CELLULITE, BUT IT'S STILL PRETTY COOL.
FREEZE, SUCKA!
SKREEE

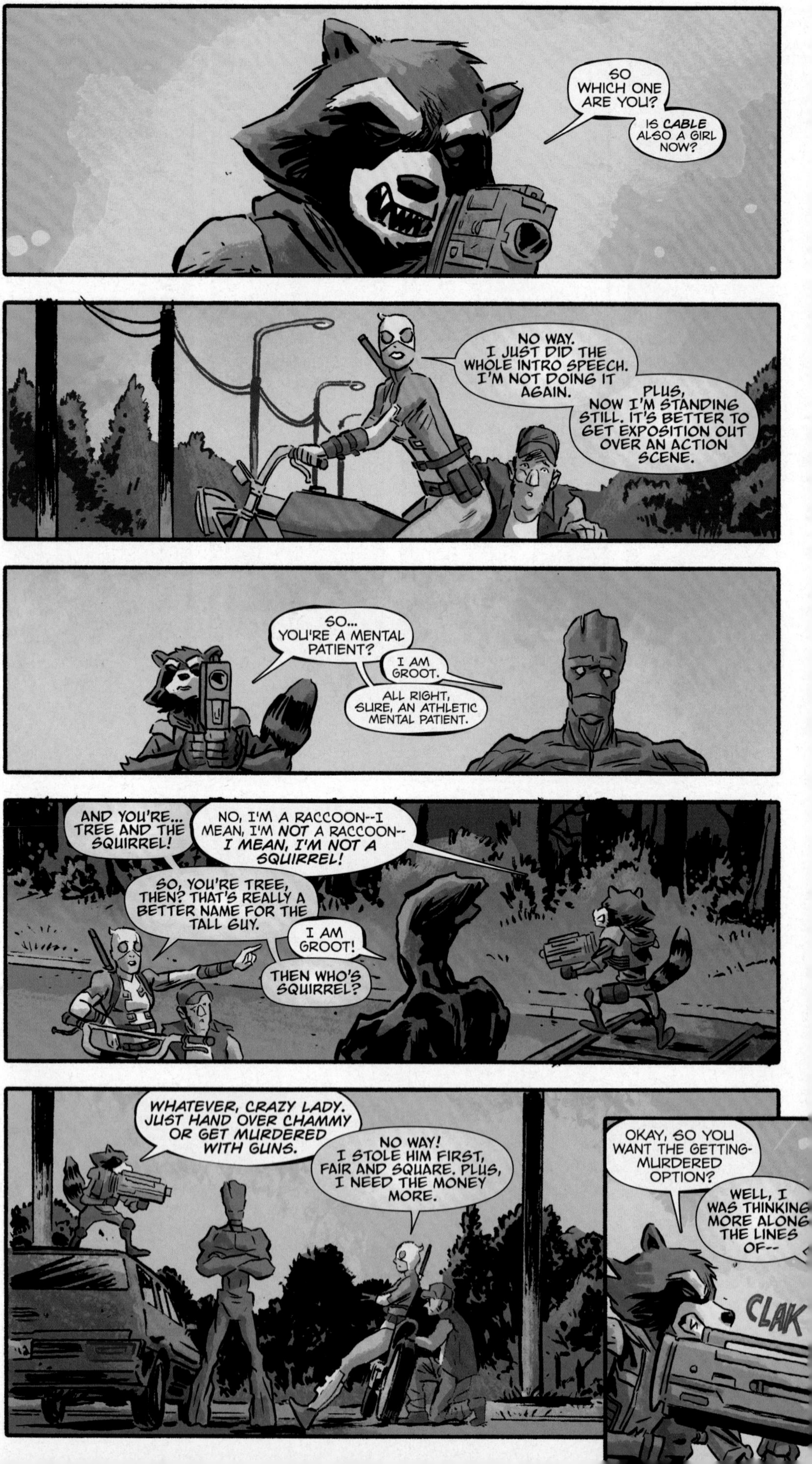
SO WHICH ONE ARE YOU?
IS CABLE ALSO A GIRL NOW?
NO WAY. I JUST DID THE WHOLE INTRO SPEECH. I'M NOT DOING IT AGAIN.
PLUS, NOW I'M STANDING STILL. IT'S BETTER TO GET EXPOSITION OUT OVER AN ACTION SCENE.
SO... YOU'RE A MENTAL PATIENT?
I AM GROOT.
ALL RIGHT, SURE, AN ATHLETIC MENTAL PATIENT.
AND YOU'RE... TREE AND THE SQUIRREL!
NO, I'M A RACCOON--I MEAN, I'M NOT A RACCOON-- I MEAN, I'M NOT A SQUIRREL!
SO, YOU'RE TREE, THEN? THAT'S REALLY A BETTER NAME FOR THE TALL GUY.
I AM GROOT!
THEN WHO'S SQUIRREL?
WHATEVER, CRAZY LADY. JUST HAND OVER CHAMMY OR GET MURDERED WITH GUNS.
NO WAY! I STOLE HIM FIRST, FAIR AND SQUARE. PLUS, I NEED THE MONEY MORE.
OKAY, SO YOU WANT THE GETTING-MURDERED OPTION?
WELL, I WAS THINKING MORE ALONG THE LINES OF--
CLAK

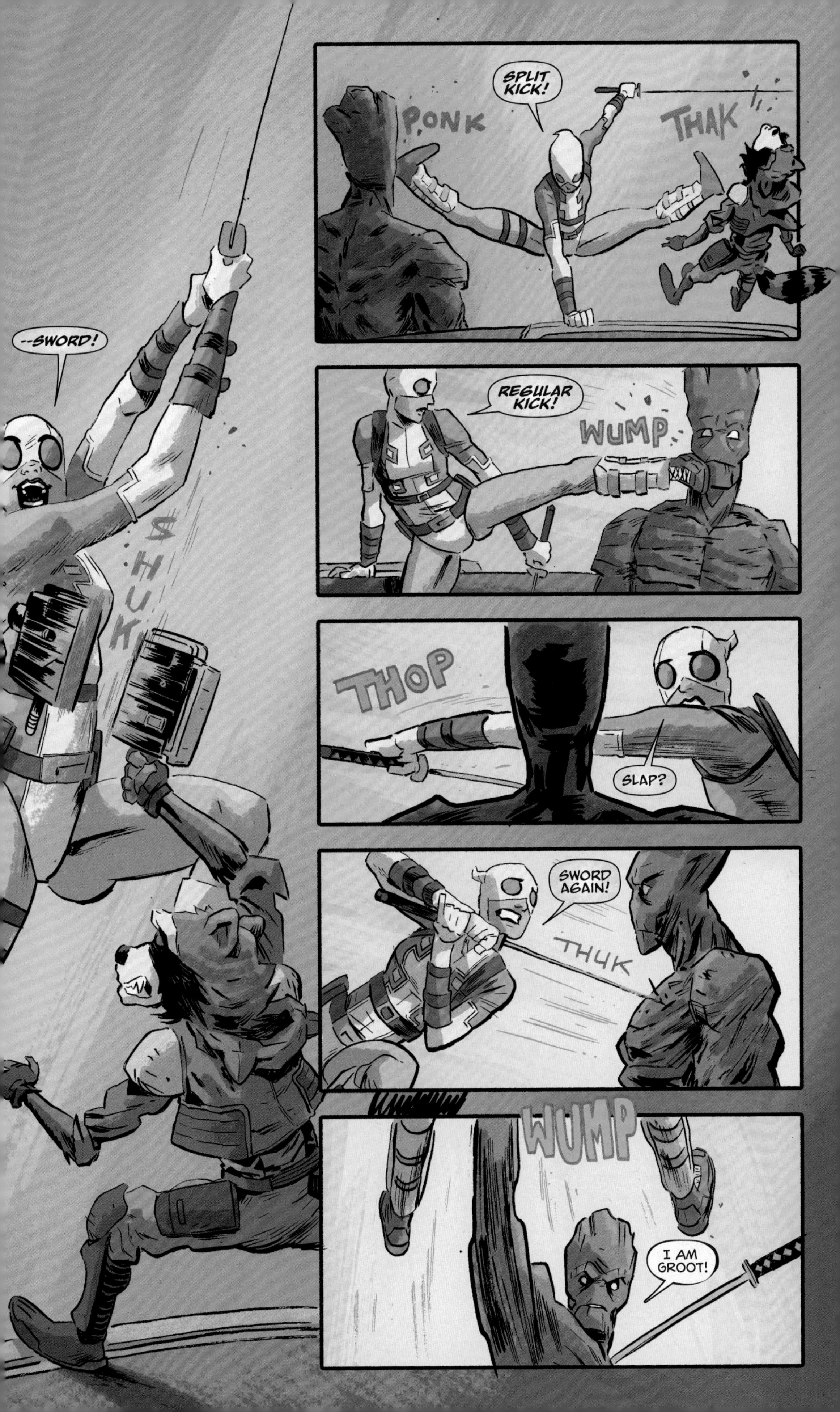
--SWORD!
SHUK
SPLIT KICK!
PONK
THAK
REGULAR KICK!
WUMP
THOP
SLAP?
SWORD AGAIN!
THUK
WUMP
I AM GROOT!

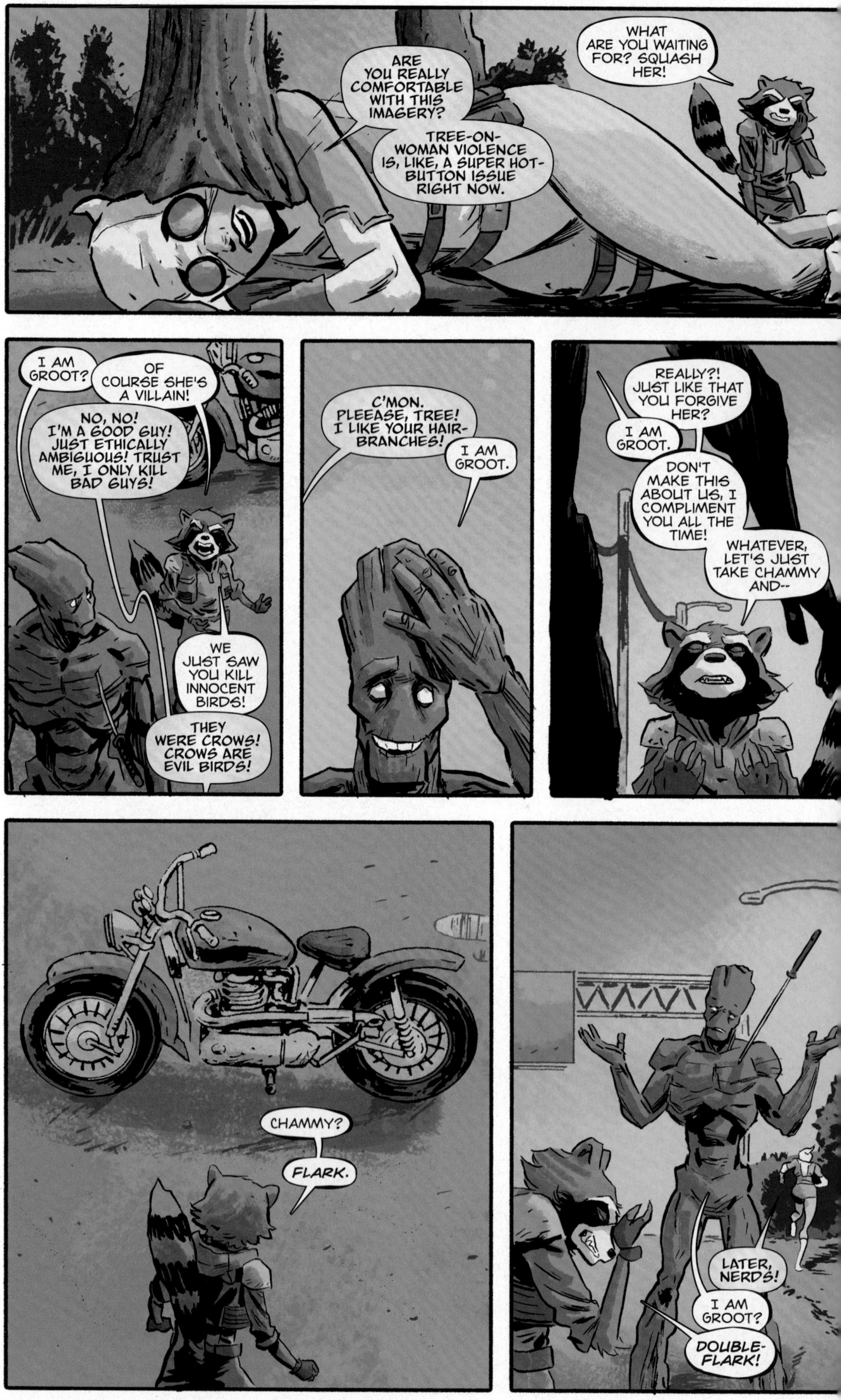
ARE YOU REALLY COMFORTABLE WITH THIS IMAGERY?
TREE-ON-WOMAN VIOLENCE IS, LIKE, A SUPER HOT-BUTTON ISSUE RIGHT NOW.
WHAT ARE YOU WAITING FOR? SQUASH HER!
I AM GROOT?
OF COURSE SHE'S A VILLAIN!
NO, NO! I'M A GOOD GUY! JUST ETHICALLY AMBIGUOUS! TRUST ME, I ONLY KILL BAD GUYS!
WE JUST SAW YOU KILL INNOCENT BIRDS!
THEY WERE CROWS! CROWS ARE EVIL BIRDS!
C'MON. PLEEASE, TREE! I LIKE YOUR HAIR-BRANCHES!
I AM GROOT.
REALLY?! JUST LIKE THAT YOU FORGIVE HER?
I AM GROOT.
DON'T MAKE THIS ABOUT US, I COMPLIMENT YOU ALL THE TIME!
WHATEVER, LET'S JUST TAKE CHAMMY AND--
CHAMMY?
FLARK.
LATER, NERDS!
I AM GROOT?
DOUBLE-FLARK!

WHERE HAVE YOU BEEN? WHAT HAPPENED TO YOUR FACE?

UH...I GOT INTO A BAR FIGHT. SORRY.

IT'S 2PM! IT'D BE EARLY TO EVEN *START* DRINKING, LET ALONE--

RIGHT. I'M HEARING YOU. I'M SORRY.

WHO WERE YOU FIGHTING WITH?

I'M SORRY. I HEAR YOU.

WHAT? ANSWER THE QUESTION!

UH... I'M HEARING YOU...AND I'M SORRY.

STOP SAYING THAT!

I NEED TO GO TO THE BATHROOM.

WHAT DO YOU DO IN THAT BATHROOM? YOU SPEND WAY TOO MUCH TIME IN THERE!

CLIK

VRRRRRRR

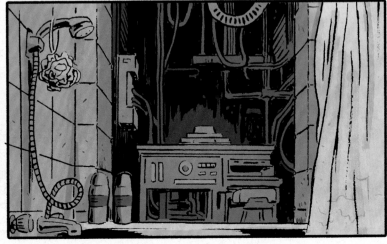

YOU DIDN'T GET THE TALCUM POWDER? WHAT HAPPENED?! WAS IT *REEVE*?

NO, NO. IT WAS-- DON'T WORRY ABOUT IT. BUT I NEED TO FIND ANOTHER WAY OFF THE PLANET!

OR A SHIP THAT'S POWERED BY SOMETHING LESS RIDICULOUS!

ALL RIGHT, I'LL SEE WHAT I CAN WORK OUT.

HAVE YOU TOLD RUTH YET?

NOT YET. BUT SHE DEFINITELY KNOWS SOMETHING'S UP.

WE'VE BEEN FIGHTING.

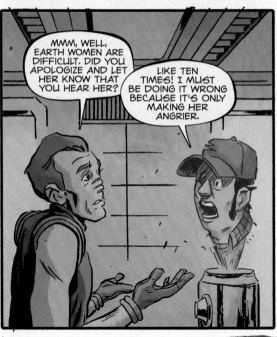

MMM, WELL, EARTH WOMEN ARE DIFFICULT. DID YOU APOLOGIZE AND LET HER KNOW THAT YOU HEAR HER?

LIKE TEN TIMES! I MUST BE DOING IT WRONG BECAUSE IT'S ONLY MAKING HER ANGRIER.

WELL, THAT'S ALL I GOT. MAYBE *BUY* HER SOME-THING?

KRUNK

KRAK

"AND THEN I FINISHED THEM OFF WITH THIS AWESOME SPLIT KICK..."

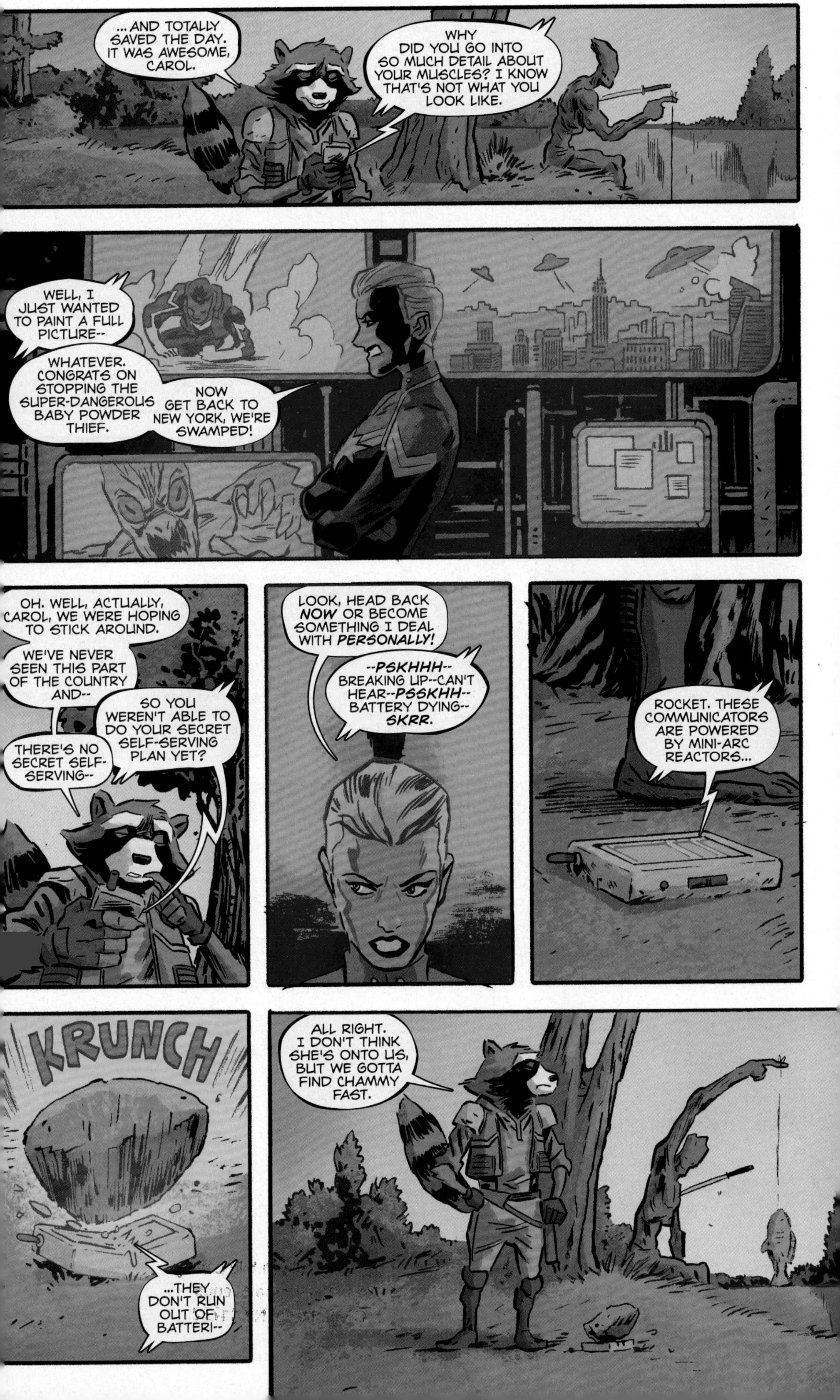
...AND TOTALLY SAVED THE DAY. IT WAS AWESOME, CAROL.
WHY DID YOU GO INTO SO MUCH DETAIL ABOUT YOUR MUSCLES? I KNOW THAT'S NOT WHAT YOU LOOK LIKE.
WELL, I JUST WANTED TO PAINT A FULL PICTURE--
WHATEVER. CONGRATS ON STOPPING THE SUPER-DANGEROUS BABY POWDER THIEF.
NOW GET BACK TO NEW YORK, WE'RE SWAMPED!
OH. WELL, ACTUALLY, CAROL, WE WERE HOPING TO STICK AROUND.
WE'VE NEVER SEEN THIS PART OF THE COUNTRY AND--
SO YOU WEREN'T ABLE TO DO YOUR SECRET SELF-SERVING PLAN YET?
THERE'S NO SECRET SELF-SERVING--
LOOK, HEAD BACK NOW OR BECOME SOMETHING I DEAL WITH PERSONALLY!
--PSKHHH-- BREAKING UP--CAN'T HEAR--PSSKHH-- BATTERY DYING-- SKRR.
ROCKET. THESE COMMUNICATORS ARE POWERED BY MINI-ARC REACTORS...
KRUNCH
...THEY DON'T RUN OUT OF BATTERI--
ALL RIGHT. I DON'T THINK SHE'S ONTO US, BUT WE GOTTA FIND CHAMMY FAST.

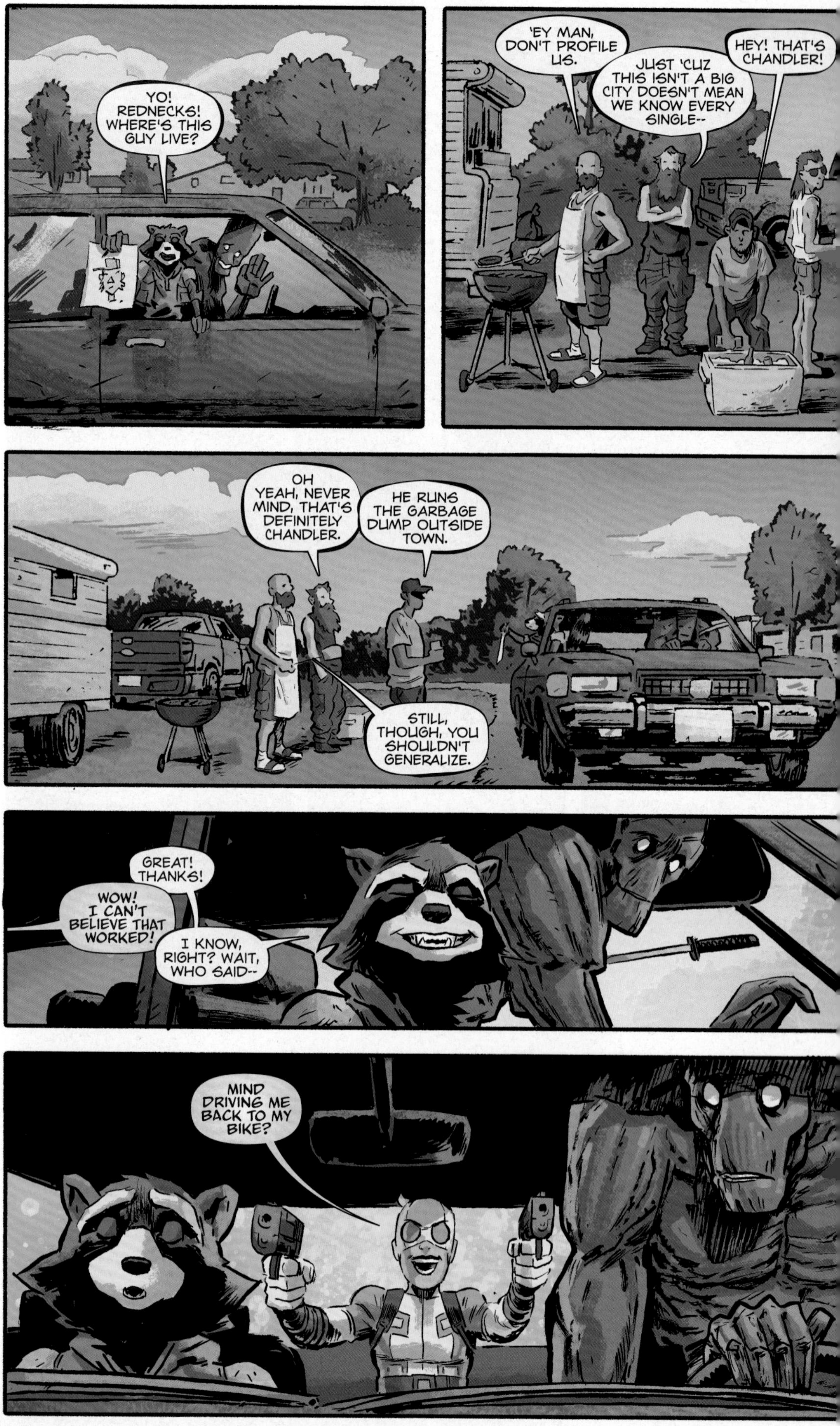

YO! REDNECKS! WHERE'S THIS GUY LIVE?
'EY MAN, DON'T PROFILE US.
JUST 'CUZ THIS ISN'T A BIG CITY DOESN'T MEAN WE KNOW EVERY SINGLE--
HEY! THAT'S CHANDLER!
OH YEAH, NEVER MIND, THAT'S DEFINITELY CHANDLER.
HE RUNS THE GARBAGE DUMP OUTSIDE TOWN.
STILL, THOUGH, YOU SHOULDN'T GENERALIZE.
GREAT! THANKS!
WOW! I CAN'T BELIEVE THAT WORKED!
I KNOW, RIGHT? WAIT, WHO SAID--
MIND DRIVING ME BACK TO MY BIKE?

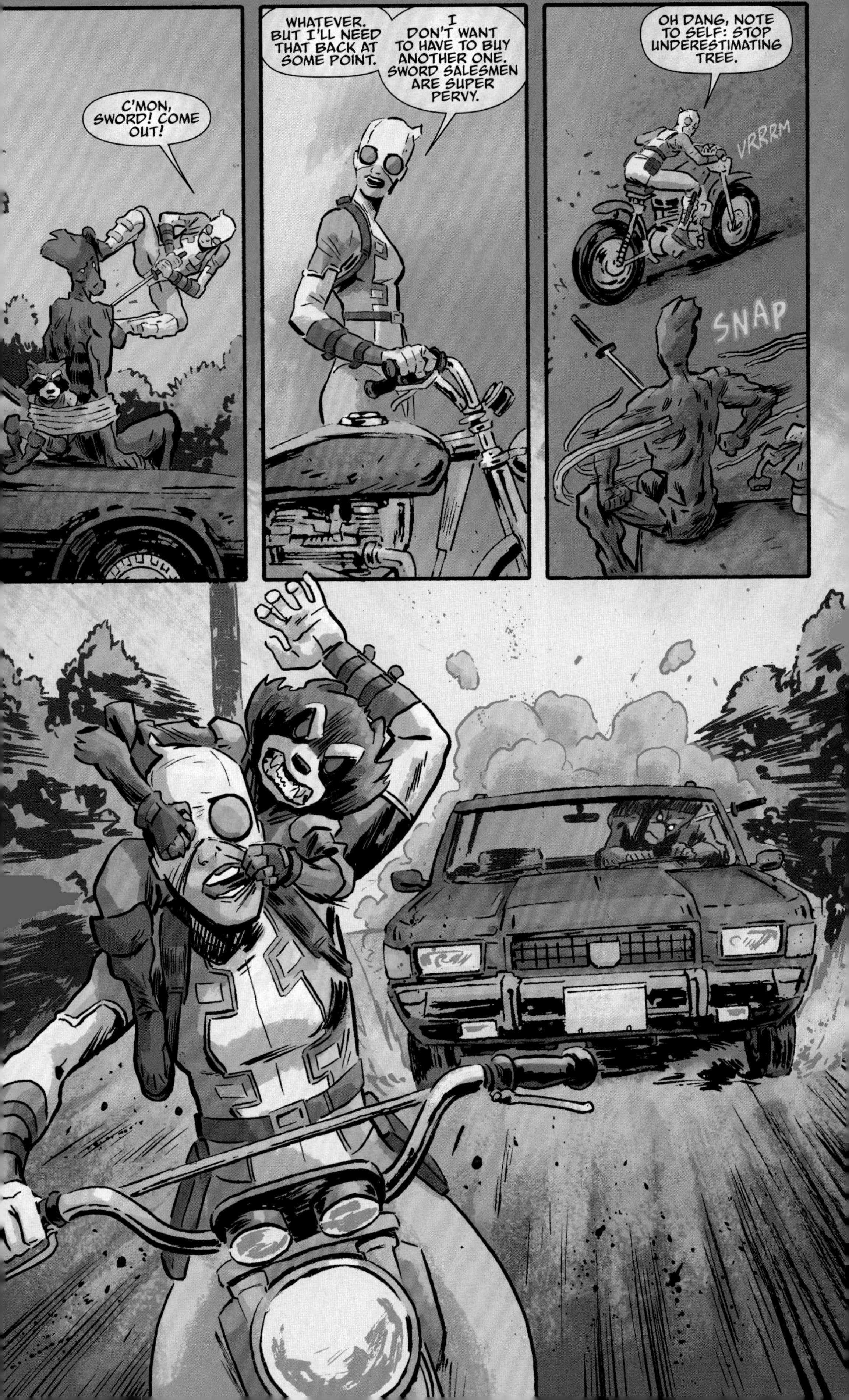
C'MON, SWORD! COME OUT!
WHATEVER. BUT I'LL NEED THAT BACK AT SOME POINT.
I DON'T WANT TO HAVE TO BUY ANOTHER ONE. SWORD SALESMEN ARE SUPER PERVY.
OH DANG, NOTE TO SELF: STOP UNDERESTIMATING TREE.
VRRRM
SNAP

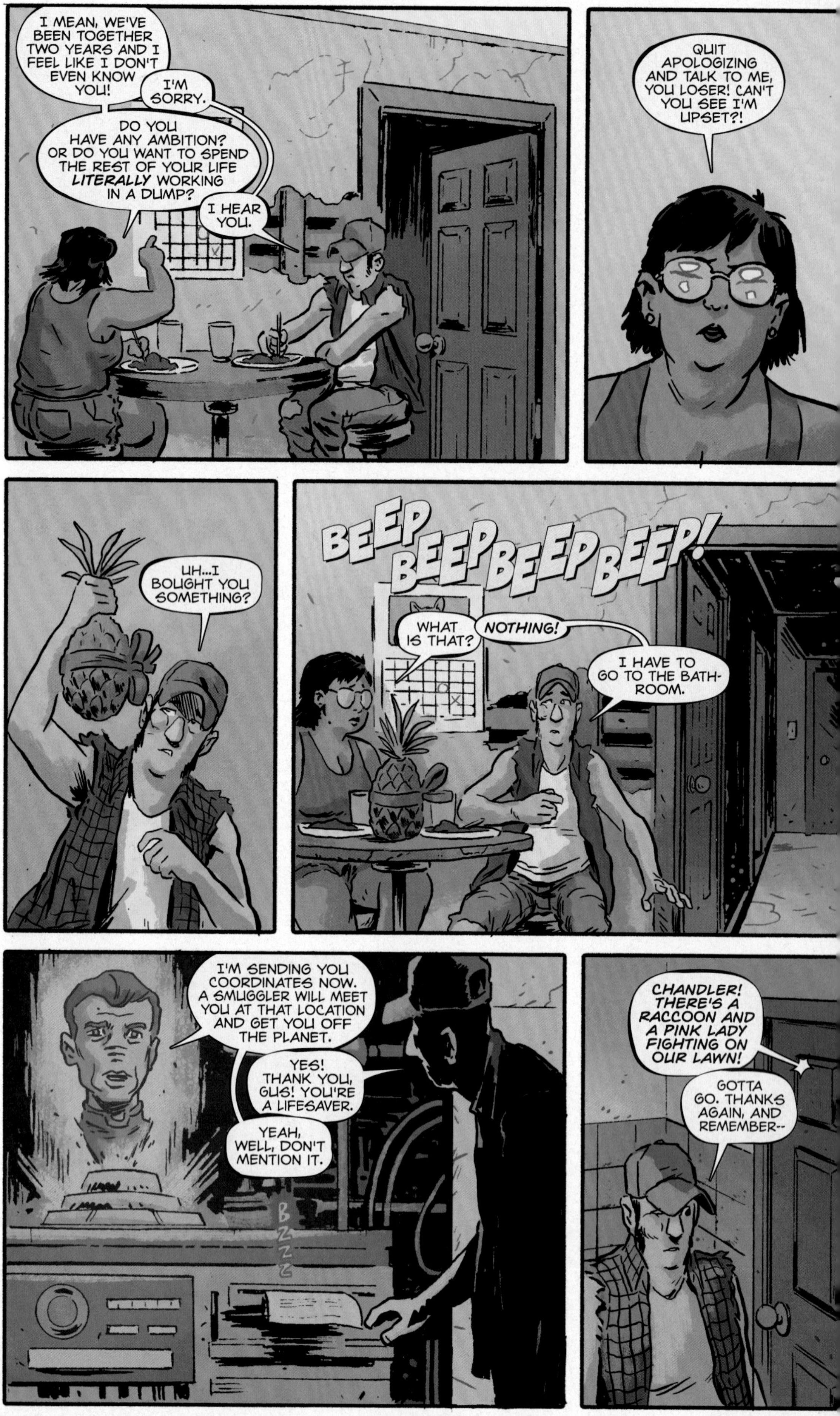

I MEAN, WE'VE BEEN TOGETHER TWO YEARS AND I FEEL LIKE I DON'T EVEN KNOW YOU!
I'M SORRY.
DO YOU HAVE ANY AMBITION? OR DO YOU WANT TO SPEND THE REST OF YOUR LIFE *LITERALLY* WORKING IN A DUMP?
I HEAR YOU.
QUIT APOLOGIZING AND TALK TO ME, YOU LOSER! CAN'T YOU SEE I'M UPSET?!
UH...I BOUGHT YOU SOMETHING?
BEEP BEEP BEEP BEEP!
WHAT IS THAT?
NOTHING!
I HAVE TO GO TO THE BATH-ROOM.
I'M SENDING YOU COORDINATES NOW. A SMUGGLER WILL MEET YOU AT THAT LOCATION AND GET YOU OFF THE PLANET.
YES! THANK YOU, GUS! YOU'RE A LIFESAVER.
YEAH, WELL, DON'T MENTION IT.
BZZZ
CHANDLER! THERE'S A RACCOON AND A PINK LADY FIGHTING ON OUR LAWN!
GOTTA GO. THANKS AGAIN, AND REMEMBER--

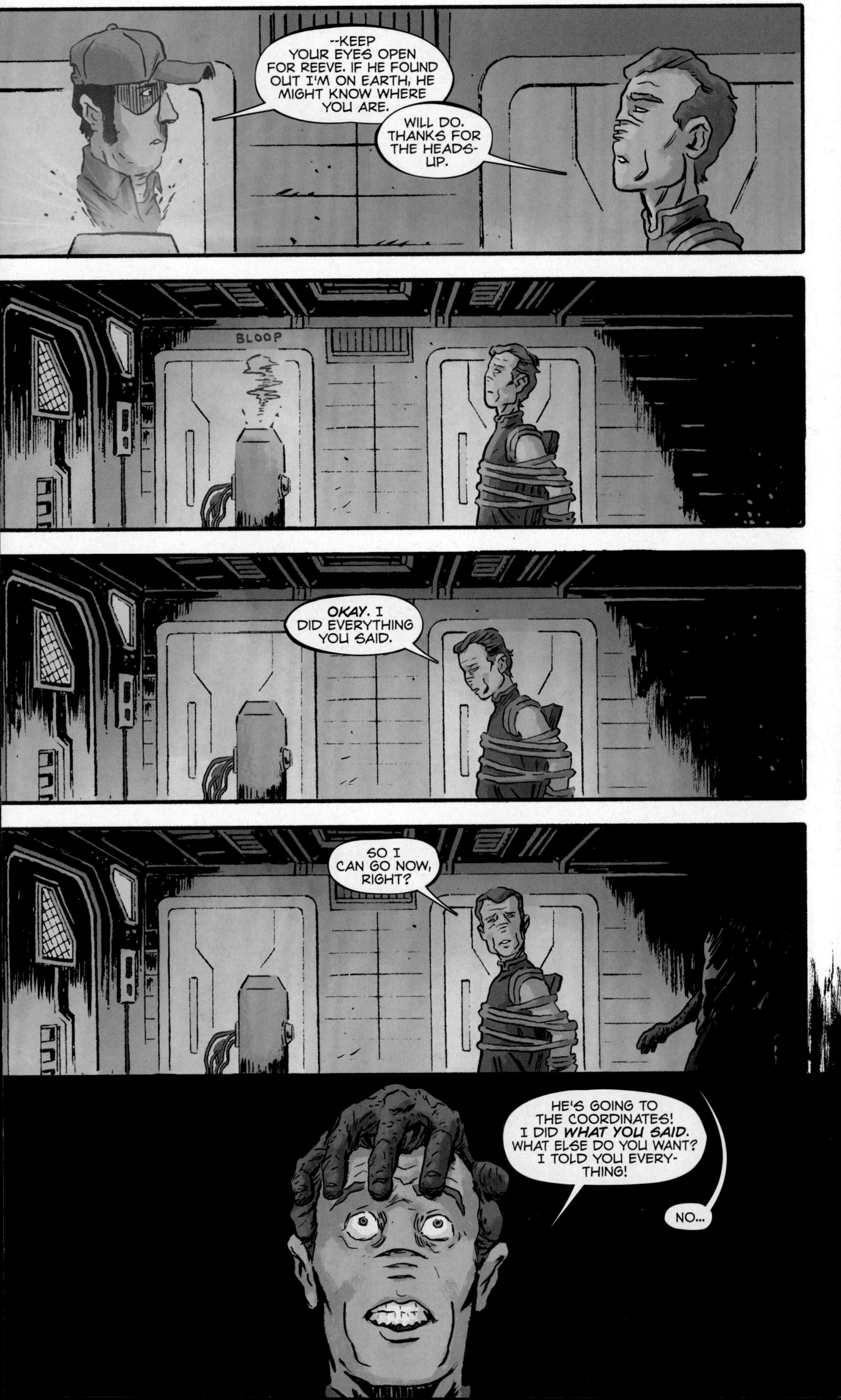
--KEEP YOUR EYES OPEN FOR REEVE. IF HE FOUND OUT I'M ON EARTH, HE MIGHT KNOW WHERE YOU ARE.
WILL DO. THANKS FOR THE HEADS-UP.
BLOOP
OKAY. I DID EVERYTHING YOU SAID.
SO I CAN GO NOW, RIGHT?
HE'S GOING TO THE COORDINATES! I DID ***WHAT YOU SAID***. WHAT ELSE DO YOU WANT? I TOLD YOU EVERY-THING!
NO...

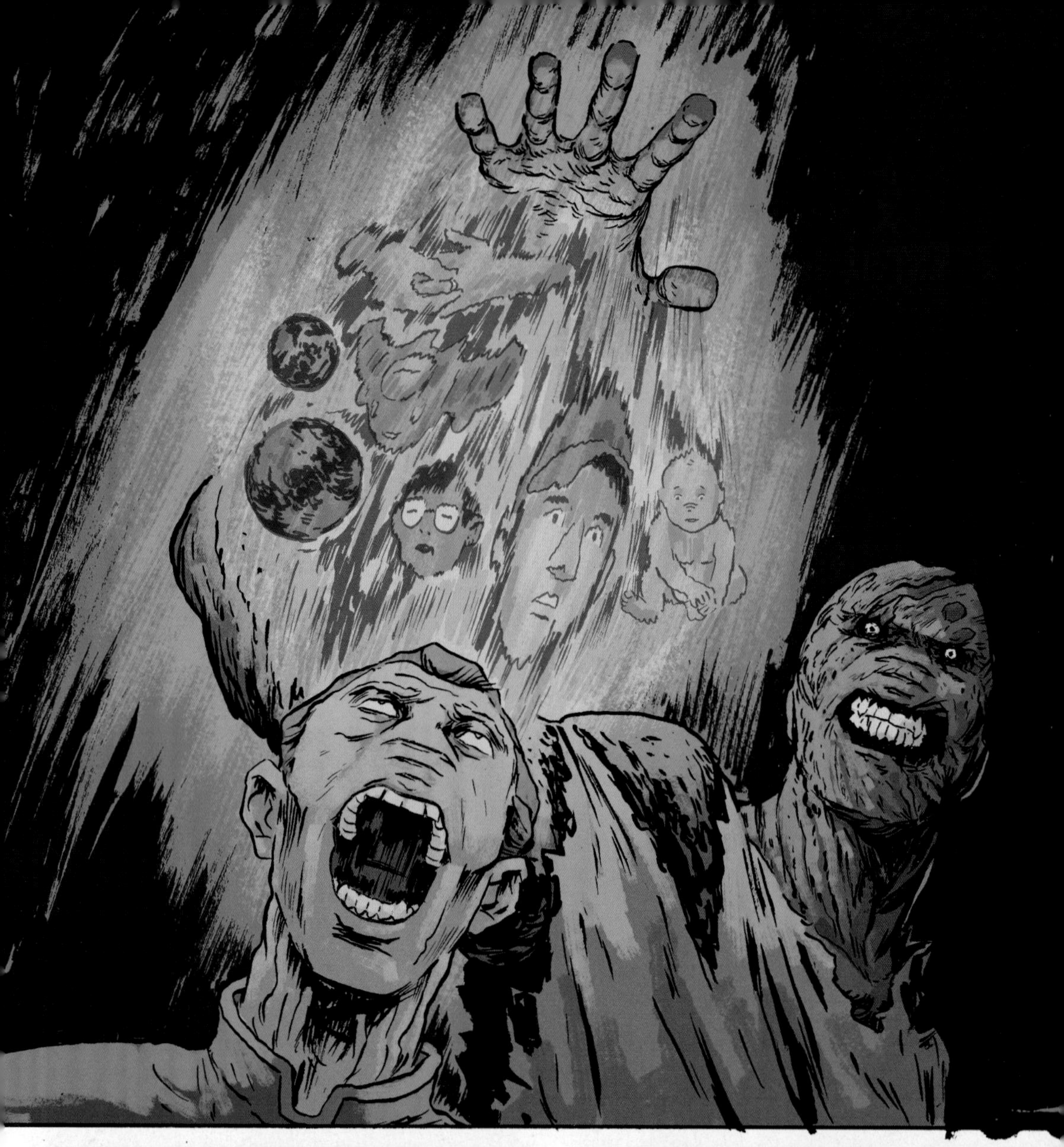

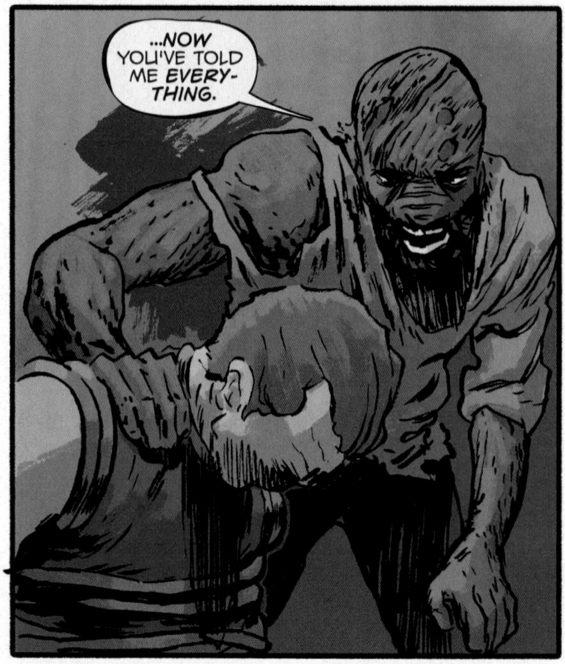
...NOW YOU'VE TOLD ME EVERY-THING.

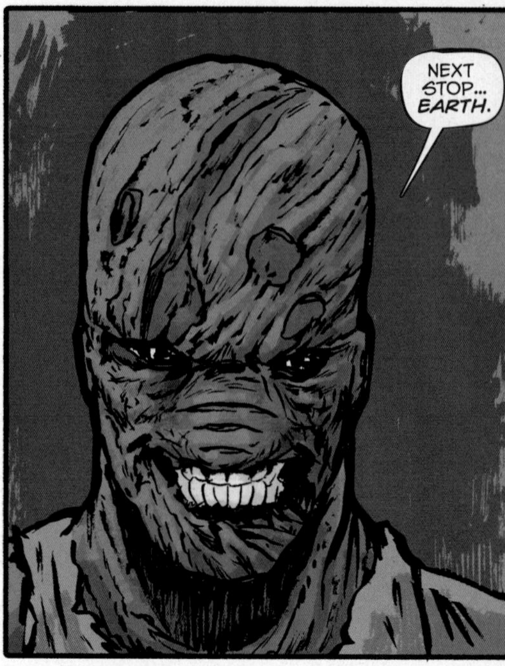
NEXT STOP... EARTH.

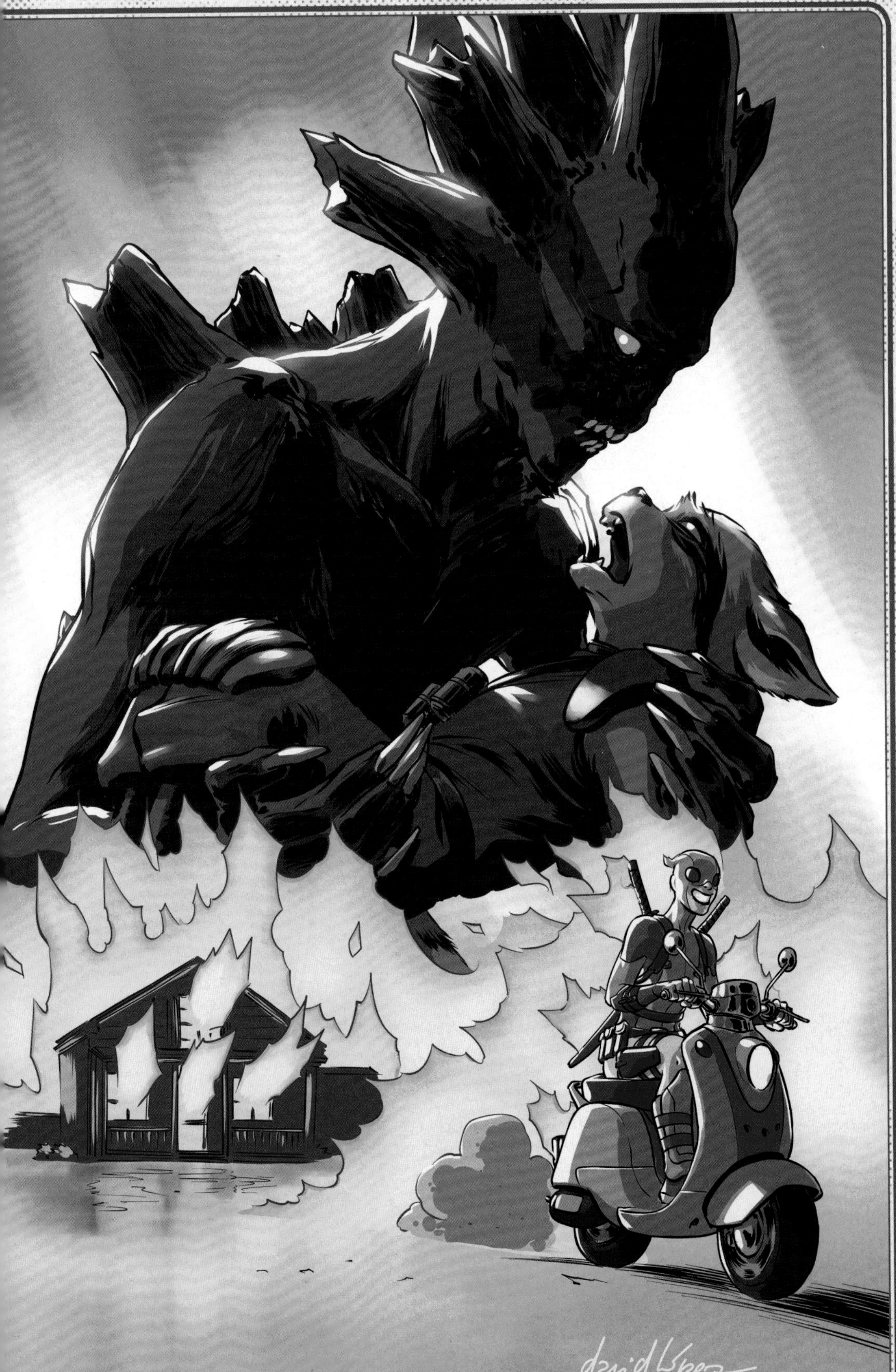
david lópez

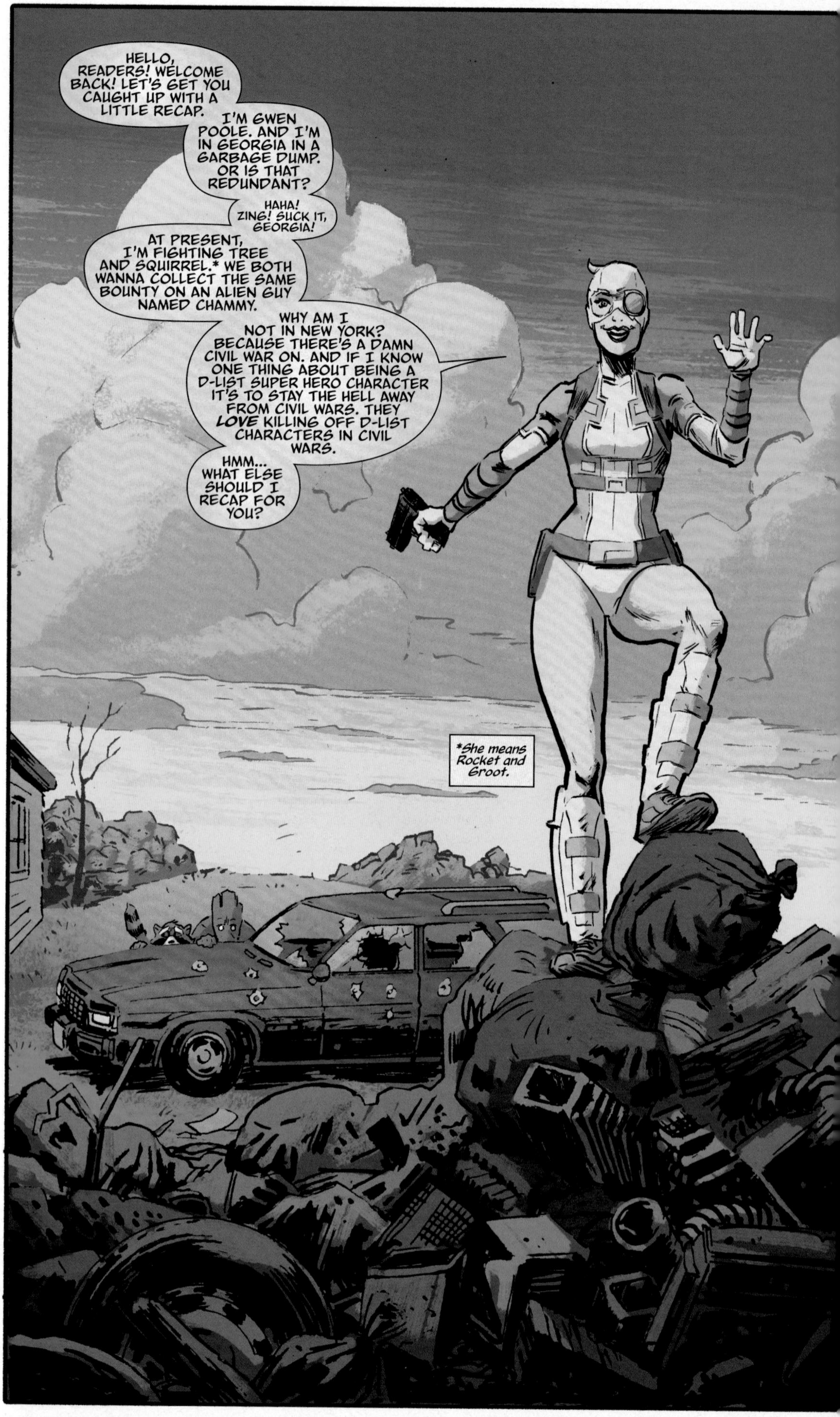
HELLO, READERS! WELCOME BACK! LET'S GET YOU CAUGHT UP WITH A LITTLE RECAP.
I'M GWEN POOLE. AND I'M IN GEORGIA IN A GARBAGE DUMP. OR IS THAT REDUNDANT?
HAHA! ZING! SUCK IT, GEORGIA!
AT PRESENT, I'M FIGHTING TREE AND SQUIRREL.* WE BOTH WANNA COLLECT THE SAME BOUNTY ON AN ALIEN GUY NAMED CHAMMY.
WHY AM I NOT IN NEW YORK? BECAUSE THERE'S A DAMN CIVIL WAR ON. AND IF I KNOW ONE THING ABOUT BEING A D-LIST SUPER HERO CHARACTER IT'S TO STAY THE HELL AWAY FROM CIVIL WARS. THEY *LOVE* KILLING OFF D-LIST CHARACTERS IN CIVIL WARS.
HMM... WHAT ELSE SHOULD I RECAP FOR YOU?
*She means Rocket and Groot.

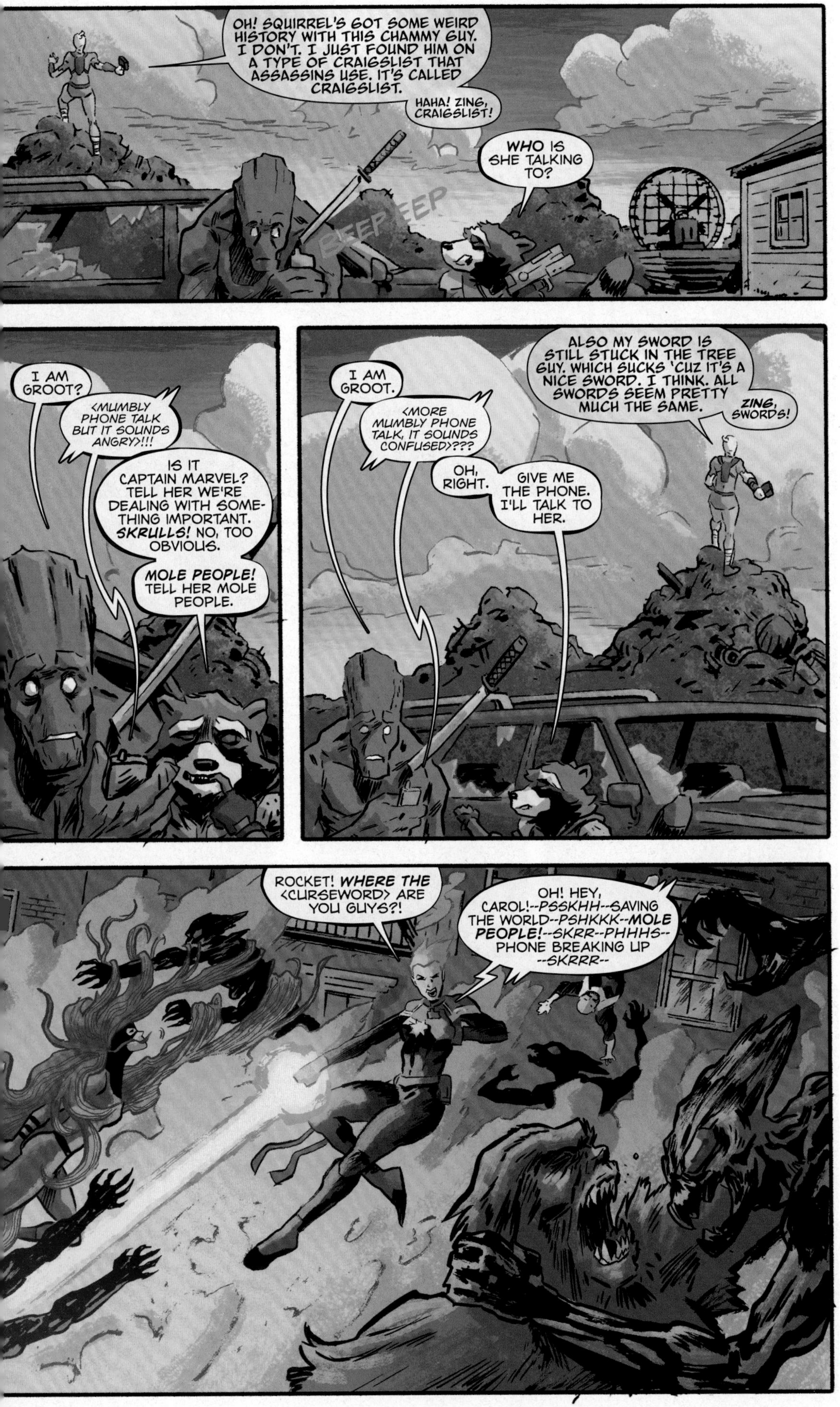
OH! SQUIRREL'S GOT SOME WEIRD HISTORY WITH THIS CHAMMY GUY. I DON'T. I JUST FOUND HIM ON A TYPE OF CRAIGSLIST THAT ASSASSINS USE. IT'S CALLED CRAIGSLIST.
HAHA! ZING, CRAIGSLIST!
WHO IS SHE TALKING TO?
BEEP BEEP
I AM GROOT?
<MUMBLY PHONE TALK BUT IT SOUNDS ANGRY>!!!
IS IT CAPTAIN MARVEL? TELL HER WE'RE DEALING WITH SOMETHING IMPORTANT. SKRULLS! NO, TOO OBVIOUS.
MOLE PEOPLE! TELL HER MOLE PEOPLE.
I AM GROOT.
<MORE MUMBLY PHONE TALK, IT SOUNDS CONFUSED>???
ALSO MY SWORD IS STILL STUCK IN THE TREE GUY. WHICH SUCKS 'CUZ IT'S A NICE SWORD. I THINK. ALL SWORDS SEEM PRETTY MUCH THE SAME.
ZING, SWORDS!
OH, RIGHT.
GIVE ME THE PHONE. I'LL TALK TO HER.
ROCKET! WHERE THE <CURSEWORD> ARE YOU GUYS?!
OH! HEY, CAROL!--PSSKHH--SAVING THE WORLD--PSHKKK--MOLE PEOPLE!--SKRR--PHHHS--PHONE BREAKING UP --SKRRR--

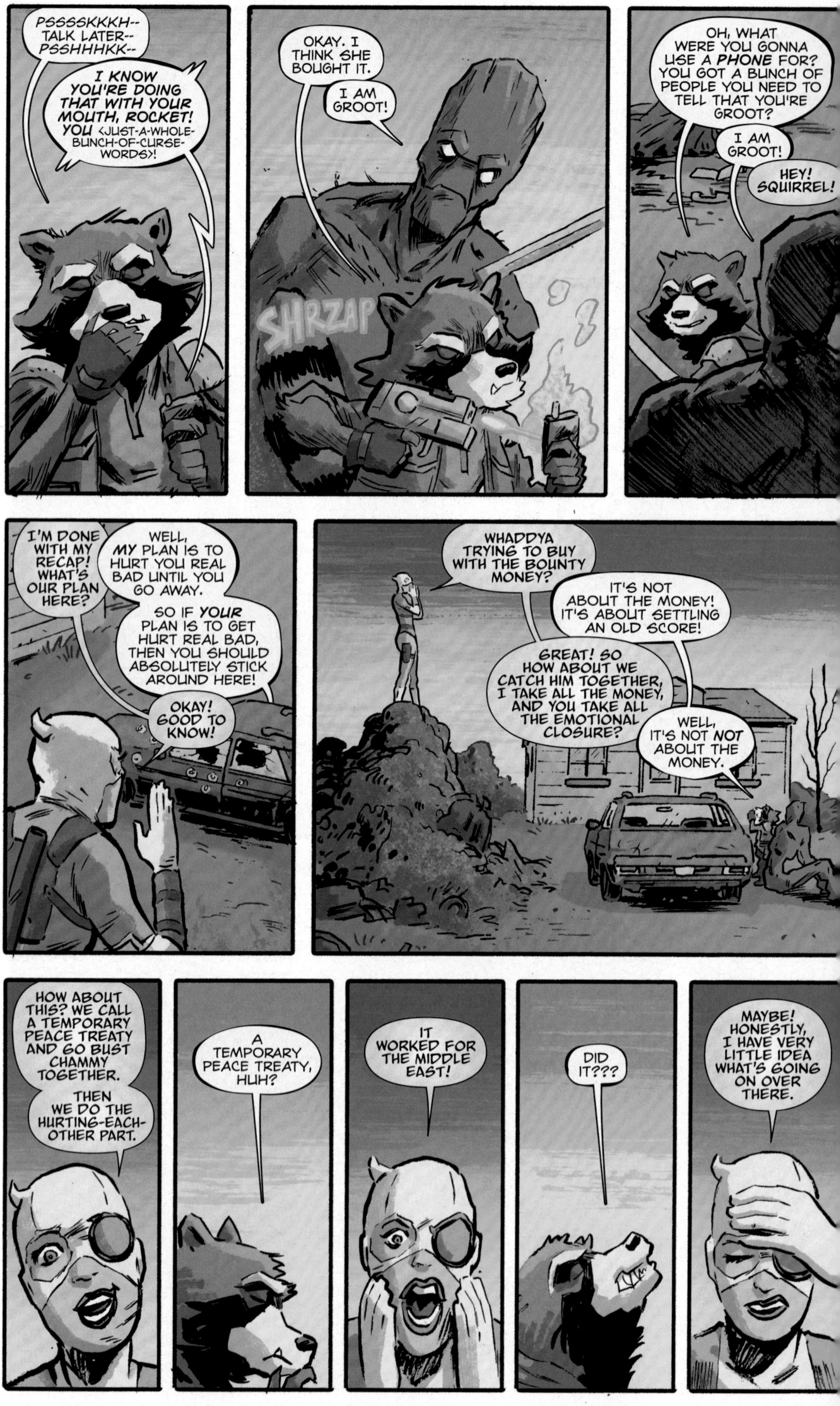
PSSSSKKKH-- TALK LATER-- PSSHHHKK--
I KNOW YOU'RE DOING THAT WITH YOUR MOUTH, ROCKET! YOU <JUST-A-WHOLE-BUNCH-OF-CURSE-WORDS>!
OKAY. I THINK SHE BOUGHT IT.
I AM GROOT!
SHRZAP
OH, WHAT WERE YOU GONNA USE A PHONE FOR? YOU GOT A BUNCH OF PEOPLE YOU NEED TO TELL THAT YOU'RE GROOT?
I AM GROOT!
HEY! SQUIRREL!
I'M DONE WITH MY RECAP! WHAT'S OUR PLAN HERE?
WELL, MY PLAN IS TO HURT YOU REAL BAD UNTIL YOU GO AWAY.
SO IF YOUR PLAN IS TO GET HURT REAL BAD, THEN YOU SHOULD ABSOLUTELY STICK AROUND HERE!
OKAY! GOOD TO KNOW!
WHADDYA TRYING TO BUY WITH THE BOUNTY MONEY?
IT'S NOT ABOUT THE MONEY! IT'S ABOUT SETTLING AN OLD SCORE!
GREAT! SO HOW ABOUT WE CATCH HIM TOGETHER, I TAKE ALL THE MONEY, AND YOU TAKE ALL THE EMOTIONAL CLOSURE?
WELL, IT'S NOT NOT ABOUT THE MONEY.
HOW ABOUT THIS? WE CALL A TEMPORARY PEACE TREATY AND GO BUST CHAMMY TOGETHER.
THEN WE DO THE HURTING-EACH-OTHER PART.
A TEMPORARY PEACE TREATY, HUH?
IT WORKED FOR THE MIDDLE EAST!
DID IT???
MAYBE! HONESTLY, I HAVE VERY LITTLE IDEA WHAT'S GOING ON OVER THERE.

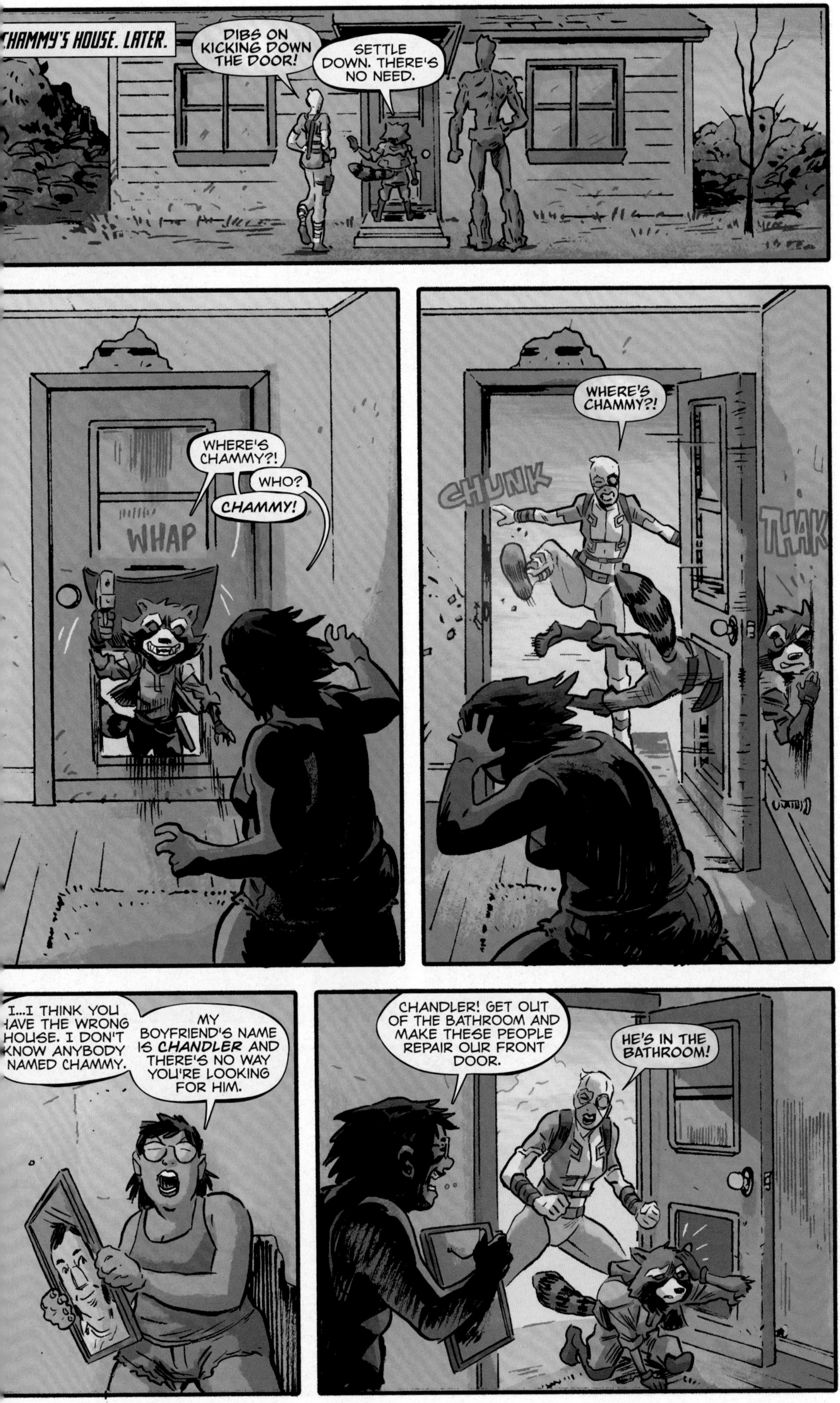

CHAMMY'S HOUSE. LATER.
DIBS ON KICKING DOWN THE DOOR!
SETTLE DOWN. THERE'S NO NEED.
WHAP
WHERE'S CHAMMY?!
WHO?
CHAMMY!
CHUNK
THAK
WHERE'S CHAMMY?!
I...I THINK YOU HAVE THE WRONG HOUSE. I DON'T KNOW ANYBODY NAMED CHAMMY.
MY BOYFRIEND'S NAME IS CHANDLER AND THERE'S NO WAY YOU'RE LOOKING FOR HIM.
CHANDLER! GET OUT OF THE BATHROOM AND MAKE THESE PEOPLE REPAIR OUR FRONT DOOR.
HE'S IN THE BATHROOM!

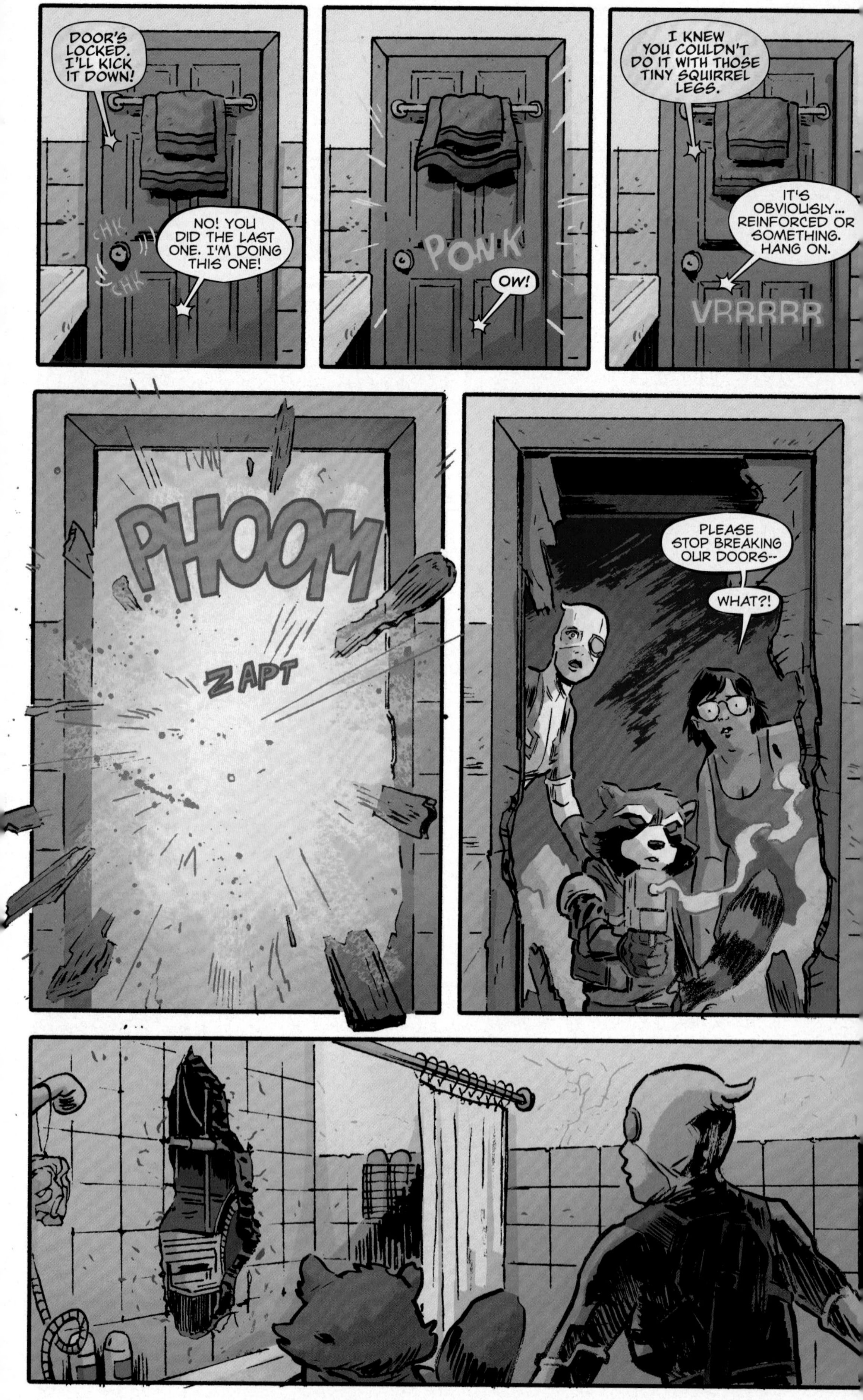
DOOR'S LOCKED. I'LL KICK IT DOWN!
CHK CHK
NO! YOU DID THE LAST ONE. I'M DOING THIS ONE!
PONK
OW!
I KNEW YOU COULDN'T DO IT WITH THOSE TINY SQUIRREL LEGS.
IT'S OBVIOUSLY... REINFORCED OR SOMETHING. HANG ON.
VRRRRR
PHOOM
ZAPT
PLEASE STOP BREAKING OUR DOORS--
WHAT?!

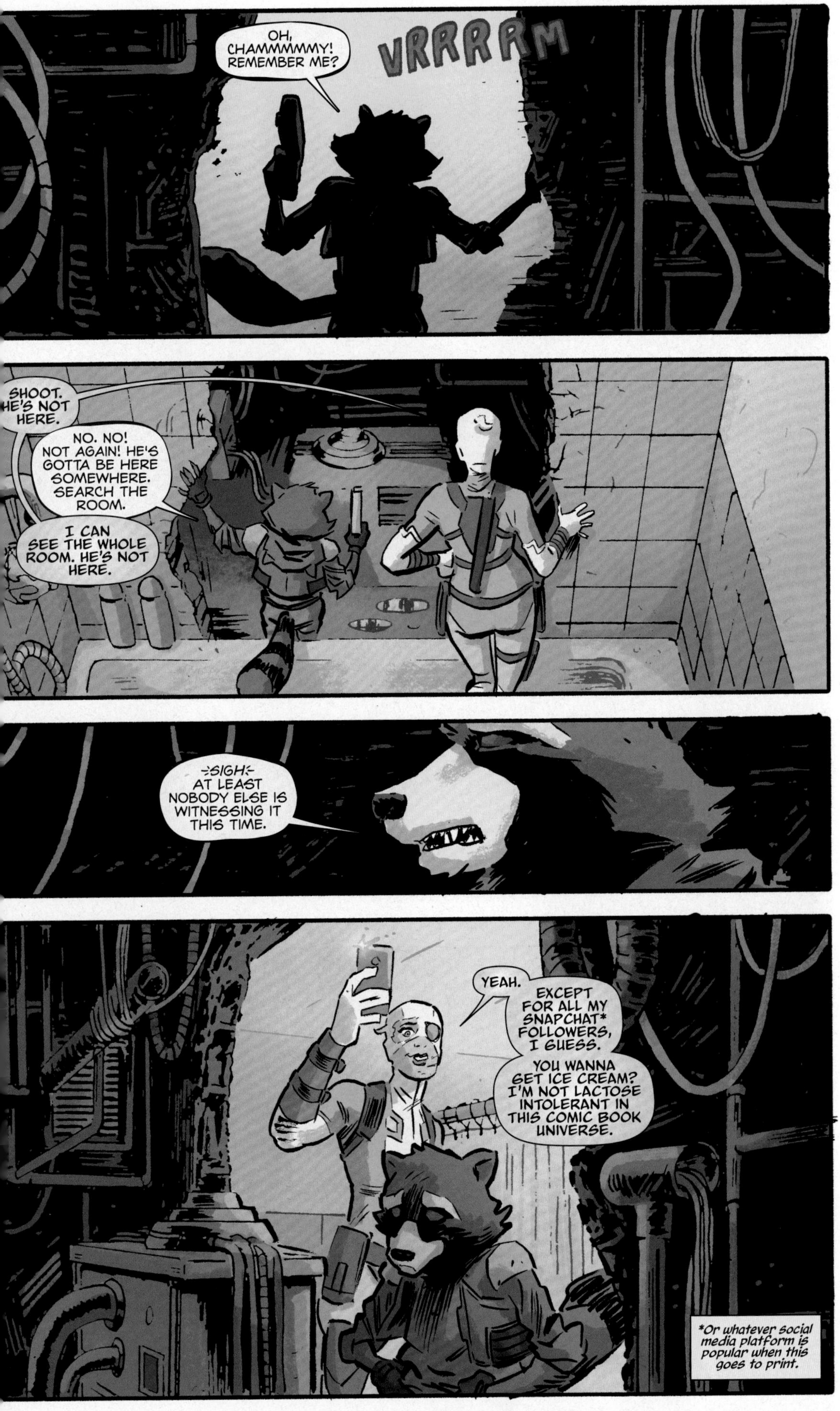
OH, CHAMMMMMY! REMEMBER ME?
VRRRRM
SHOOT. HE'S NOT HERE.
NO. NO! NOT AGAIN! HE'S GOTTA BE HERE SOMEWHERE. SEARCH THE ROOM.
I CAN SEE THE WHOLE ROOM. HE'S NOT HERE.
SIGH AT LEAST NOBODY ELSE IS WITNESSING IT THIS TIME.
YEAH.
EXCEPT FOR ALL MY SNAPCHAT* FOLLOWERS, I GUESS.
YOU WANNA GET ICE CREAM? I'M NOT LACTOSE INTOLERANT IN THIS COMIC BOOK UNIVERSE.
*Or whatever social media platform is popular when this goes to print.

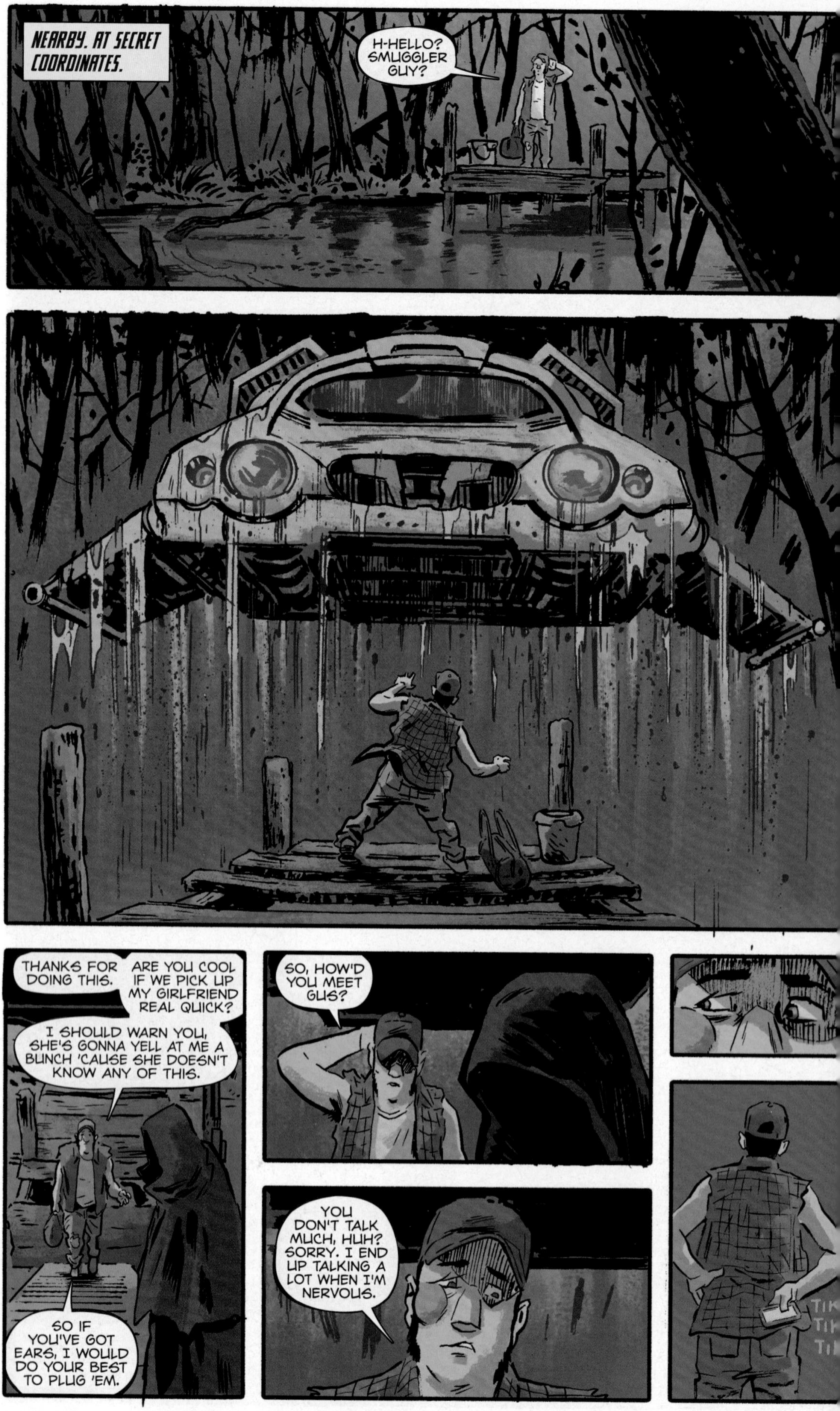
NEARBY. AT SECRET COORDINATES.
H-HELLO? SMUGGLER GUY?
THANKS FOR DOING THIS.
ARE YOU COOL IF WE PICK UP MY GIRLFRIEND REAL QUICK?
I SHOULD WARN YOU, SHE'S GONNA YELL AT ME A BUNCH 'CAUSE SHE DOESN'T KNOW ANY OF THIS.
SO IF YOU'VE GOT EARS, I WOULD DO YOUR BEST TO PLUG 'EM.
SO, HOW'D YOU MEET GUS?
YOU DON'T TALK MUCH, HUH? SORRY. I END UP TALKING A LOT WHEN I'M NERVOUS.
TIK
TIK
TI

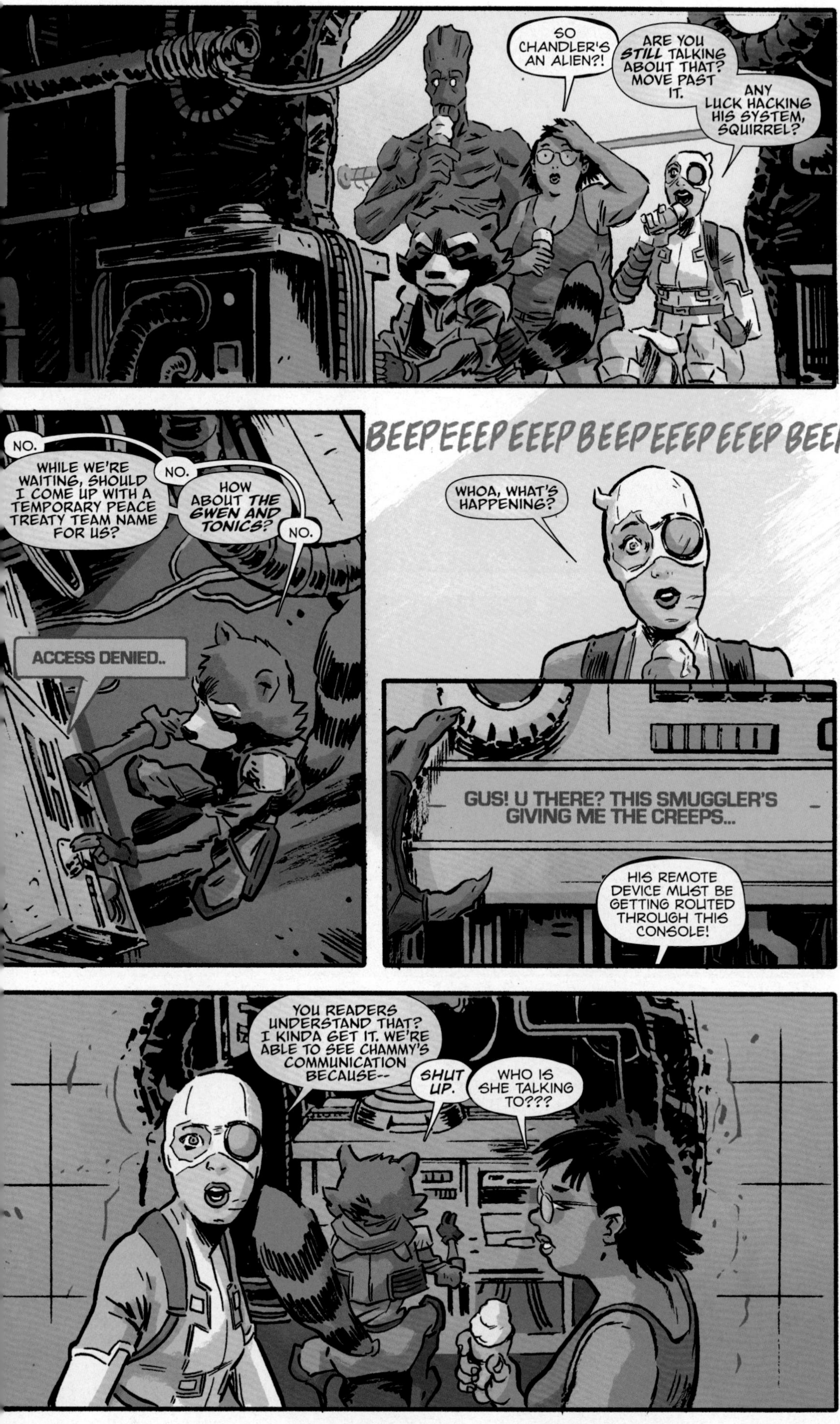
SO CHANDLER'S AN ALIEN?!
ARE YOU STILL TALKING ABOUT THAT? MOVE PAST IT.
ANY LUCK HACKING HIS SYSTEM, SQUIRREL?
NO.
WHILE WE'RE WAITING, SHOULD I COME UP WITH A TEMPORARY PEACE TREATY TEAM NAME FOR US?
NO.
HOW ABOUT THE GWEN AND TONICS?
NO.
ACCESS DENIED..
BEEPEEEPEEEPBEEPEEEPEEEPBEEPE
WHOA, WHAT'S HAPPENING?
GUS! U THERE? THIS SMUGGLER'S GIVING ME THE CREEPS...
HIS REMOTE DEVICE MUST BE GETTING ROUTED THROUGH THIS CONSOLE!
YOU READERS UNDERSTAND THAT? I KINDA GET IT. WE'RE ABLE TO SEE CHAMMY'S COMMUNICATION BECAUSE--
SHUT UP.
WHO IS SHE TALKING TO???

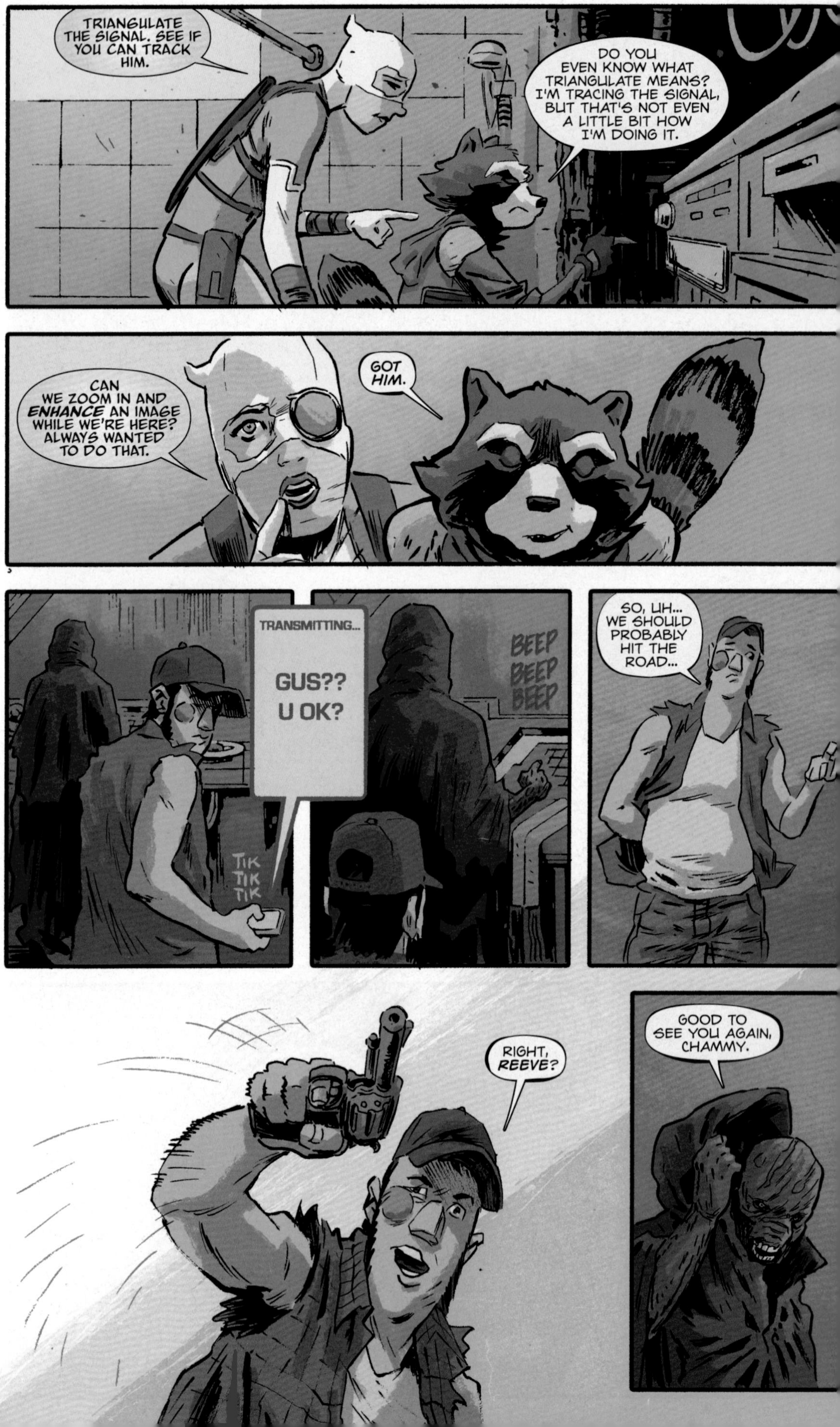
TRIANGULATE THE SIGNAL. SEE IF YOU CAN TRACK HIM.
DO YOU EVEN KNOW WHAT TRIANGULATE MEANS? I'M TRACING THE SIGNAL, BUT THAT'S NOT EVEN A LITTLE BIT HOW I'M DOING IT.
CAN WE ZOOM IN AND *ENHANCE* AN IMAGE WHILE WE'RE HERE? ALWAYS WANTED TO DO THAT.
GOT *HIM.*
TRANSMITTING...
GUS?? U OK?
TIK TIK TIK
BEEP BEEP BEEP
SO, UH... WE SHOULD PROBABLY HIT THE ROAD...
RIGHT, *REEVE?*
GOOD TO SEE YOU AGAIN, CHAMMY.

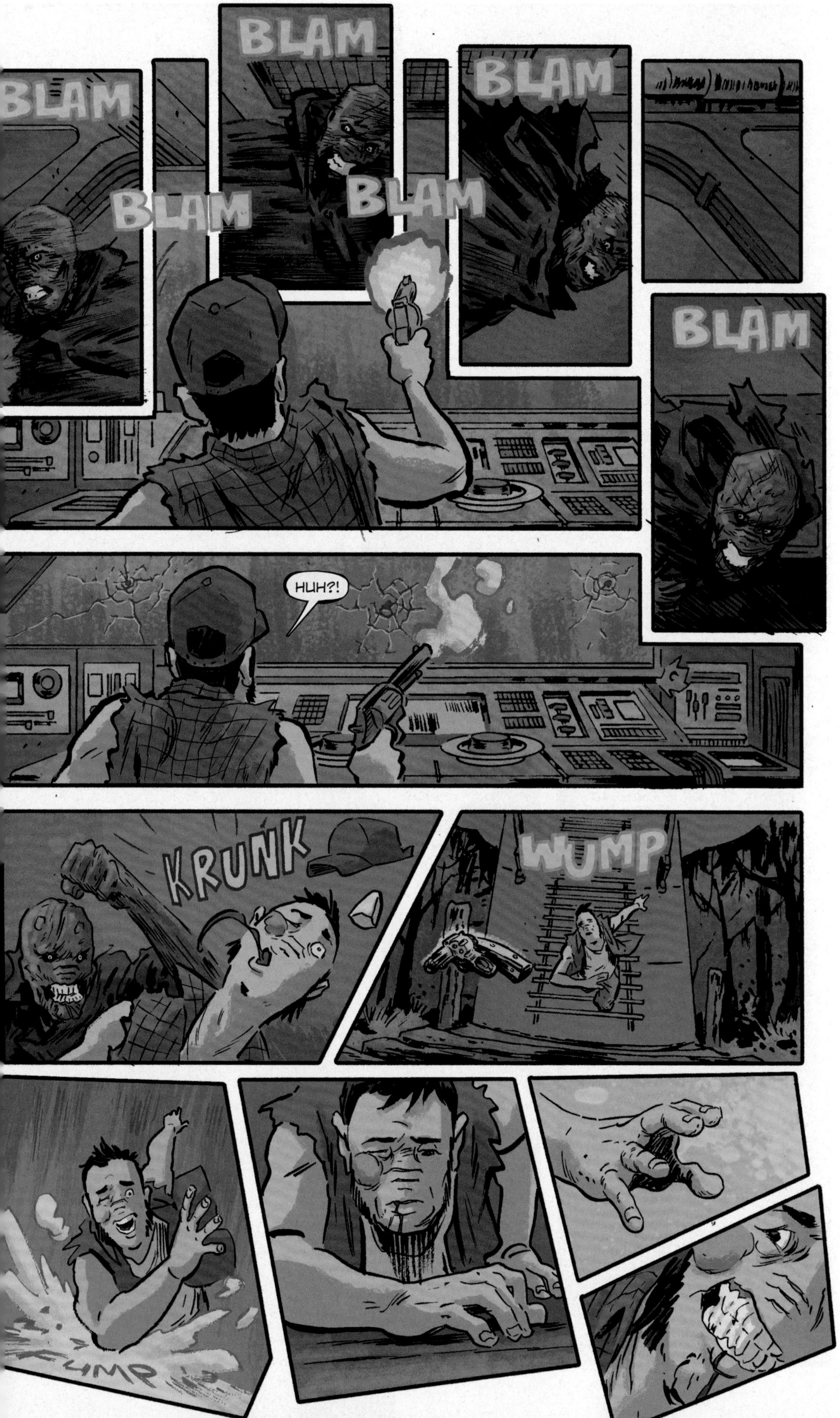
BLAM
BLAM
BLAM
BLAM
BLAM
BLAM
HUH?!
KRUNK
WUMP
FUMP

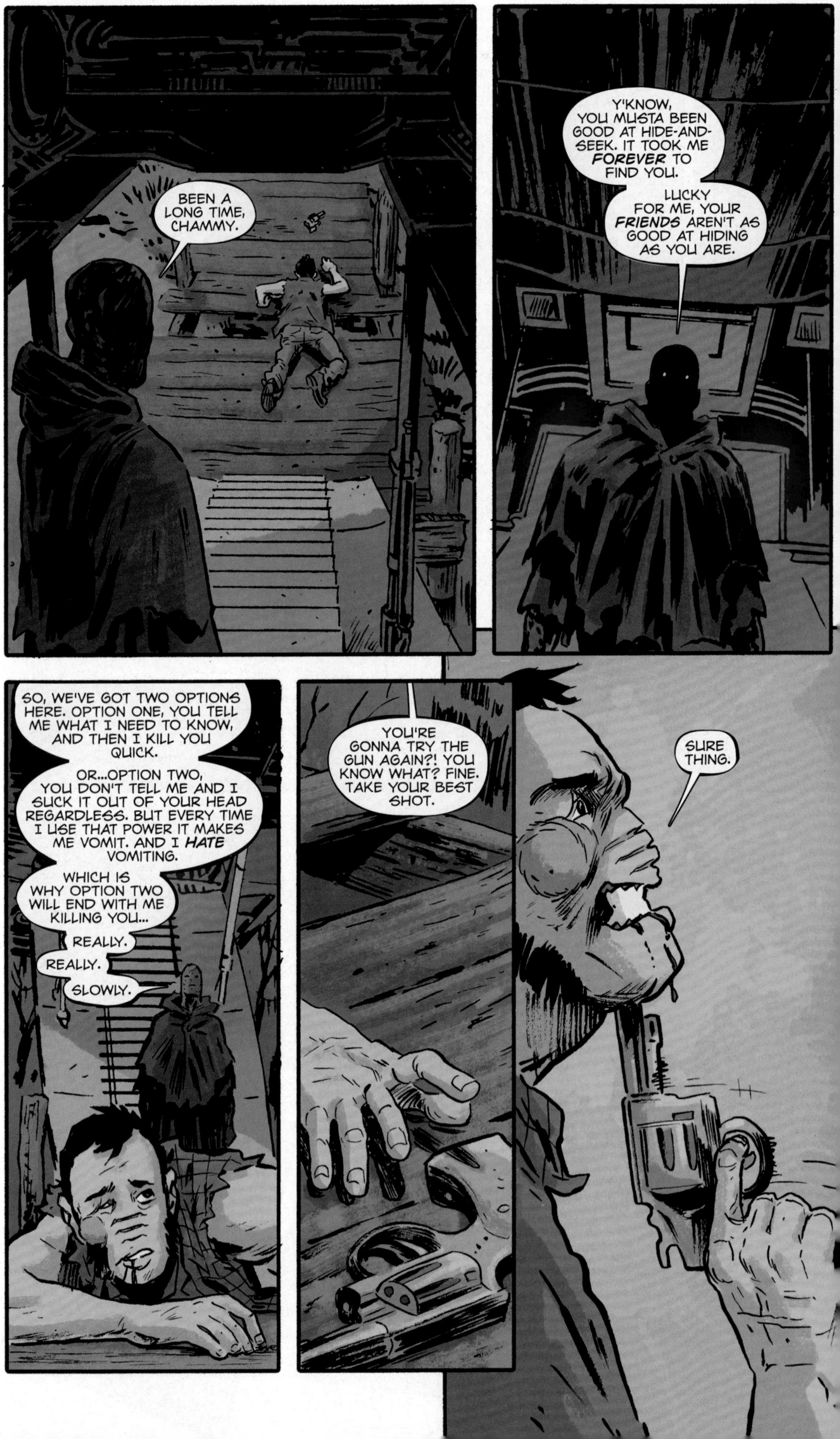
BEEN A LONG TIME, CHAMMY.
Y'KNOW, YOU MUSTA BEEN GOOD AT HIDE-AND-SEEK. IT TOOK ME *FOREVER* TO FIND YOU.
LUCKY FOR ME, YOUR *FRIENDS* AREN'T AS GOOD AT HIDING AS YOU ARE.
SO, WE'VE GOT TWO OPTIONS HERE. OPTION ONE, YOU TELL ME WHAT I NEED TO KNOW, AND THEN I KILL YOU QUICK.
OR...OPTION TWO, YOU DON'T TELL ME AND I SUCK IT OUT OF YOUR HEAD REGARDLESS. BUT EVERY TIME I USE THAT POWER IT MAKES ME VOMIT. AND I *HATE* VOMITING.
WHICH IS WHY OPTION TWO WILL END WITH ME KILLING YOU...
REALLY.
REALLY.
SLOWLY.
YOU'RE GONNA TRY THE GUN AGAIN?! YOU KNOW WHAT? FINE. TAKE YOUR BEST SHOT.
SURE THING.

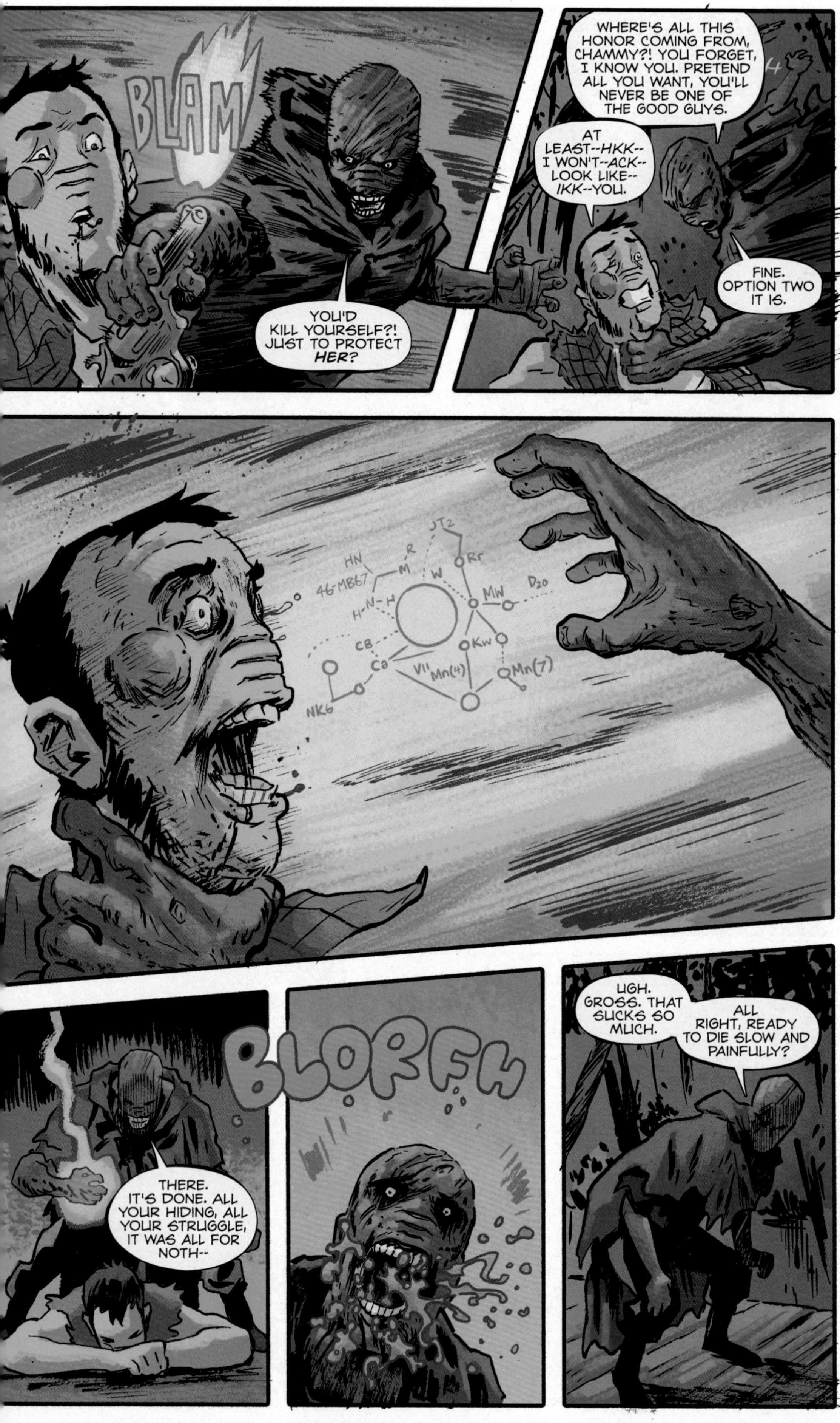
BLAM
YOU'D KILL YOURSELF?! JUST TO PROTECT *HER*?
WHERE'S ALL THIS HONOR COMING FROM, CHAMMY?! YOU FORGET, I KNOW YOU. PRETEND ALL YOU WANT, YOU'LL NEVER BE ONE OF THE GOOD GUYS.
AT LEAST--*HKK*-- I WON'T--*ACK*-- LOOK LIKE-- *IKK*--YOU.
FINE. OPTION TWO IT IS.
HN
R
M
46-MB67
H-N-H
W
Rr
MW
D20
CB
Ca
Kw
VII
Mn(4)
Mn(7)
NK6
THERE. IT'S DONE. ALL YOUR HIDING, ALL YOUR STRUGGLE, IT WAS ALL FOR NOTH--
BLORFH
UGH. GROSS. THAT SUCKS SO MUCH.
ALL RIGHT, READY TO DIE SLOW AND PAINFULLY?

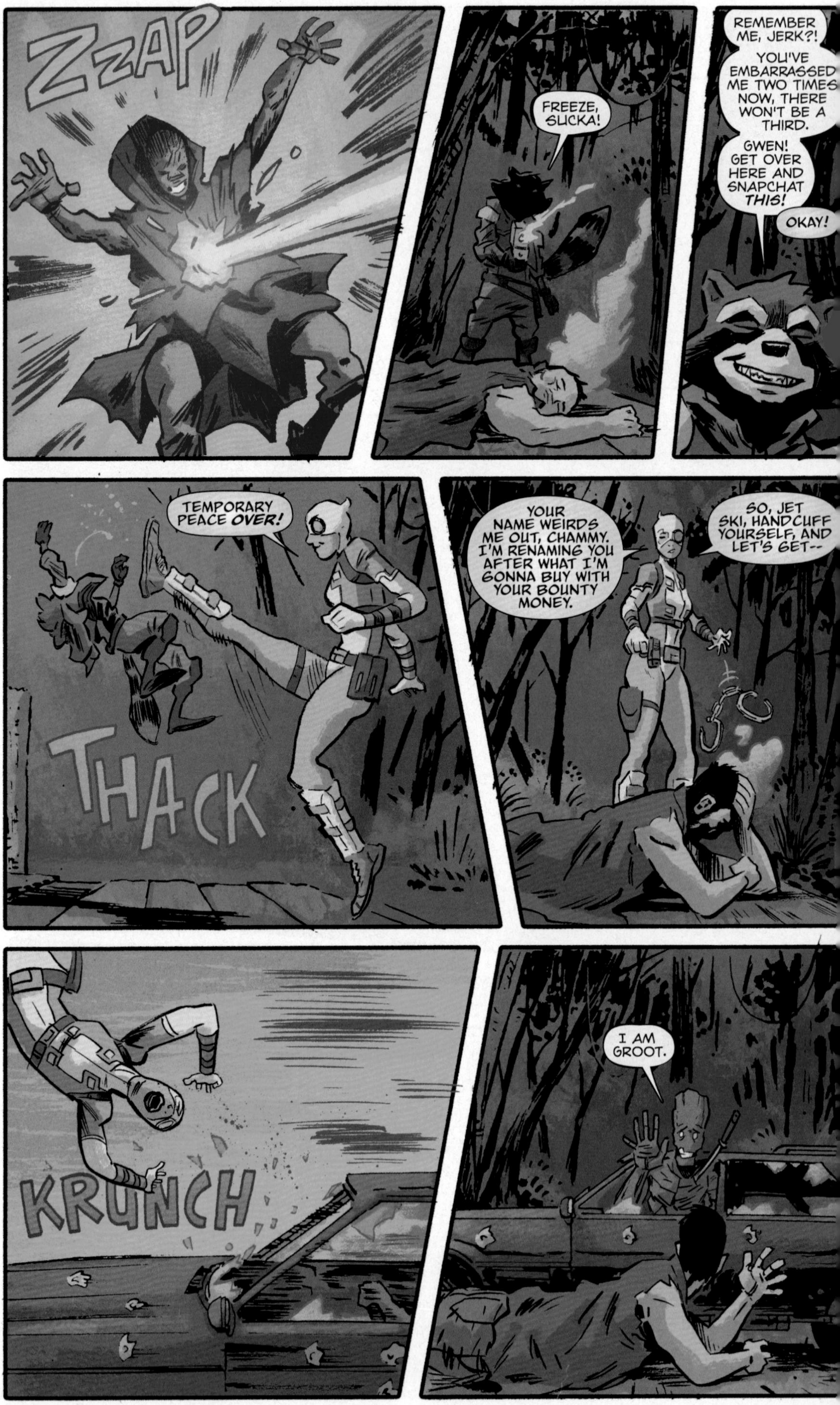
ZZAP
FREEZE, SUCKA!
REMEMBER ME, JERK?!
YOU'VE EMBARRASSED ME TWO TIMES NOW, THERE WON'T BE A THIRD.
GWEN! GET OVER HERE AND SNAPCHAT *THIS!*
OKAY!
TEMPORARY PEACE **OVER!**
THACK
YOUR NAME WEIRDS ME OUT, CHAMMY. I'M RENAMING YOU AFTER WHAT I'M GONNA BUY WITH YOUR BOUNTY MONEY.
SO, JET SKI, HANDCUFF YOURSELF, AND LET'S GET--
KRUNCH
I AM GROOT.

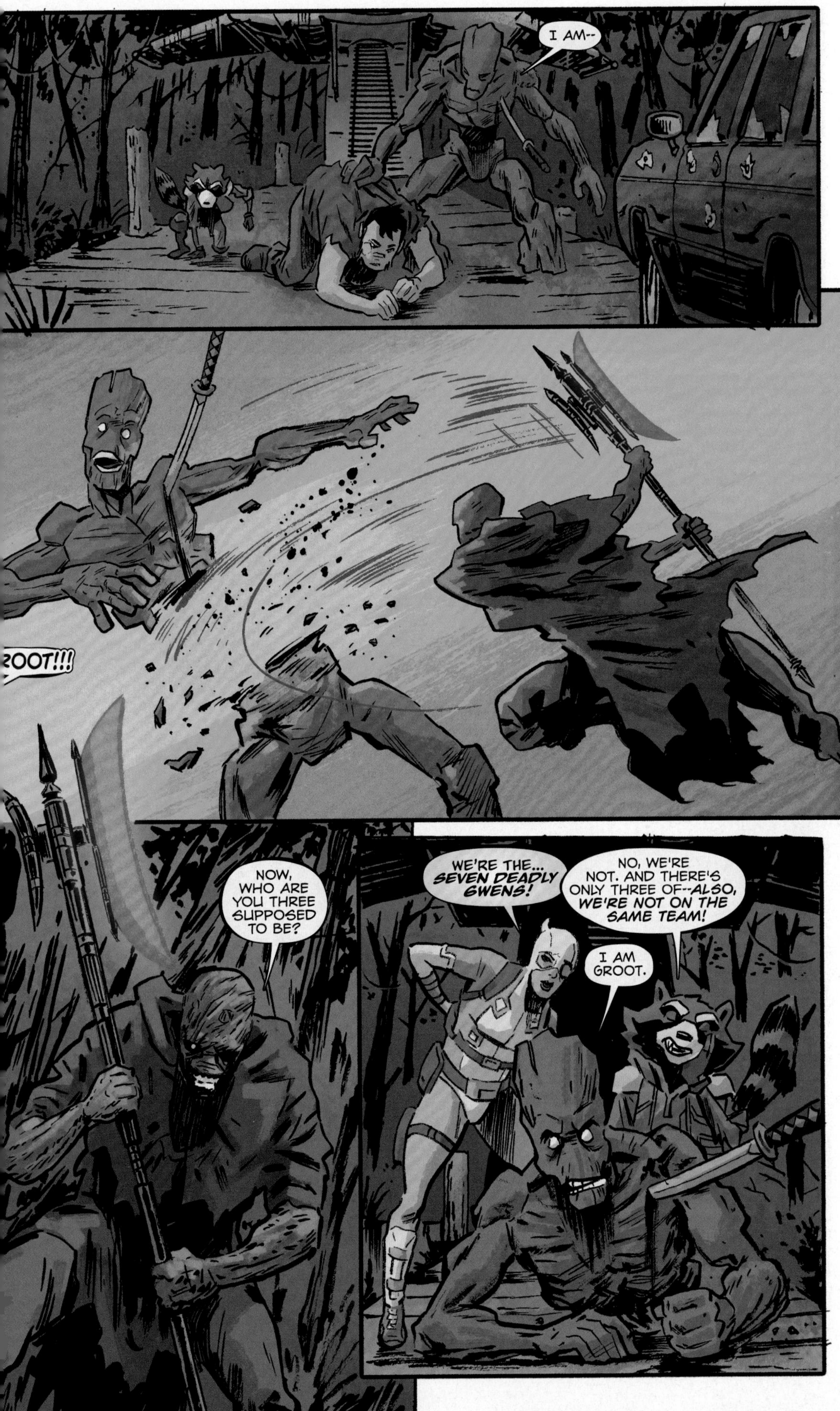
I AM--
GROOT!!!
NOW, WHO ARE YOU THREE SUPPOSED TO BE?
WE'RE THE... SEVEN DEADLY GWENS!
NO, WE'RE NOT. AND THERE'S ONLY THREE OF--ALSO, WE'RE NOT ON THE SAME TEAM!
I AM GROOT.

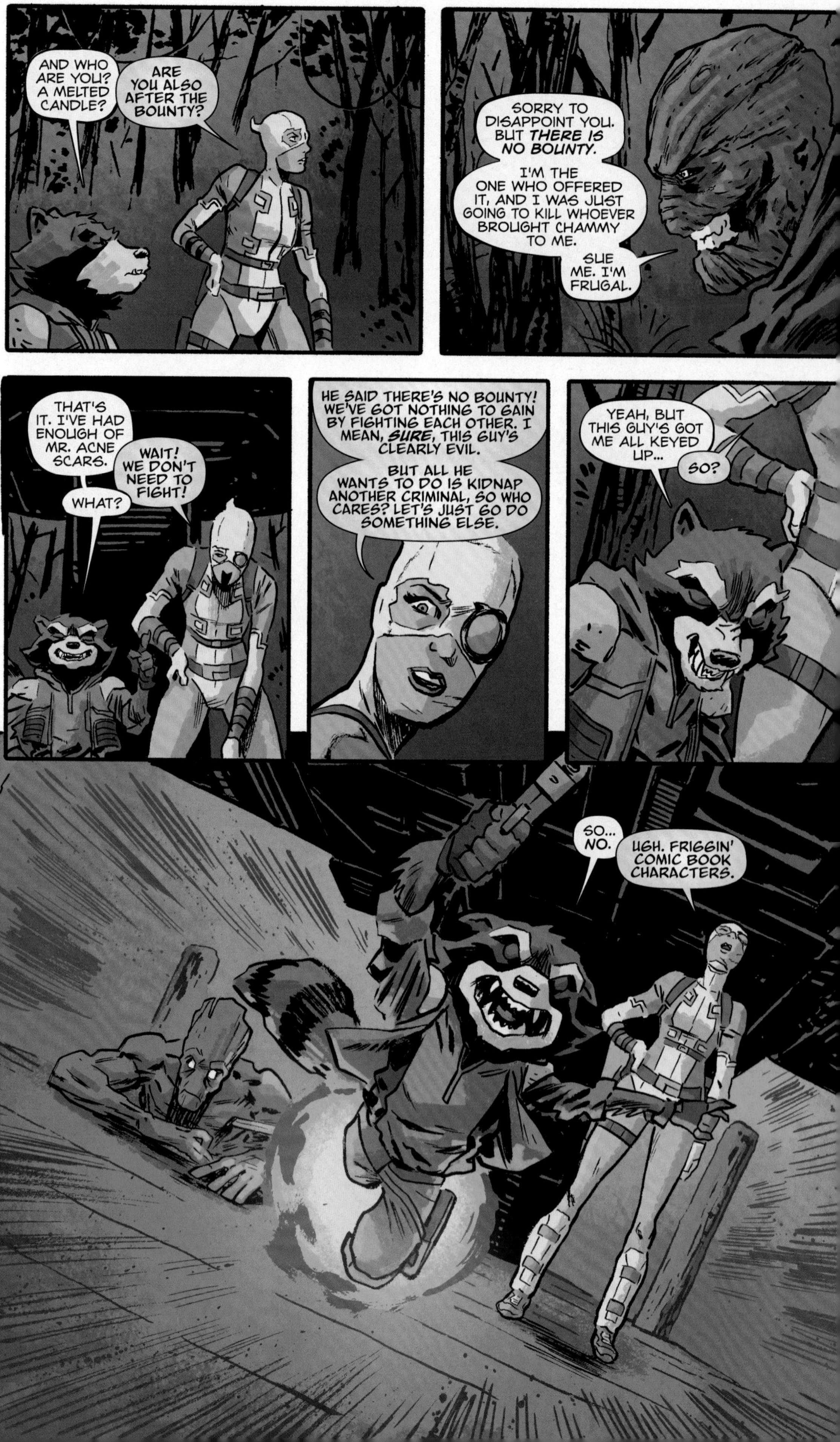
AND WHO ARE YOU? A MELTED CANDLE?
ARE YOU ALSO AFTER THE BOUNTY?
SORRY TO DISAPPOINT YOU. BUT THERE IS NO BOUNTY.
I'M THE ONE WHO OFFERED IT, AND I WAS JUST GOING TO KILL WHOEVER BROUGHT CHAMMY TO ME.
SUE ME. I'M FRUGAL.
THAT'S IT. I'VE HAD ENOUGH OF MR. ACNE SCARS.
WAIT! WE DON'T NEED TO FIGHT!
WHAT?
HE SAID THERE'S NO BOUNTY! WE'VE GOT NOTHING TO GAIN BY FIGHTING EACH OTHER. I MEAN, SURE, THIS GUY'S CLEARLY EVIL.
BUT ALL HE WANTS TO DO IS KIDNAP ANOTHER CRIMINAL, SO WHO CARES? LET'S JUST GO DO SOMETHING ELSE.
YEAH, BUT THIS GUY'S GOT ME ALL KEYED UP...
SO?
SO... NO.
UGH. FRIGGIN' COMIC BOOK CHARACTERS.

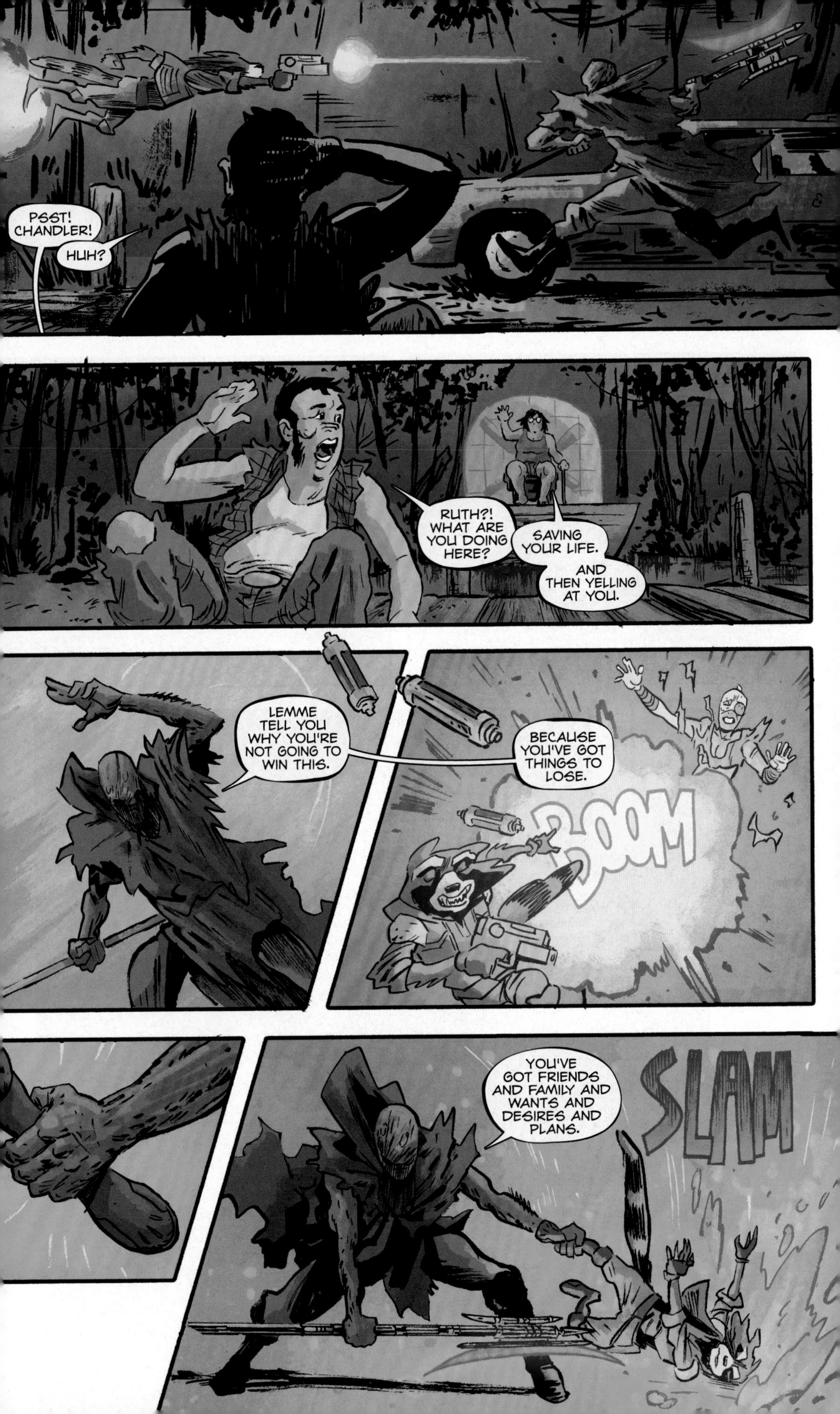
PSST! CHANDLER!
HUH?
RUTH?! WHAT ARE YOU DOING HERE?
SAVING YOUR LIFE.
AND THEN YELLING AT YOU.
LEMME TELL YOU WHY YOU'RE NOT GOING TO WIN THIS.
BECAUSE YOU'VE GOT THINGS TO LOSE.
BOOM
YOU'VE GOT FRIENDS AND FAMILY AND WANTS AND DESIRES AND PLANS.
SLAM

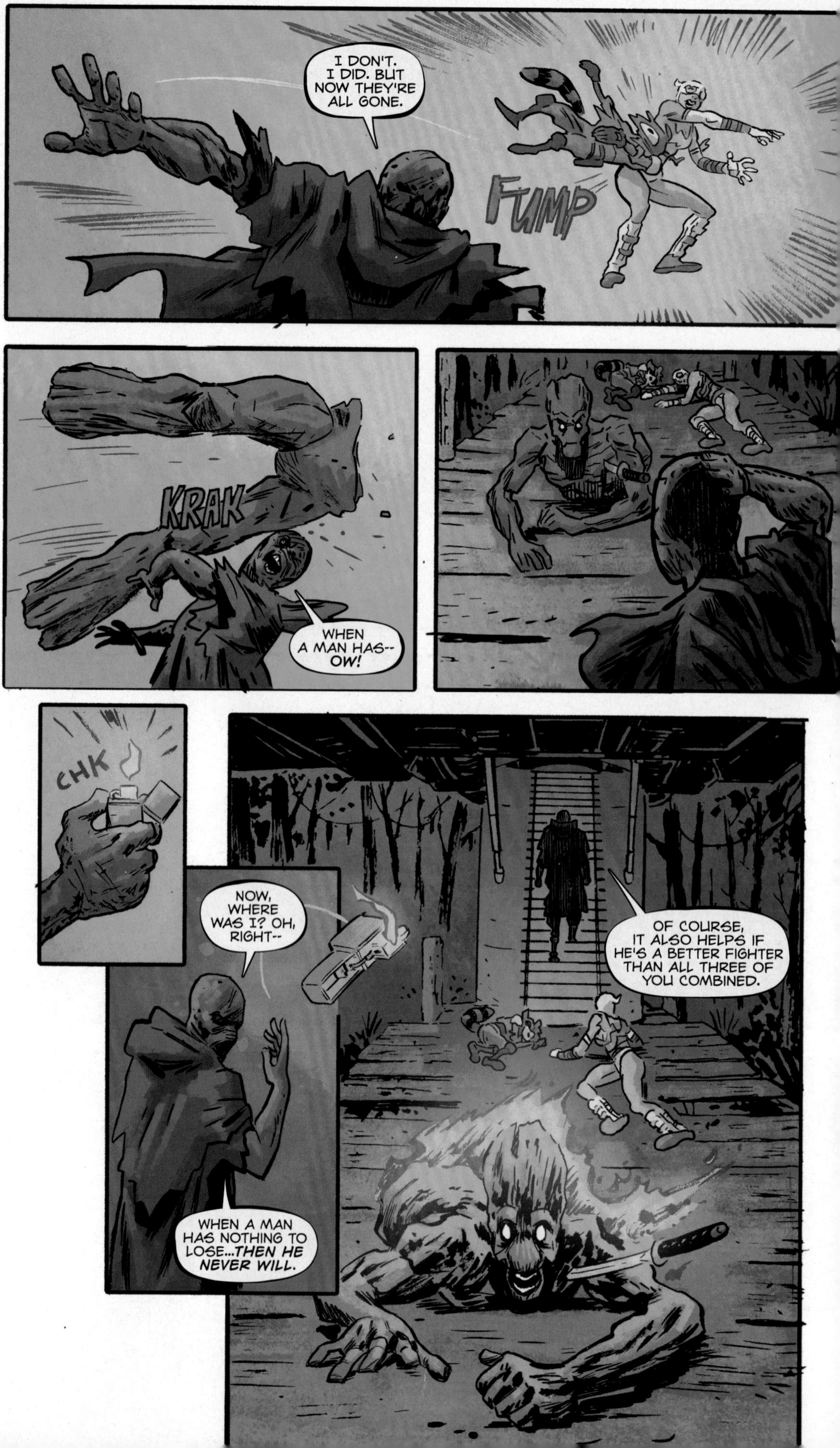
I DON'T. I DID. BUT NOW THEY'RE ALL GONE.
FUMP
KRAK
WHEN A MAN HAS-- OW!
CHK
NOW, WHERE WAS I? OH, RIGHT--
WHEN A MAN HAS NOTHING TO LOSE...THEN HE NEVER WILL.
OF COURSE, IT ALSO HELPS IF HE'S A BETTER FIGHTER THAN ALL THREE OF YOU COMBINED.

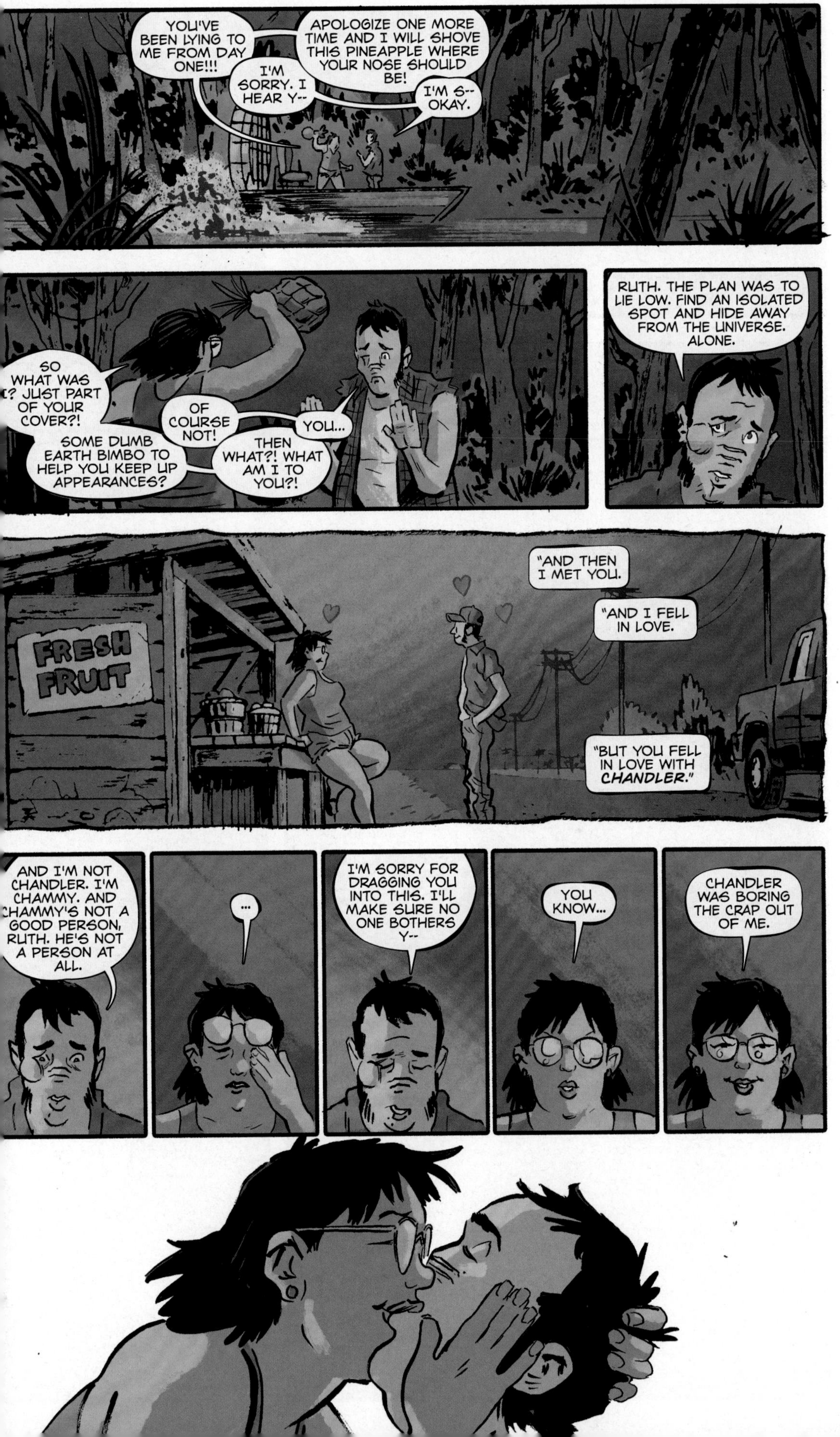
YOU'VE BEEN LYING TO ME FROM DAY ONE!!!
I'M SORRY. I HEAR Y--
APOLOGIZE ONE MORE TIME AND I WILL SHOVE THIS PINEAPPLE WHERE YOUR NOSE SHOULD BE!
I'M S-- OKAY.
SO WHAT WAS I? JUST PART OF YOUR COVER?!
SOME DUMB EARTH BIMBO TO HELP YOU KEEP UP APPEARANCES?
OF COURSE NOT!
THEN WHAT?! WHAT AM I TO YOU?!
YOU...
RUTH. THE PLAN WAS TO LIE LOW. FIND AN ISOLATED SPOT AND HIDE AWAY FROM THE UNIVERSE. ALONE.
FRESH FRUIT
"AND THEN I MET YOU.
"AND I FELL IN LOVE.
"BUT YOU FELL IN LOVE WITH CHANDLER."
AND I'M NOT CHANDLER. I'M CHAMMY. AND CHAMMY'S NOT A GOOD PERSON, RUTH. HE'S NOT A PERSON AT ALL.
...
I'M SORRY FOR DRAGGING YOU INTO THIS. I'LL MAKE SURE NO ONE BOTHERS Y--
YOU KNOW...
CHANDLER WAS BORING THE CRAP OUT OF ME.

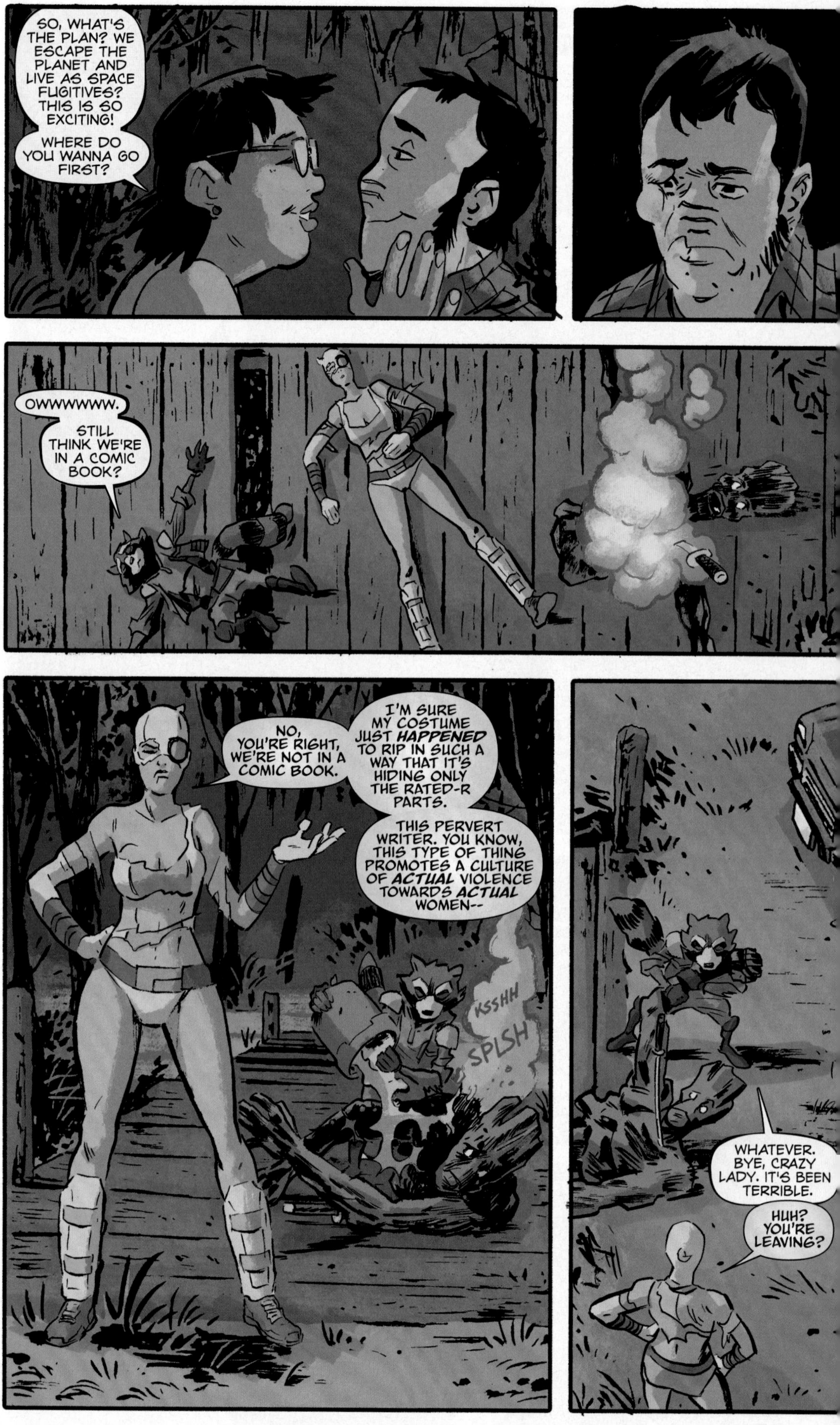
SO, WHAT'S THE PLAN? WE ESCAPE THE PLANET AND LIVE AS SPACE FUGITIVES? THIS IS SO EXCITING!
WHERE DO YOU WANNA GO FIRST?
OWWWWWW.
STILL THINK WE'RE IN A COMIC BOOK?
NO, YOU'RE RIGHT, WE'RE NOT IN A COMIC BOOK.
I'M SURE MY COSTUME JUST **HAPPENED** TO RIP IN SUCH A WAY THAT IT'S HIDING ONLY THE RATED-R PARTS.
THIS PERVERT WRITER. YOU KNOW, THIS TYPE OF THING PROMOTES A CULTURE OF **ACTUAL** VIOLENCE TOWARDS **ACTUAL** WOMEN--
KSSHH
SPLSH
WHATEVER. BYE, CRAZY LADY. IT'S BEEN TERRIBLE.
HUH? YOU'RE LEAVING?

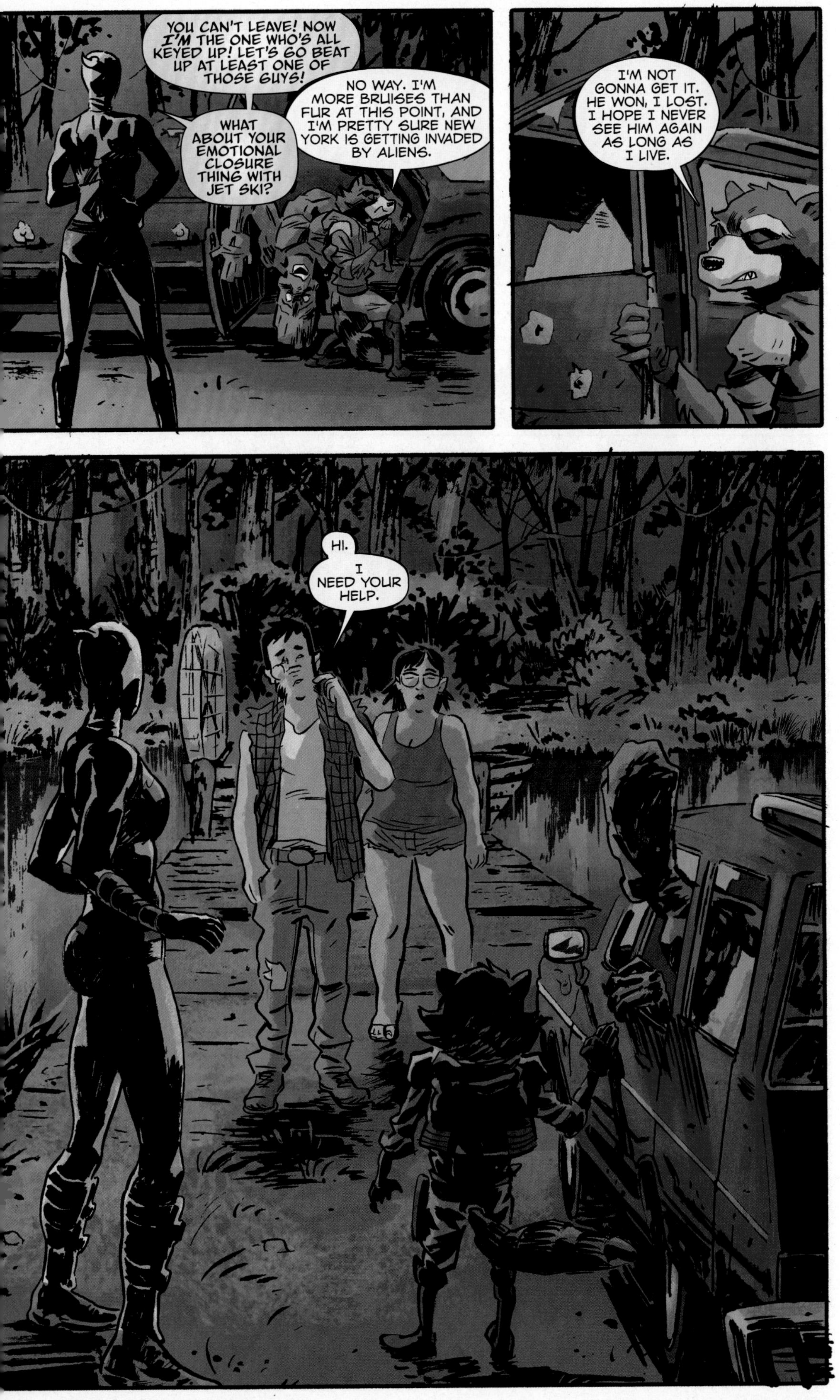
YOU CAN'T LEAVE! NOW *I'M* THE ONE WHO'S ALL KEYED UP! LET'S GO BEAT UP AT LEAST ONE OF THOSE GUYS!
WHAT ABOUT YOUR EMOTIONAL CLOSURE THING WITH JET SKI?
NO WAY. I'M MORE BRUISES THAN FUR AT THIS POINT, AND I'M PRETTY SURE NEW YORK IS GETTING INVADED BY ALIENS.
I'M NOT GONNA GET IT. HE WON, I LOST. I HOPE I NEVER SEE HIM AGAIN AS LONG AS I LIVE.
HI.
I NEED YOUR HELP.

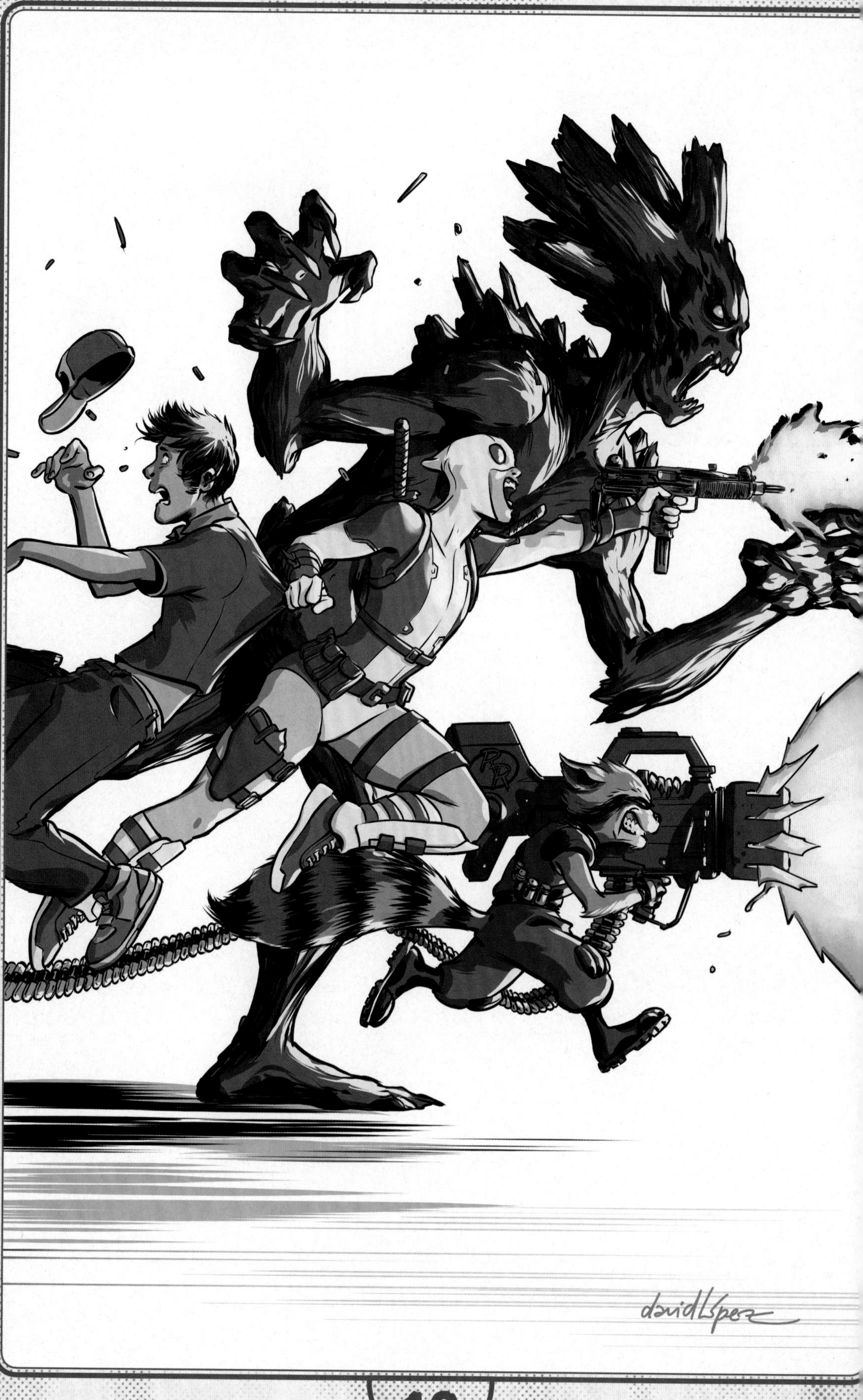
davidLópez

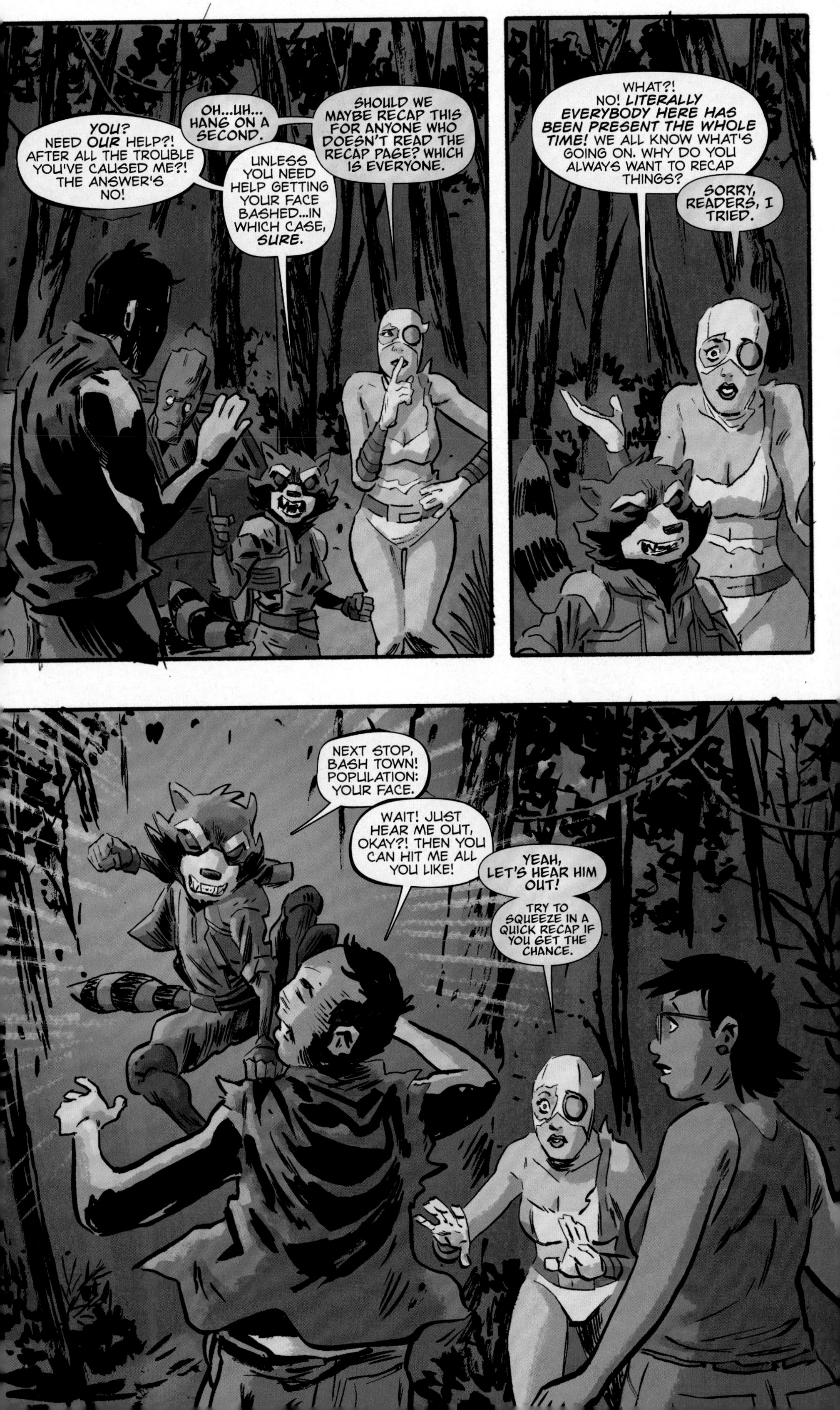
YOU? NEED OUR HELP?! AFTER ALL THE TROUBLE YOU'VE CAUSED ME?! THE ANSWER'S NO!
OH...UH... HANG ON A SECOND.
UNLESS YOU NEED HELP GETTING YOUR FACE BASHED...IN WHICH CASE, SURE.
SHOULD WE MAYBE RECAP THIS FOR ANYONE WHO DOESN'T READ THE RECAP PAGE? WHICH IS EVERYONE.
WHAT?! NO! LITERALLY EVERYBODY HERE HAS BEEN PRESENT THE WHOLE TIME! WE ALL KNOW WHAT'S GOING ON. WHY DO YOU ALWAYS WANT TO RECAP THINGS?
SORRY, READERS, I TRIED.
NEXT STOP, BASH TOWN! POPULATION: YOUR FACE.
WAIT! JUST HEAR ME OUT, OKAY?! THEN YOU CAN HIT ME ALL YOU LIKE!
YEAH, LET'S HEAR HIM OUT!
TRY TO SQUEEZE IN A QUICK RECAP IF YOU GET THE CHANCE.

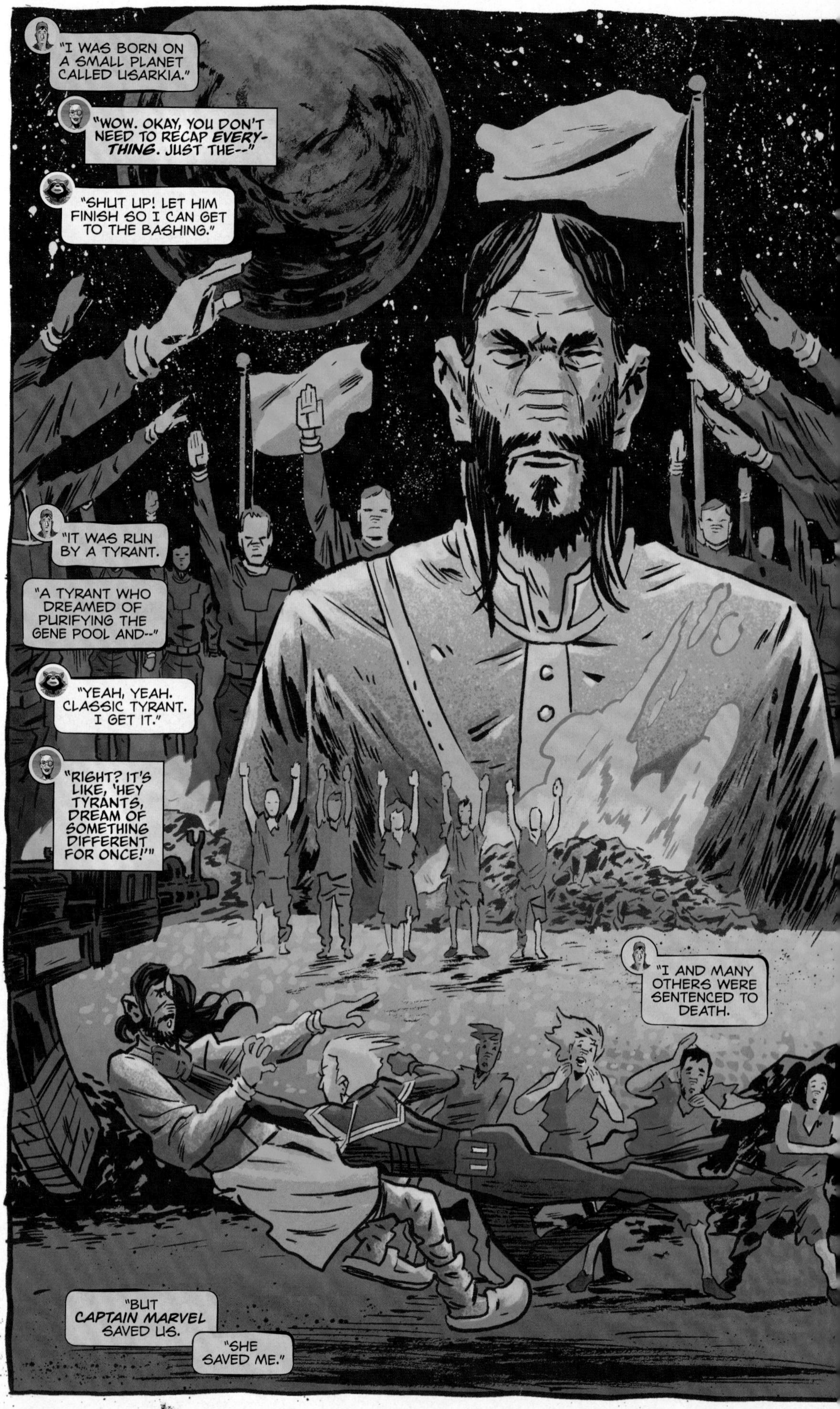

"I WAS BORN ON A SMALL PLANET CALLED USARKIA."
"WOW. OKAY, YOU DON'T NEED TO RECAP EVERY-THING. JUST THE--"
"SHUT UP! LET HIM FINISH SO I CAN GET TO THE BASHING."
"IT WAS RUN BY A TYRANT.
"A TYRANT WHO DREAMED OF PURIFYING THE GENE POOL AND--"
"YEAH, YEAH. CLASSIC TYRANT. I GET IT."
"RIGHT? IT'S LIKE, 'HEY TYRANTS, DREAM OF SOMETHING DIFFERENT FOR ONCE!'"
"I AND MANY OTHERS WERE SENTENCED TO DEATH.
"BUT CAPTAIN MARVEL SAVED US.
"SHE SAVED ME."

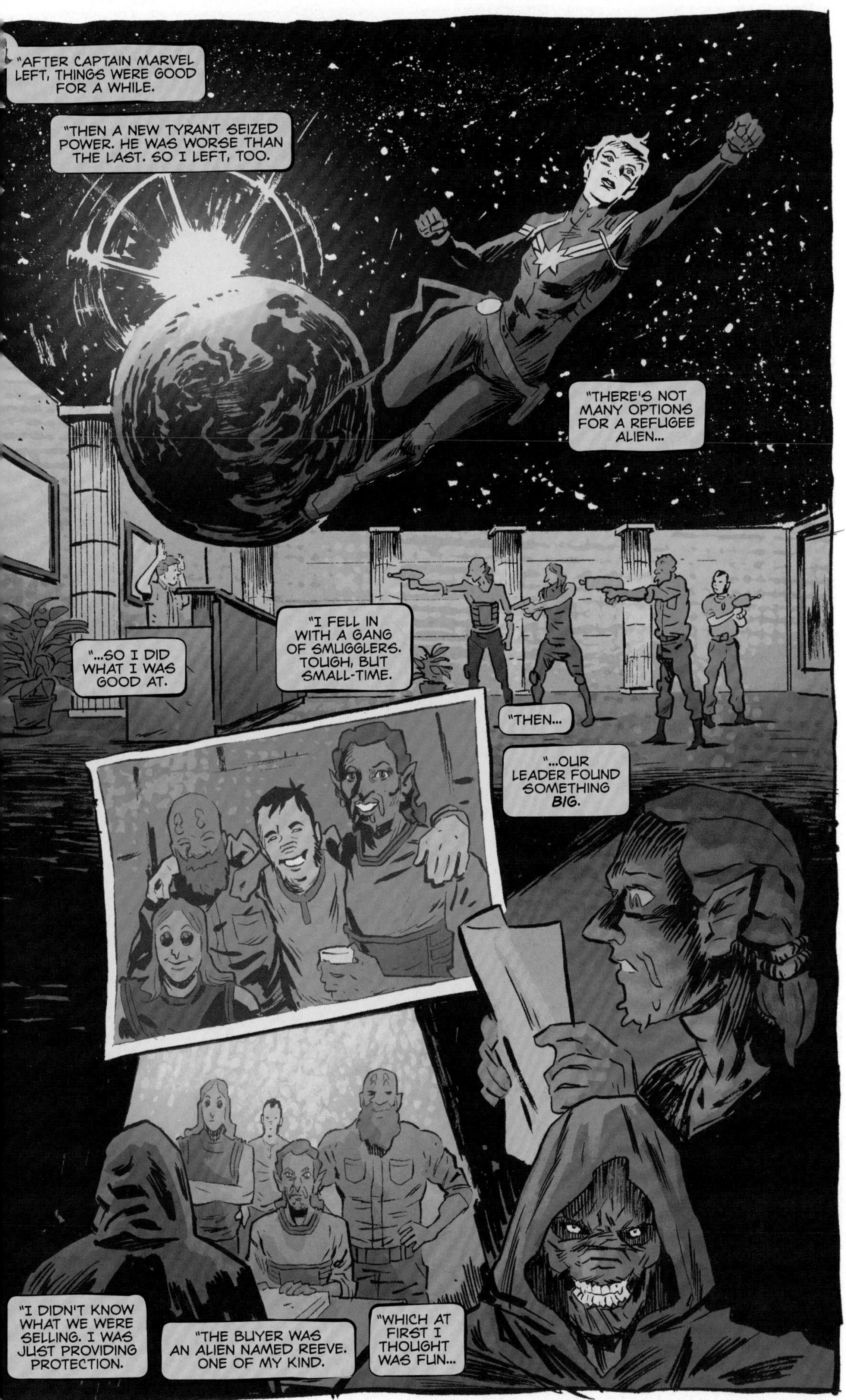
"AFTER CAPTAIN MARVEL LEFT, THINGS WERE GOOD FOR A WHILE.
"THEN A NEW TYRANT SEIZED POWER. HE WAS WORSE THAN THE LAST. SO I LEFT, TOO.
"THERE'S NOT MANY OPTIONS FOR A REFUGEE ALIEN...
"...SO I DID WHAT I WAS GOOD AT.
"I FELL IN WITH A GANG OF SMUGGLERS. TOUGH, BUT SMALL-TIME.
"THEN...
"...OUR LEADER FOUND SOMETHING *BIG*.
"I DIDN'T KNOW WHAT WE WERE SELLING. I WAS JUST PROVIDING PROTECTION.
"THE BUYER WAS AN ALIEN NAMED REEVE. ONE OF MY KIND.
"WHICH AT FIRST I THOUGHT WAS FUN...

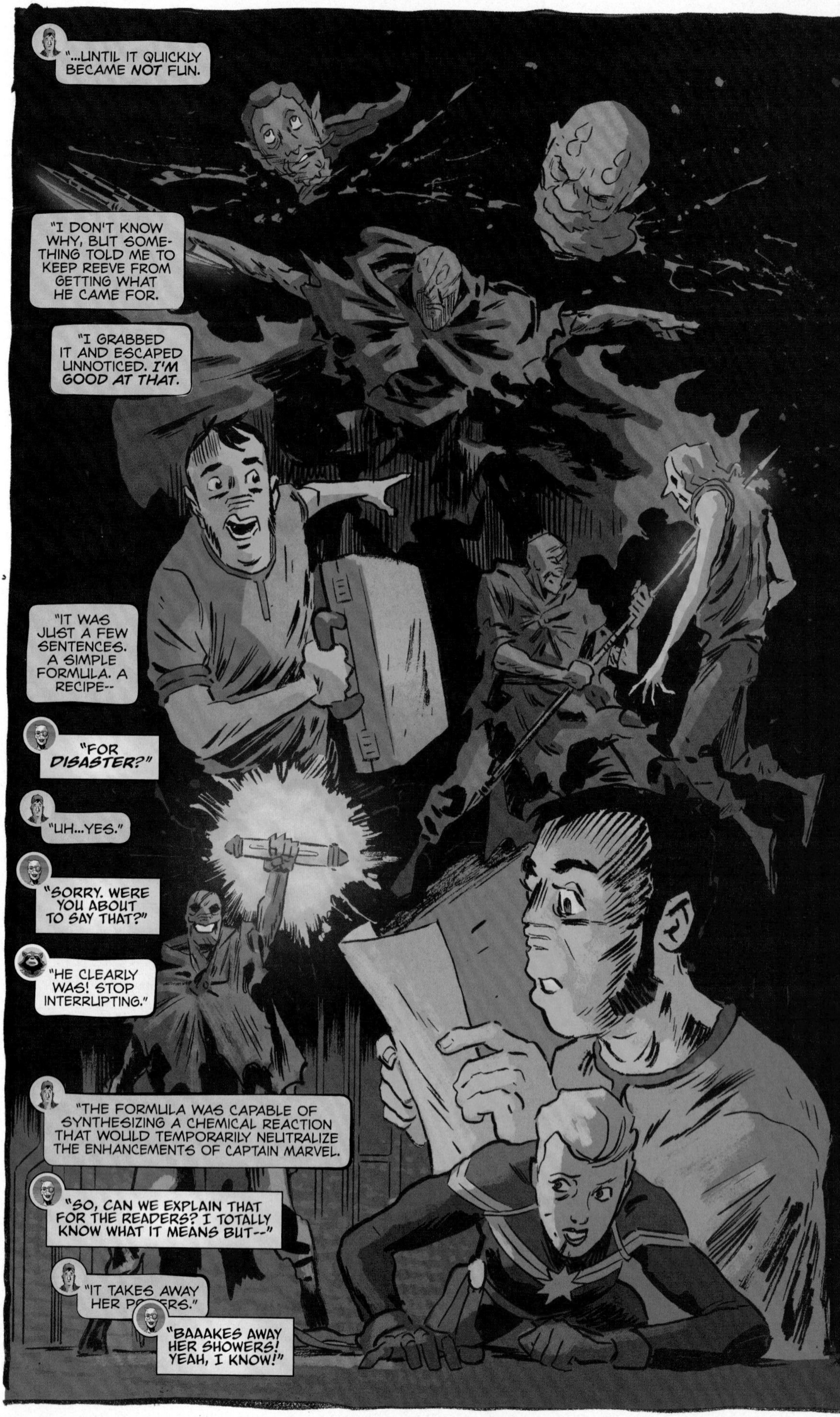
"...UNTIL IT QUICKLY BECAME *NOT* FUN.
"I DON'T KNOW WHY, BUT SOMETHING TOLD ME TO KEEP REEVE FROM GETTING WHAT HE CAME FOR.
"I GRABBED IT AND ESCAPED UNNOTICED. *I'M GOOD AT THAT.*
"IT WAS JUST A FEW SENTENCES. A SIMPLE FORMULA. A RECIPE--
"FOR *DISASTER?*"
"UH...YES."
"SORRY. WERE YOU ABOUT TO SAY THAT?"
"HE CLEARLY WAS! STOP INTERRUPTING."
"THE FORMULA WAS CAPABLE OF SYNTHESIZING A CHEMICAL REACTION THAT WOULD TEMPORARILY NEUTRALIZE THE ENHANCEMENTS OF CAPTAIN MARVEL.
"SO, CAN WE EXPLAIN THAT FOR THE READERS? I TOTALLY KNOW WHAT IT MEANS BUT--"
"IT TAKES AWAY HER PO ERS."
"BAAAKES AWAY HER SHOWERS! YEAH, I KNOW!"

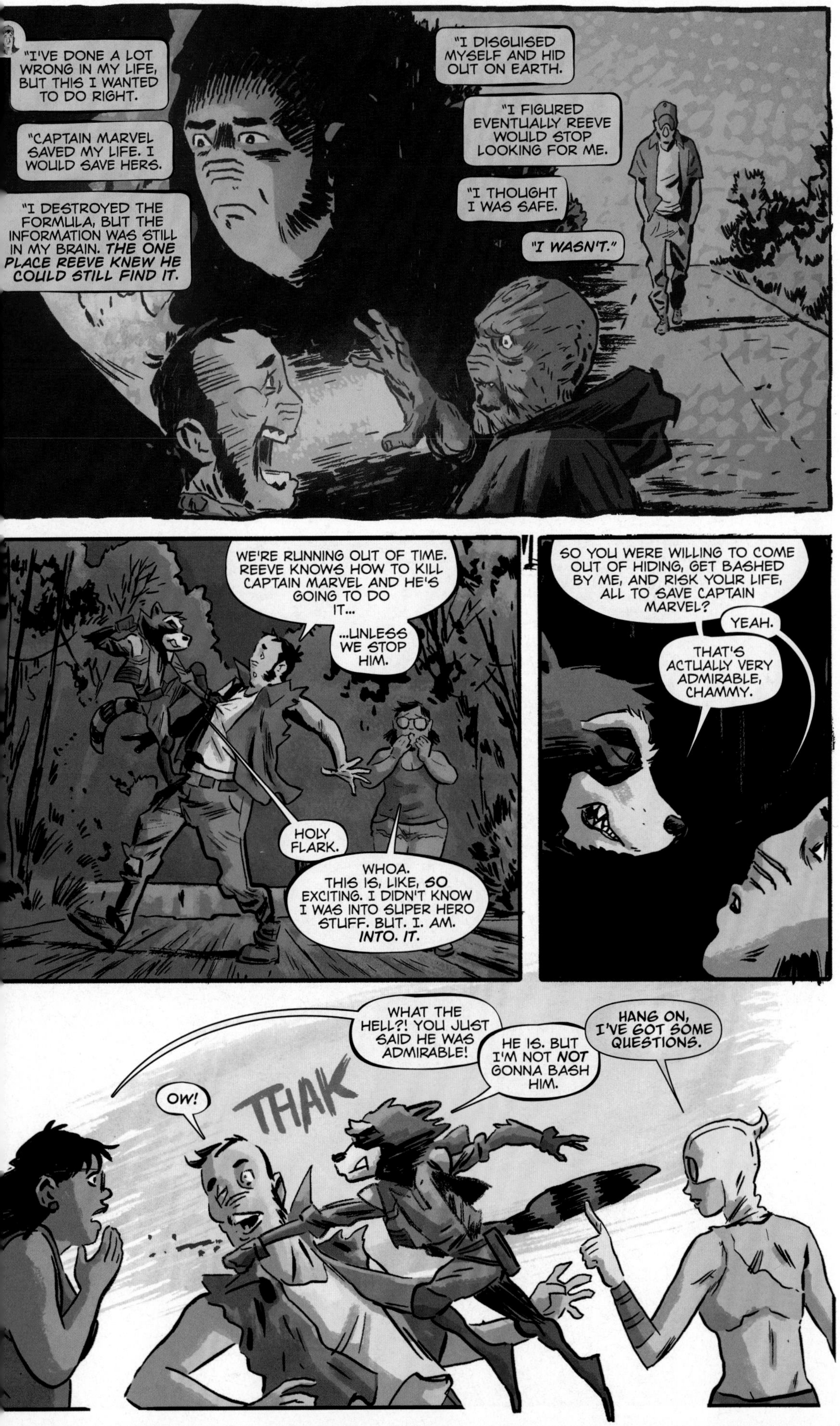
"I'VE DONE A LOT WRONG IN MY LIFE, BUT THIS I WANTED TO DO RIGHT.
"CAPTAIN MARVEL SAVED MY LIFE. I WOULD SAVE HERS.
"I DESTROYED THE FORMULA, BUT THE INFORMATION WAS STILL IN MY BRAIN. *THE ONE PLACE REEVE KNEW HE COULD STILL FIND IT.*
"I DISGUISED MYSELF AND HID OUT ON EARTH.
"I FIGURED EVENTUALLY REEVE WOULD STOP LOOKING FOR ME.
"I THOUGHT I WAS SAFE.
"I WASN'T."
WE'RE RUNNING OUT OF TIME. REEVE KNOWS HOW TO KILL CAPTAIN MARVEL AND HE'S GOING TO DO IT...
...UNLESS WE STOP HIM.
HOLY FLARK.
WHOA. THIS IS, LIKE, *SO* EXCITING. I DIDN'T KNOW I WAS INTO SUPER HERO STUFF. BUT. I. AM. *INTO. IT.*
SO YOU WERE WILLING TO COME OUT OF HIDING, GET BASHED BY ME, AND RISK YOUR LIFE, ALL TO SAVE CAPTAIN MARVEL?
YEAH.
THAT'S ACTUALLY VERY ADMIRABLE, CHAMMY.
OW!
THAK
WHAT THE HELL?! YOU JUST SAID HE WAS ADMIRABLE!
HE IS. BUT I'M NOT *NOT* GONNA BASH HIM.
HANG ON, I'VE GOT SOME QUESTIONS.

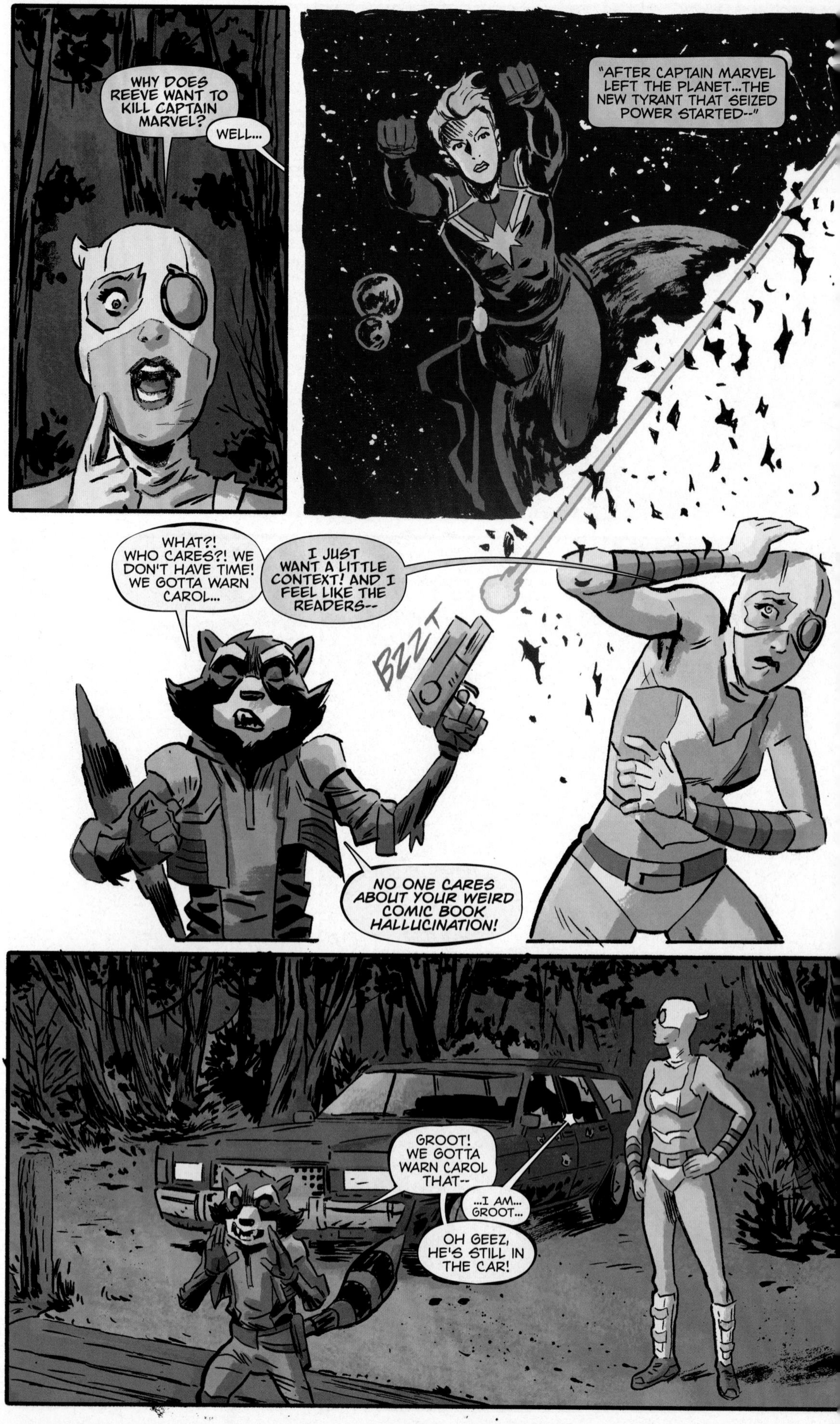
WHY DOES REEVE WANT TO KILL CAPTAIN MARVEL?
WELL...
"AFTER CAPTAIN MARVEL LEFT THE PLANET...THE NEW TYRANT THAT SEIZED POWER STARTED--"
WHAT?! WHO CARES?! WE DON'T HAVE TIME! WE GOTTA WARN CAROL...
I JUST WANT A LITTLE CONTEXT! AND I FEEL LIKE THE READERS--
BZZT
NO ONE CARES ABOUT YOUR WEIRD COMIC BOOK HALLUCINATION!
GROOT! WE GOTTA WARN CAROL THAT--
...I AM... GROOT...
OH GEEZ, HE'S STILL IN THE CAR!

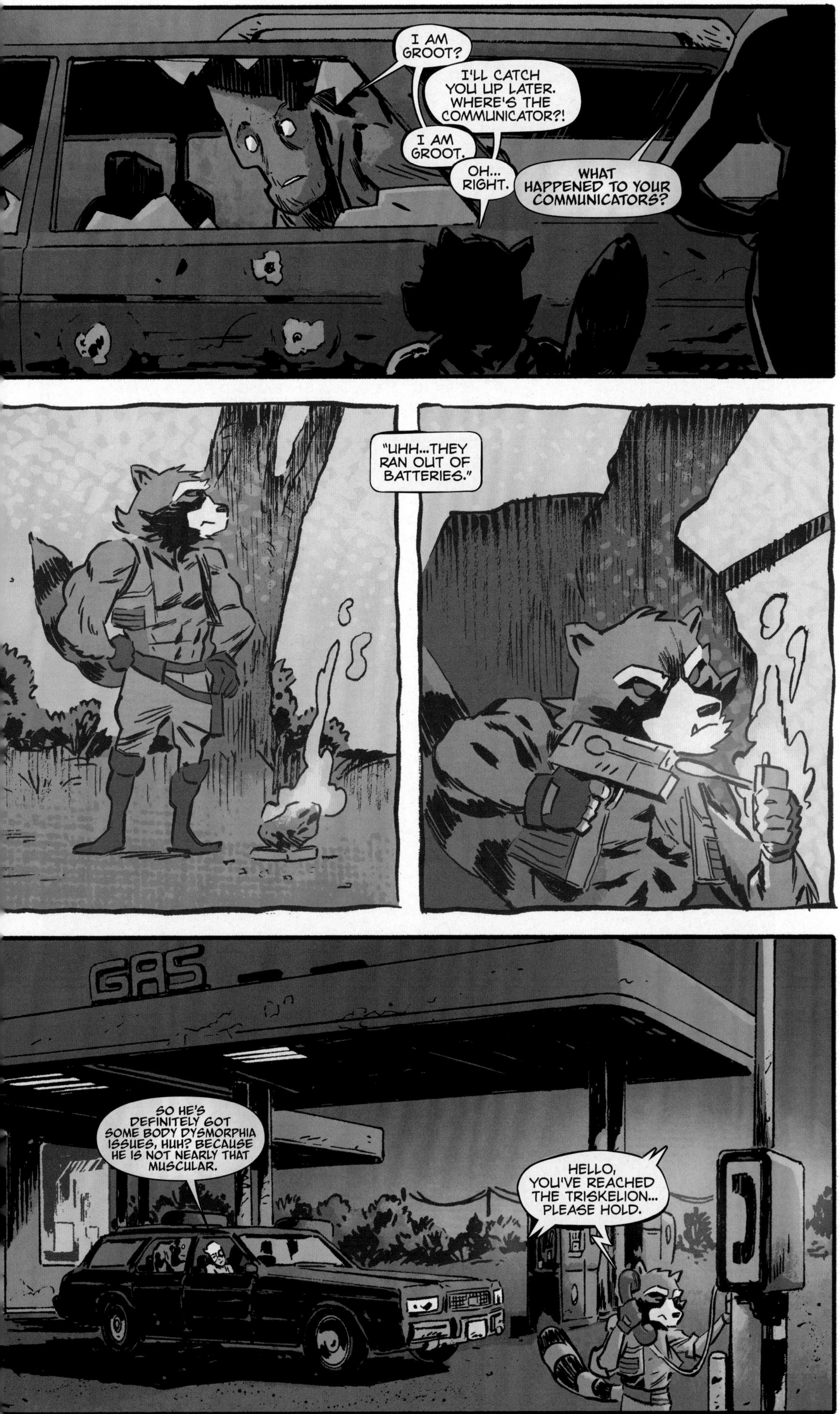
I AM GROOT?
I'LL CATCH YOU UP LATER. WHERE'S THE COMMUNICATOR?!
I AM GROOT.
OH... RIGHT.
WHAT HAPPENED TO YOUR COMMUNICATORS?
"UHH...THEY RAN OUT OF BATTERIES."
GAS
SO HE'S DEFINITELY GOT SOME BODY DYSMORPHIA ISSUES, HUH? BECAUSE HE IS NOT NEARLY THAT MUSCULAR.
HELLO, YOU'VE REACHED THE TRISKELION... PLEASE HOLD.

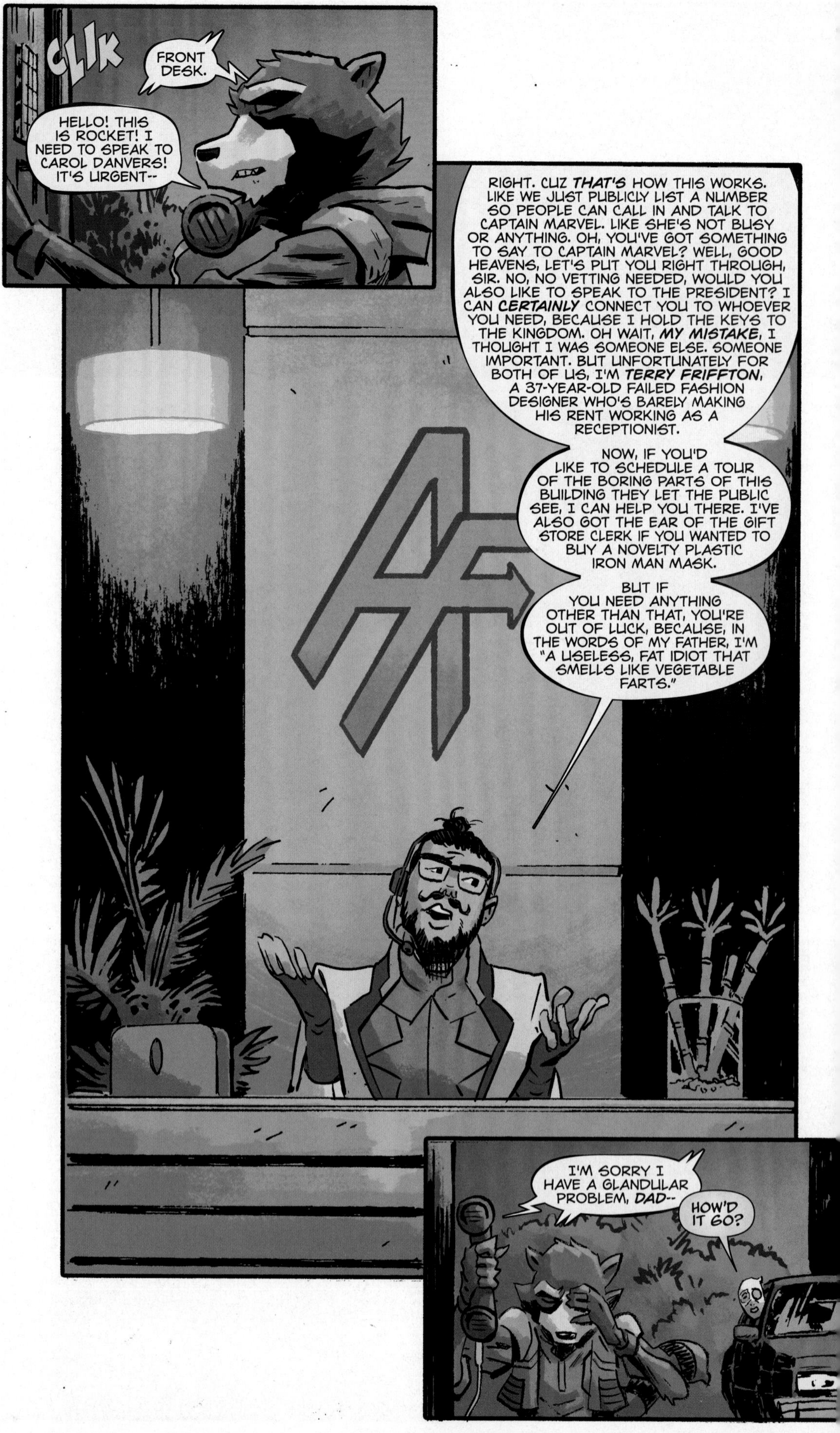
CLIK
FRONT DESK.
HELLO! THIS IS ROCKET! I NEED TO SPEAK TO CAROL DANVERS! IT'S URGENT--
RIGHT. CUZ THAT'S HOW THIS WORKS. LIKE WE JUST PUBLICLY LIST A NUMBER SO PEOPLE CAN CALL IN AND TALK TO CAPTAIN MARVEL. LIKE SHE'S NOT BUSY OR ANYTHING. OH, YOU'VE GOT SOMETHING TO SAY TO CAPTAIN MARVEL? WELL, GOOD HEAVENS, LET'S PUT YOU RIGHT THROUGH, SIR. NO, NO VETTING NEEDED, WOULD YOU ALSO LIKE TO SPEAK TO THE PRESIDENT? I CAN CERTAINLY CONNECT YOU TO WHOEVER YOU NEED, BECAUSE I HOLD THE KEYS TO THE KINGDOM. OH WAIT, MY MISTAKE, I THOUGHT I WAS SOMEONE ELSE. SOMEONE IMPORTANT. BUT UNFORTUNATELY FOR BOTH OF US, I'M TERRY FRIFFTON, A 37-YEAR-OLD FAILED FASHION DESIGNER WHO'S BARELY MAKING HIS RENT WORKING AS A RECEPTIONIST.
NOW, IF YOU'D LIKE TO SCHEDULE A TOUR OF THE BORING PARTS OF THIS BUILDING THEY LET THE PUBLIC SEE, I CAN HELP YOU THERE. I'VE ALSO GOT THE EAR OF THE GIFT STORE CLERK IF YOU WANTED TO BUY A NOVELTY PLASTIC IRON MAN MASK.
BUT IF YOU NEED ANYTHING OTHER THAN THAT, YOU'RE OUT OF LUCK, BECAUSE, IN THE WORDS OF MY FATHER, I'M "A USELESS, FAT IDIOT THAT SMELLS LIKE VEGETABLE FARTS."
I'M SORRY I HAVE A GLANDULAR PROBLEM, DAD--
HOW'D IT GO?

SKREEEE

ALL RIGHT, EVERY-BODY! QUICK AS YOU CAN!

GWEN! LET'S GO!

I'M NOT GOING.

COME ON! THAT LUNATIC'S GONNA KILL CAPTAIN MARVEL!

NO, HE'S NOT.

WHAT DO YOU MEAN, HE'S NOT?!

BECAUSE THEY'RE NOT GONNA KILL OFF CAPTAIN MARVEL IN A COMIC BOOK STARRING SQUIRREL AND THE TALKING TREE!

WHAT?

WHAT'S SHE TALKING ABOUT?

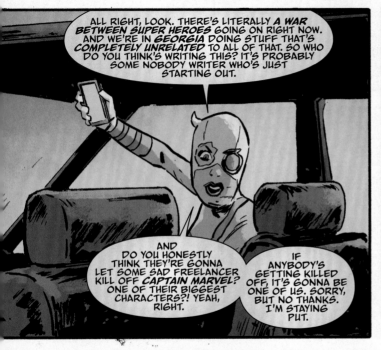

ALL RIGHT, LOOK. THERE'S LITERALLY *A WAR BETWEEN SUPER HEROES* GOING ON RIGHT NOW. AND WE'RE IN *GEORGIA* DOING STUFF THAT'S *COMPLETELY UNRELATED* TO ALL OF THAT. SO WHO DO YOU THINK'S WRITING THIS? IT'S PROBABLY SOME NOBODY WRITER WHO'S JUST STARTING OUT.

AND DO YOU HONESTLY THINK THEY'RE GONNA LET SOME SAD FREELANCER KILL OFF *CAPTAIN MARVEL?* ONE OF THEIR BIGGEST CHARACTERS?! YEAH, RIGHT.

IF ANYBODY'S GETTING KILLED OFF, IT'S GONNA BE ONE OF US. SORRY, BUT NO THANKS. I'M STAYING PUT.

I AM GROOT?

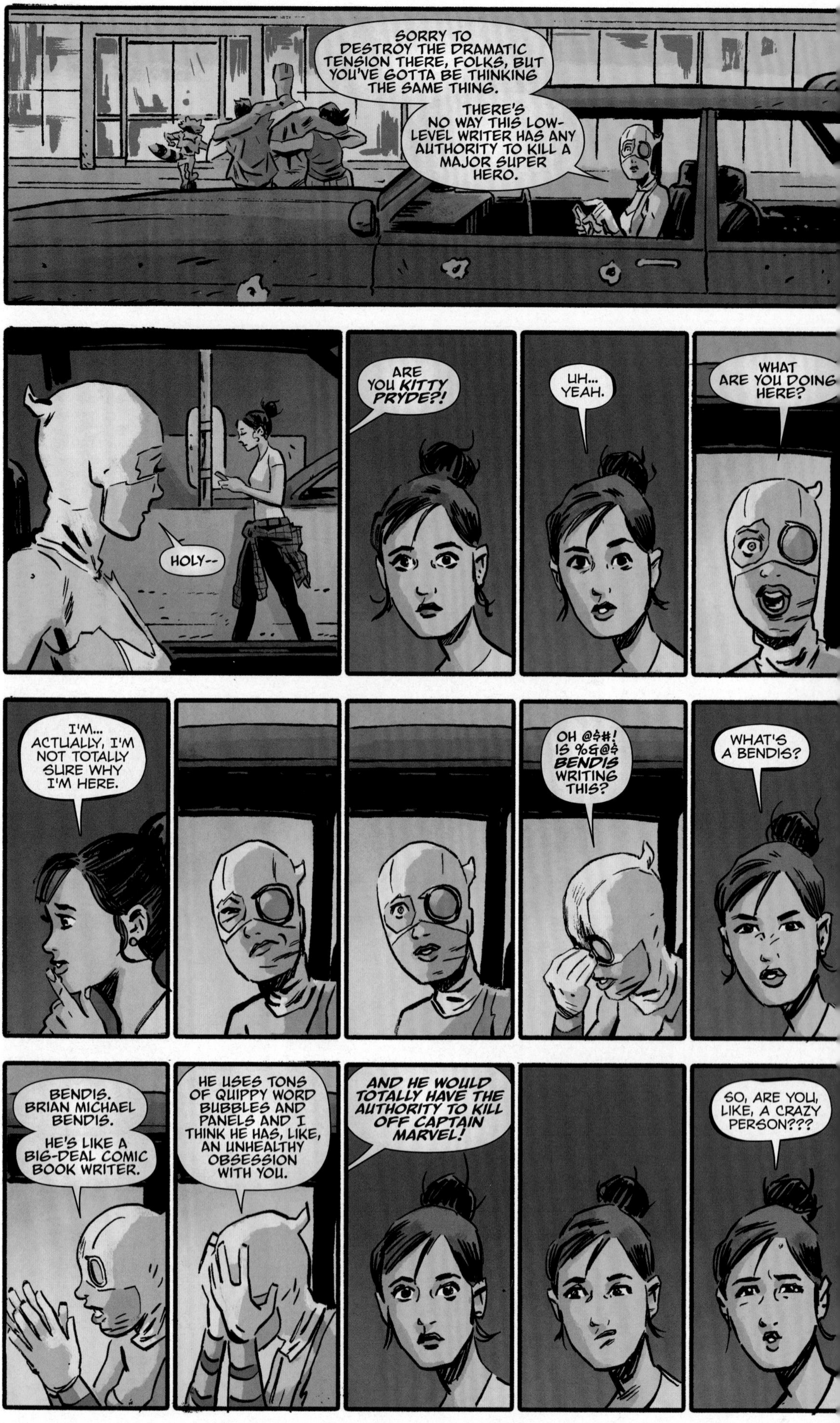
SORRY TO DESTROY THE DRAMATIC TENSION THERE, FOLKS, BUT YOU'VE GOTTA BE THINKING THE SAME THING.
THERE'S NO WAY THIS LOW-LEVEL WRITER HAS ANY AUTHORITY TO KILL A MAJOR SUPER HERO.
HOLY--
ARE YOU *KITTY PRYDE?!*
UH... YEAH.
WHAT ARE YOU DOING HERE?
I'M... ACTUALLY, I'M NOT TOTALLY SURE WHY I'M HERE.
OH @$#! IS %&@$ *BENDIS* WRITING THIS?
WHAT'S A BENDIS?
BENDIS. BRIAN MICHAEL BENDIS.
HE'S LIKE A BIG-DEAL COMIC BOOK WRITER.
HE USES TONS OF QUIPPY WORD BUBBLES AND PANELS AND I THINK HE HAS, LIKE, AN UNHEALTHY OBSESSION WITH YOU.
AND HE WOULD TOTALLY HAVE THE AUTHORITY TO KILL OFF CAPTAIN MARVEL!
SO, ARE YOU, LIKE, A CRAZY PERSON???

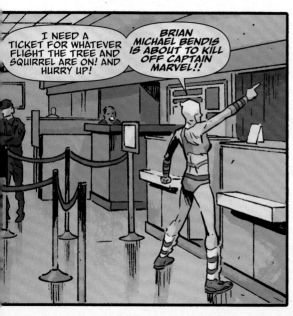

I NEED A TICKET FOR WHATEVER FLIGHT THE TREE AND SQUIRREL ARE ON! AND HURRY UP!

BRIAN MICHAEL BENDIS IS ABOUT TO KILL OFF CAPTAIN MARVEL!!

OKAY, I'VE GOT ONE TICKET LEFT, BUT IT'S A MIDDLE SEAT.

OH... YUCK.

HMM...IS THIS REALLY WORTH IT? I DON'T KNOW HER PERSONALLY...

I JUST DON'T SEE WHY YOU SHOULD GET THE AISLE, YOU HAVE THE SHORTEST LEGS OF ANY OF US!

THE TRISKELION.

GOOD WORK TODAY, GUYS. GET SOME REST.

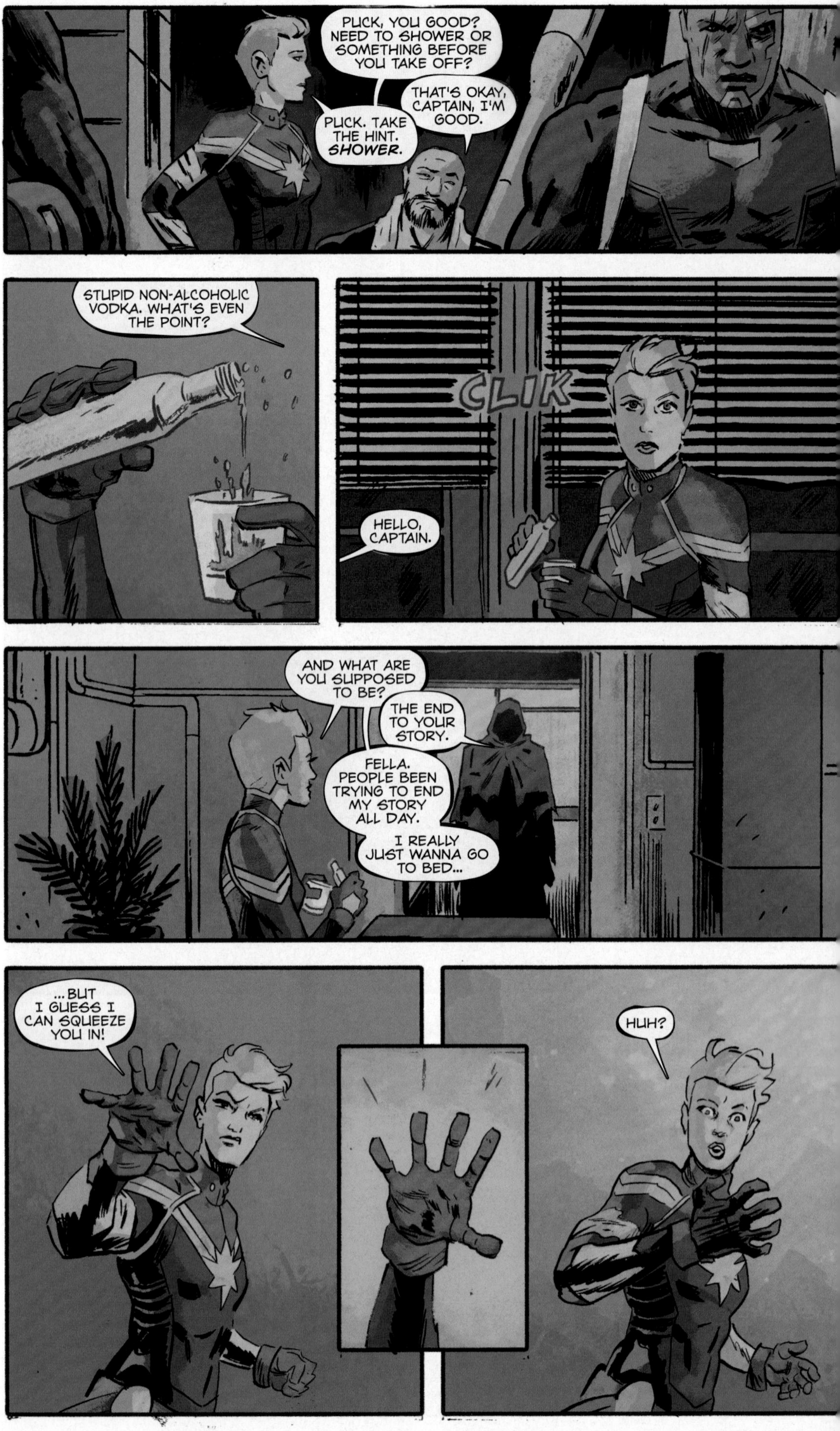
PUCK, YOU GOOD? NEED TO SHOWER OR SOMETHING BEFORE YOU TAKE OFF?
PUCK. TAKE THE HINT. *SHOWER*.
THAT'S OKAY, CAPTAIN, I'M GOOD.
STUPID NON-ALCOHOLIC VODKA. WHAT'S EVEN THE POINT?
CLIK
HELLO, CAPTAIN.
AND WHAT ARE YOU SUPPOSED TO BE?
THE END TO YOUR STORY.
FELLA. PEOPLE BEEN TRYING TO END MY STORY ALL DAY.
I REALLY JUST WANNA GO TO BED...
...BUT I GUESS I CAN SQUEEZE YOU IN!
HUH?

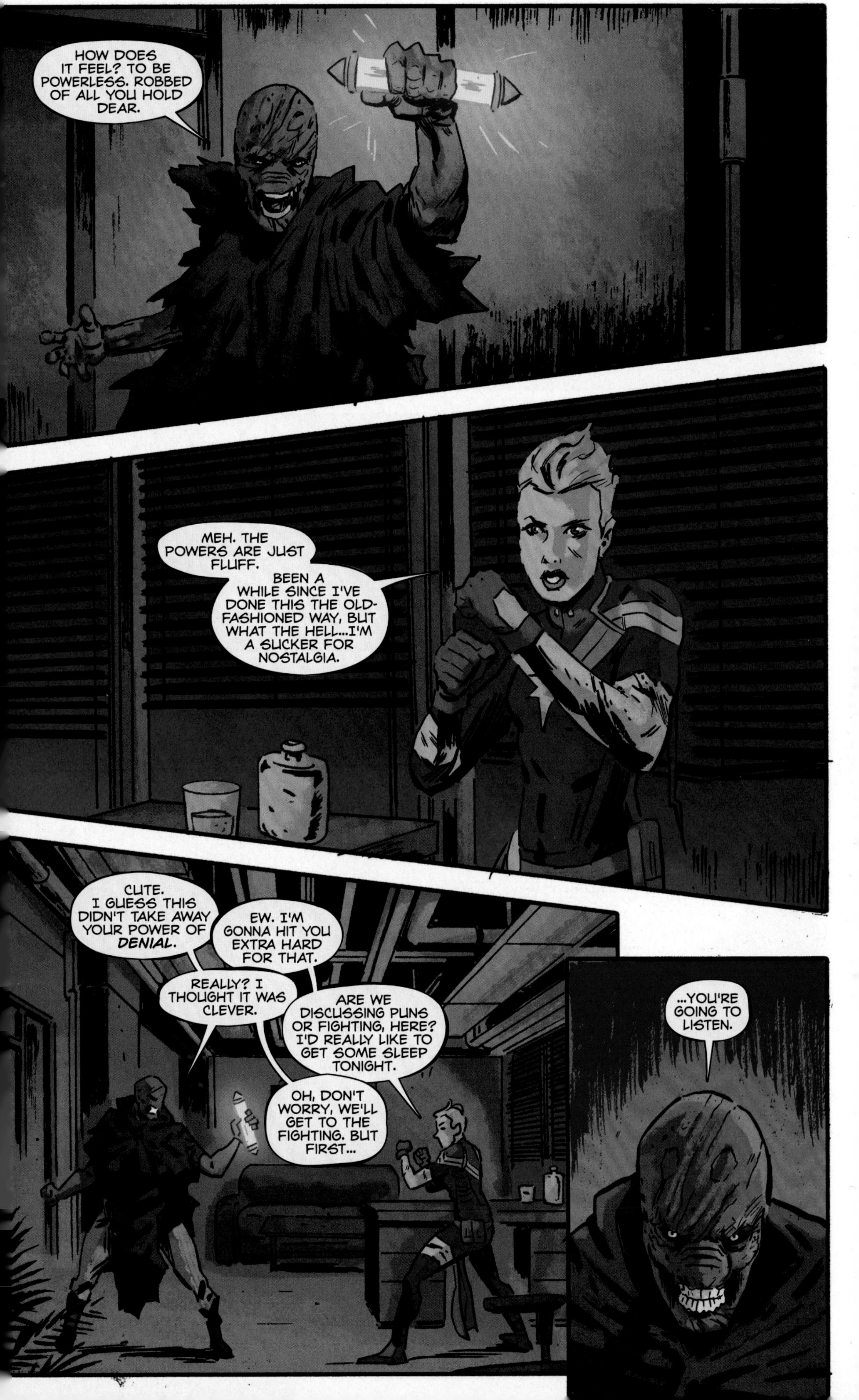
HOW DOES IT FEEL? TO BE POWERLESS. ROBBED OF ALL YOU HOLD DEAR.
MEH. THE POWERS ARE JUST FLUFF.
BEEN A WHILE SINCE I'VE DONE THIS THE OLD-FASHIONED WAY, BUT WHAT THE HELL...I'M A SUCKER FOR NOSTALGIA.
CUTE. I GUESS THIS DIDN'T TAKE AWAY YOUR POWER OF *DENIAL*.
EW. I'M GONNA HIT YOU EXTRA HARD FOR THAT.
REALLY? I THOUGHT IT WAS CLEVER.
ARE WE DISCUSSING PUNS OR FIGHTING, HERE? I'D REALLY LIKE TO GET SOME SLEEP TONIGHT.
OH, DON'T WORRY, WE'LL GET TO THE FIGHTING. BUT FIRST...
...YOU'RE GOING TO LISTEN.

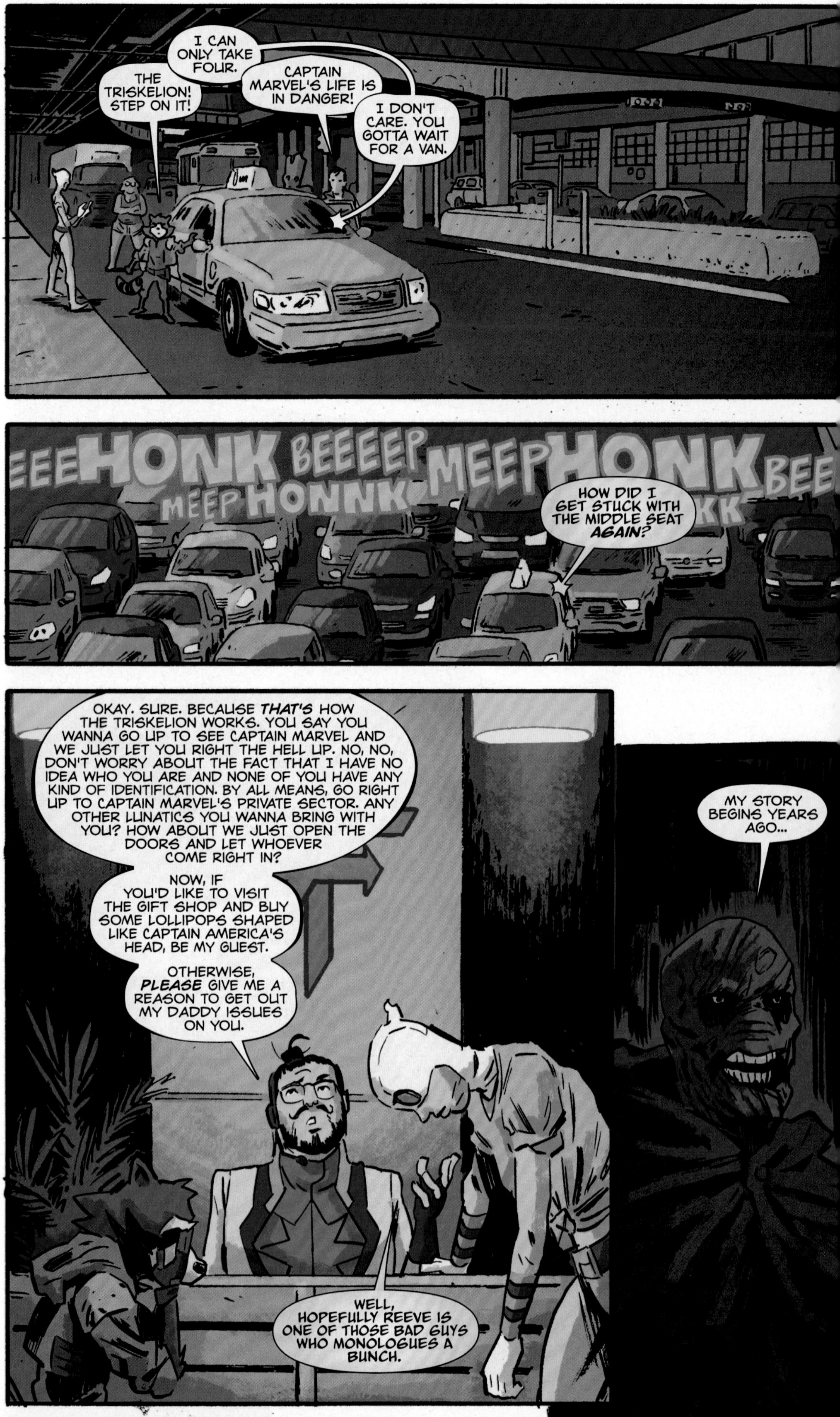
THE TRISKELION! STEP ON IT!
I CAN ONLY TAKE FOUR.
CAPTAIN MARVEL'S LIFE IS IN DANGER!
I DON'T CARE. YOU GOTTA WAIT FOR A VAN.
EEEHONK BEEEEP MEEPHONK BEE
MEEP HONNK
KK
HOW DID I GET STUCK WITH THE MIDDLE SEAT *AGAIN?*
OKAY. SURE. BECAUSE *THAT'S* HOW THE TRISKELION WORKS. YOU SAY YOU WANNA GO UP TO SEE CAPTAIN MARVEL AND WE JUST LET YOU RIGHT THE HELL UP. NO, NO, DON'T WORRY ABOUT THE FACT THAT I HAVE NO IDEA WHO YOU ARE AND NONE OF YOU HAVE ANY KIND OF IDENTIFICATION. BY ALL MEANS, GO RIGHT UP TO CAPTAIN MARVEL'S PRIVATE SECTOR. ANY OTHER LUNATICS YOU WANNA BRING WITH YOU? HOW ABOUT WE JUST OPEN THE DOORS AND LET WHOEVER COME RIGHT IN?
NOW, IF YOU'D LIKE TO VISIT THE GIFT SHOP AND BUY SOME LOLLIPOPS SHAPED LIKE CAPTAIN AMERICA'S HEAD, BE MY GUEST.
OTHERWISE, *PLEASE* GIVE ME A REASON TO GET OUT MY DADDY ISSUES ON YOU.
WELL, HOPEFULLY REEVE IS ONE OF THOSE BAD GUYS WHO MONOLOGUES A BUNCH.
MY STORY BEGINS YEARS AGO...

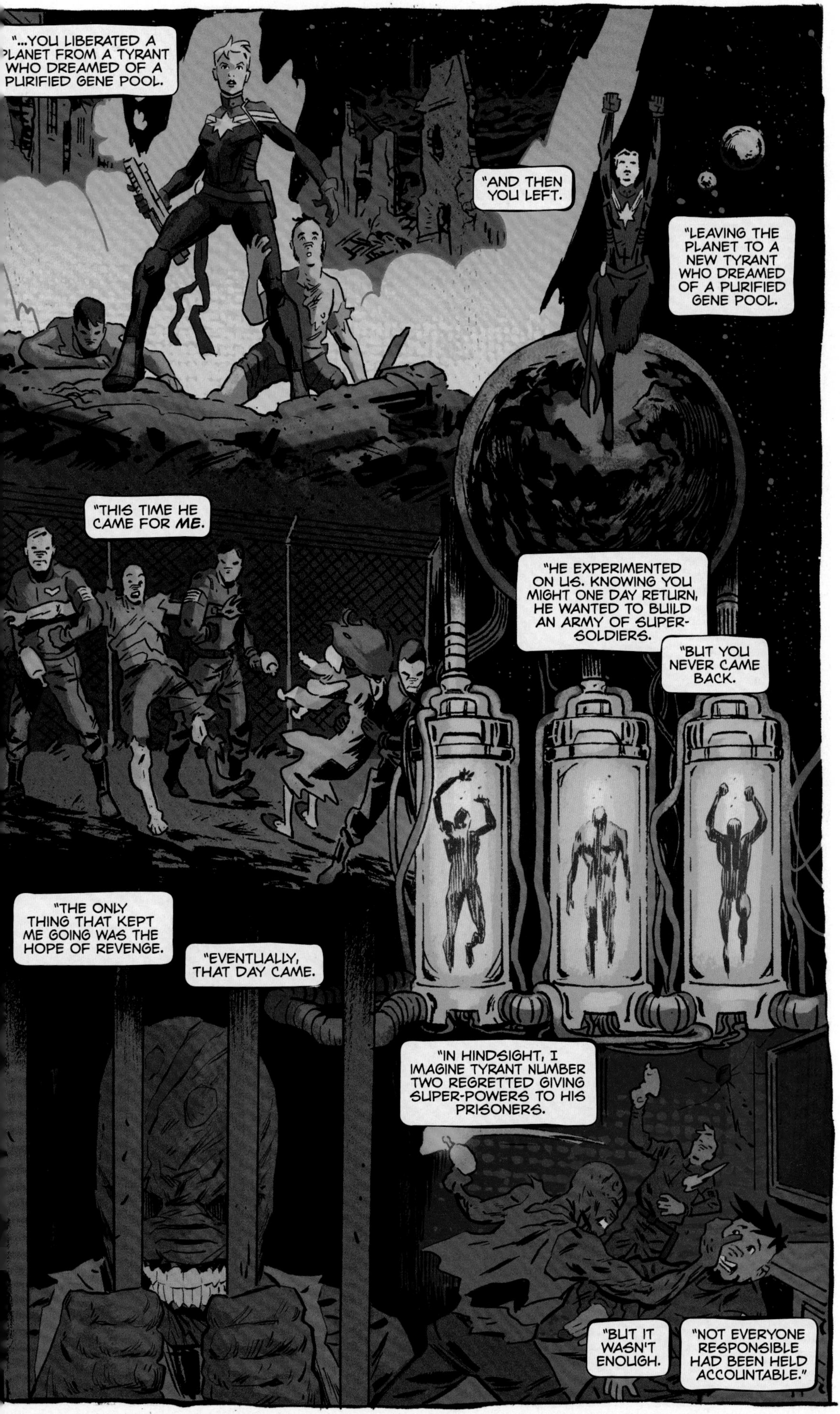
"...YOU LIBERATED A PLANET FROM A TYRANT WHO DREAMED OF A PURIFIED GENE POOL.
"AND THEN YOU LEFT.
"LEAVING THE PLANET TO A NEW TYRANT WHO DREAMED OF A PURIFIED GENE POOL.
"THIS TIME HE CAME FOR *ME*.
"HE EXPERIMENTED ON US. KNOWING YOU MIGHT ONE DAY RETURN, HE WANTED TO BUILD AN ARMY OF SUPER-SOLDIERS.
"BUT YOU NEVER CAME BACK.
"THE ONLY THING THAT KEPT ME GOING WAS THE HOPE OF REVENGE.
"EVENTUALLY, THAT DAY CAME.
"IN HINDSIGHT, I IMAGINE TYRANT NUMBER TWO REGRETTED GIVING SUPER-POWERS TO HIS PRISONERS.
"BUT IT WASN'T ENOUGH.
"NOT EVERYONE RESPONSIBLE HAD BEEN HELD ACCOUNTABLE."

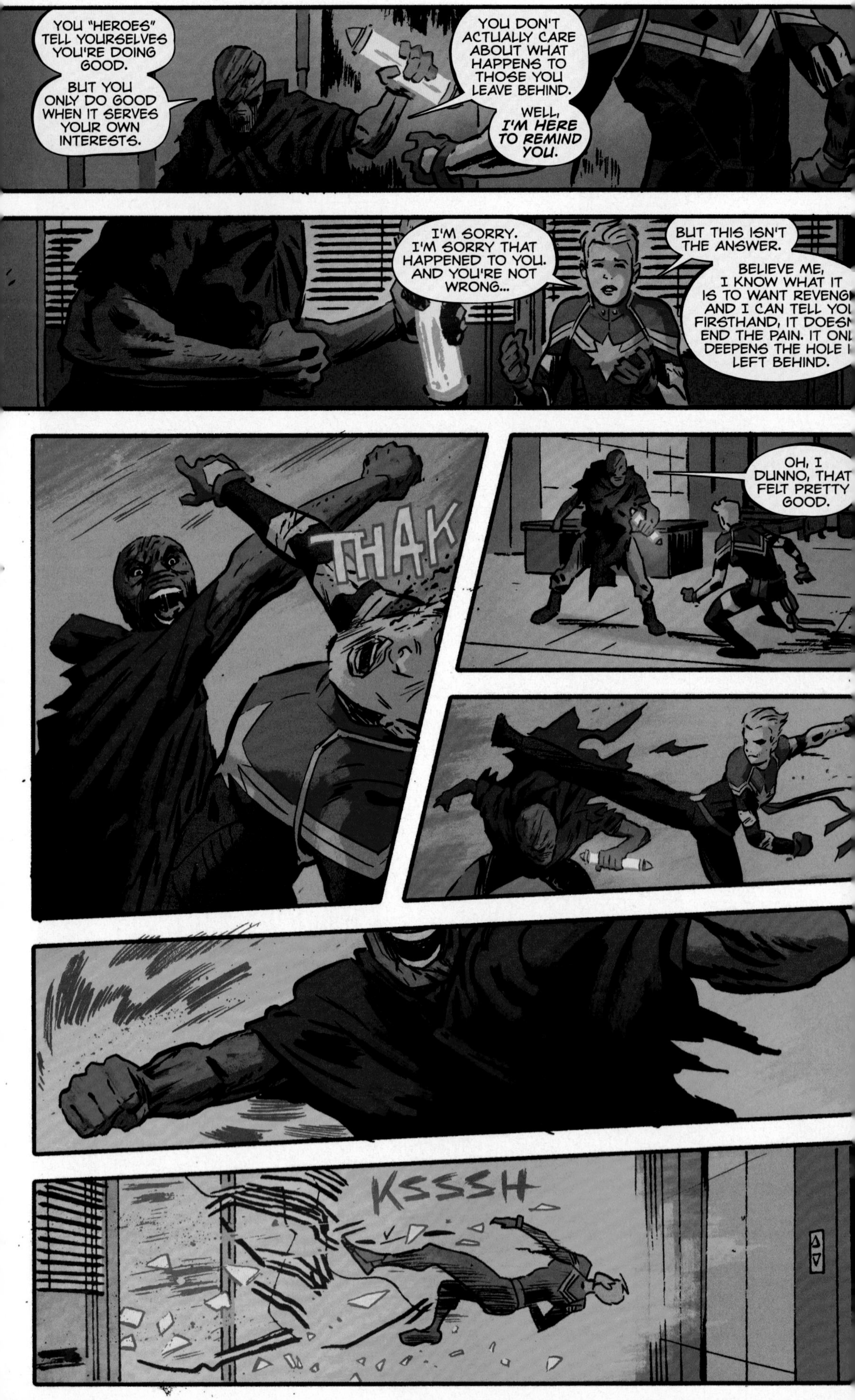

YOU "HEROES" TELL YOURSELVES YOU'RE DOING GOOD.
BUT YOU ONLY DO GOOD WHEN IT SERVES YOUR OWN INTERESTS.
YOU DON'T ACTUALLY CARE ABOUT WHAT HAPPENS TO THOSE YOU LEAVE BEHIND.
WELL, *I'M HERE TO REMIND* YOU.
I'M SORRY. I'M SORRY THAT HAPPENED TO YOU. AND YOU'RE NOT WRONG...
BUT THIS ISN'T THE ANSWER.
BELIEVE ME, I KNOW WHAT IT IS TO WANT REVENG AND I CAN TELL YO FIRSTHAND, IT DOES END THE PAIN. IT ON DEEPENS THE HOLE LEFT BEHIND.
THAK
OH, I DUNNO, THAT FELT PRETTY GOOD.
KSSSH

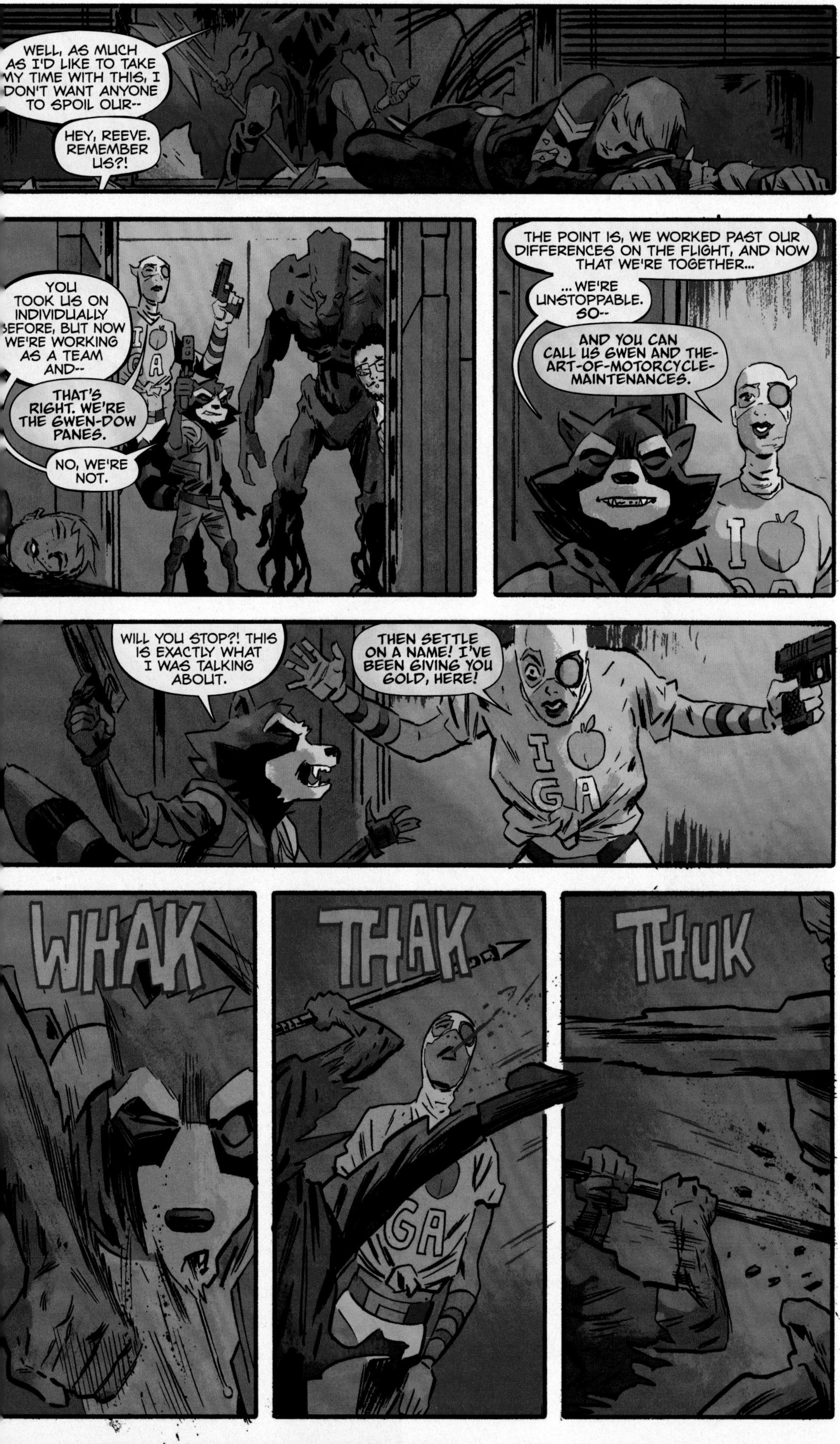
WELL, AS MUCH AS I'D LIKE TO TAKE MY TIME WITH THIS, I DON'T WANT ANYONE TO SPOIL OUR--
HEY, REEVE. REMEMBER US?!
YOU TOOK US ON INDIVIDUALLY BEFORE, BUT NOW WE'RE WORKING AS A TEAM AND--
THAT'S RIGHT. WE'RE THE GWEN-DOW PANES.
NO, WE'RE NOT.
THE POINT IS, WE WORKED PAST OUR DIFFERENCES ON THE FLIGHT, AND NOW THAT WE'RE TOGETHER...
...WE'RE UNSTOPPABLE. SO--
AND YOU CAN CALL US GWEN AND THE-ART-OF-MOTORCYCLE-MAINTENANCES.
WILL YOU STOP?! THIS IS EXACTLY WHAT I WAS TALKING ABOUT.
THEN SETTLE ON A NAME! I'VE BEEN GIVING YOU GOLD, HERE!
WHAK
THAK
THUK

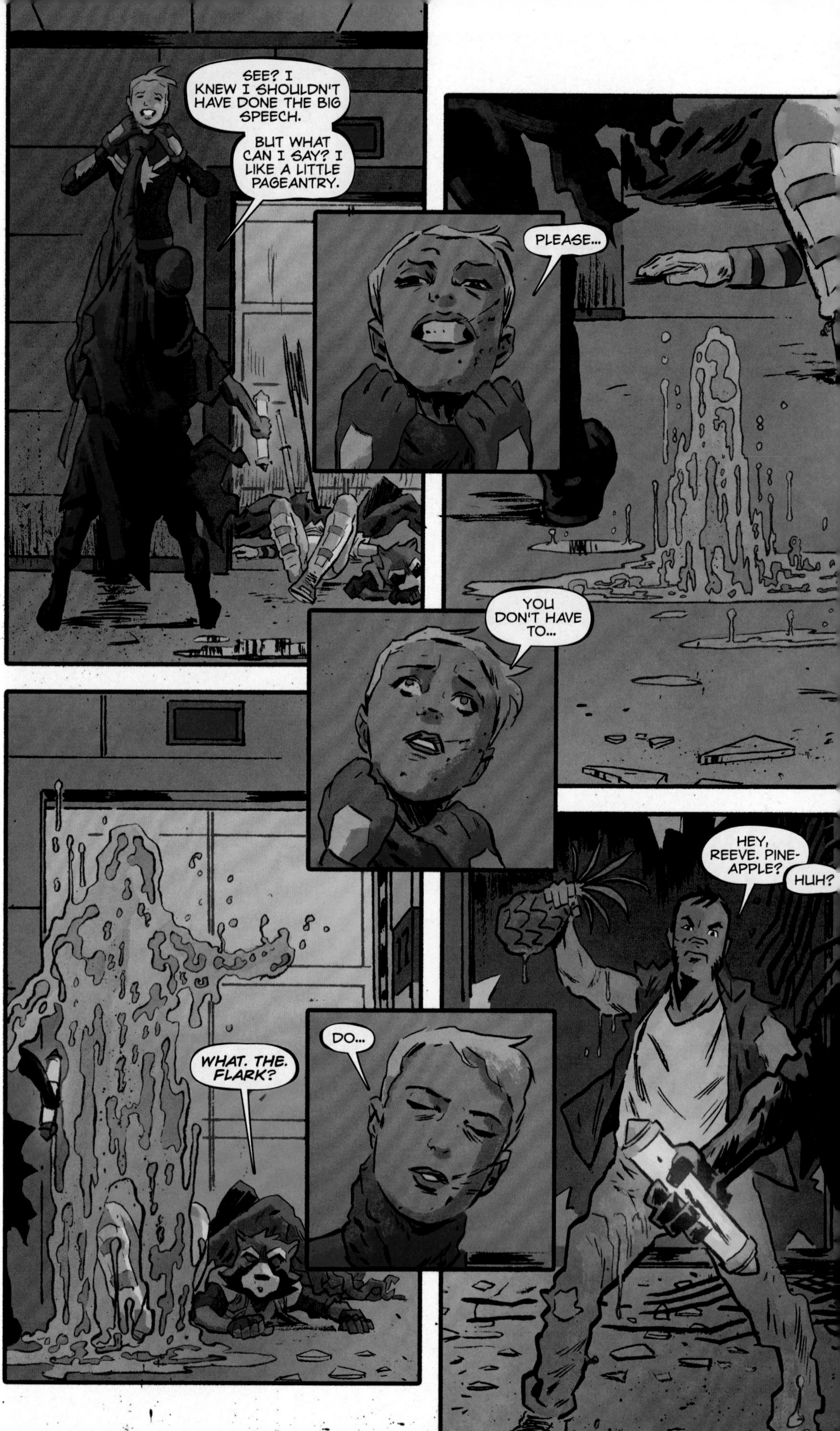

SEE? I KNEW I SHOULDN'T HAVE DONE THE BIG SPEECH.
BUT WHAT CAN I SAY? I LIKE A LITTLE PAGEANTRY.
PLEASE...
YOU DON'T HAVE TO...
DO...
WHAT. THE. FLARK?
HEY, REEVE. PINE-APPLE?
HUH?

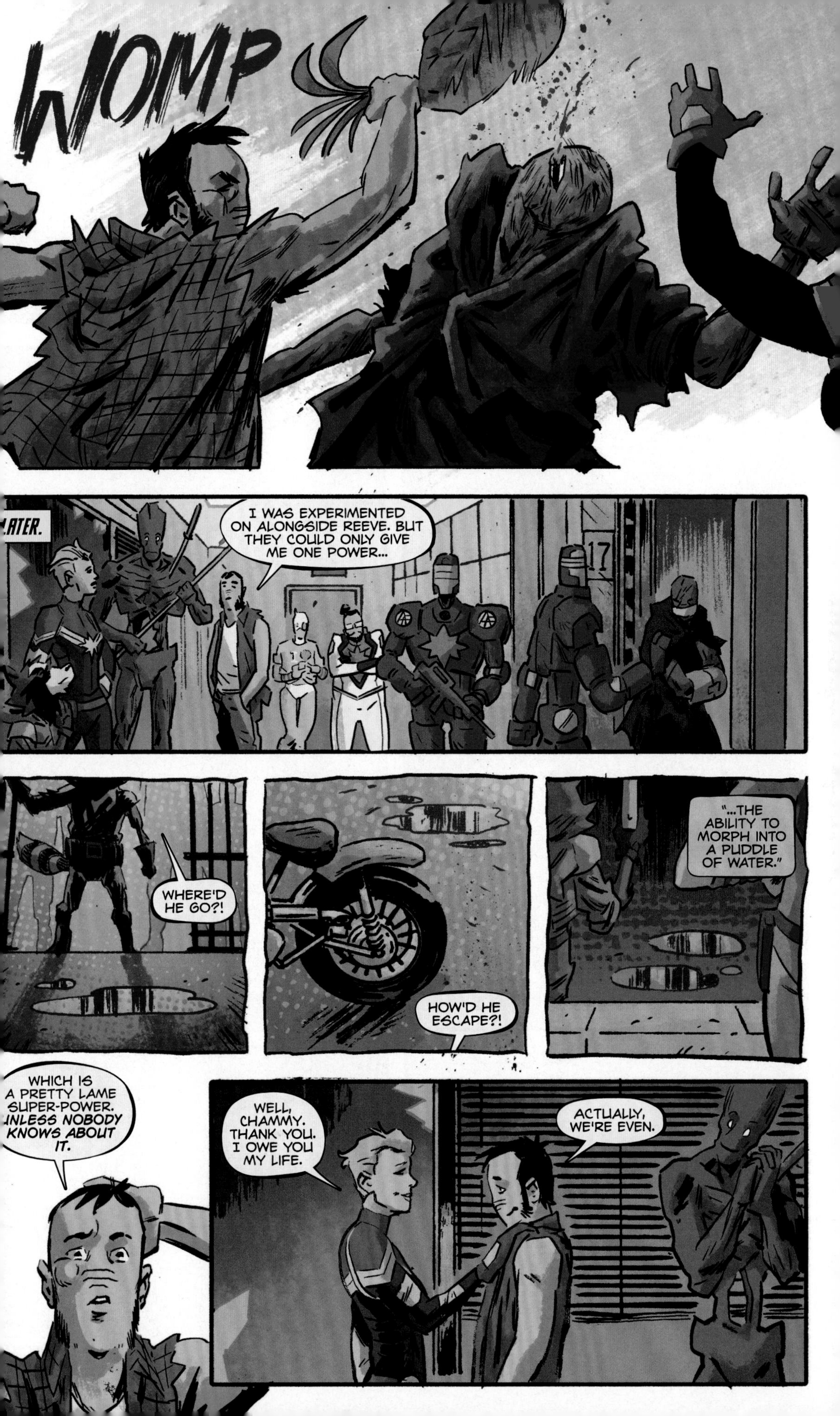
WOMP
LATER.
I WAS EXPERIMENTED ON ALONGSIDE REEVE. BUT THEY COULD ONLY GIVE ME ONE POWER...
17
WHERE'D HE GO?!
HOW'D HE ESCAPE?!
"...THE ABILITY TO MORPH INTO A PUDDLE OF WATER."
WHICH IS A PRETTY LAME SUPER-POWER. UNLESS NOBODY KNOWS ABOUT IT.
WELL, CHAMMY. THANK YOU. I OWE YOU MY LIFE.
ACTUALLY, WE'RE EVEN.

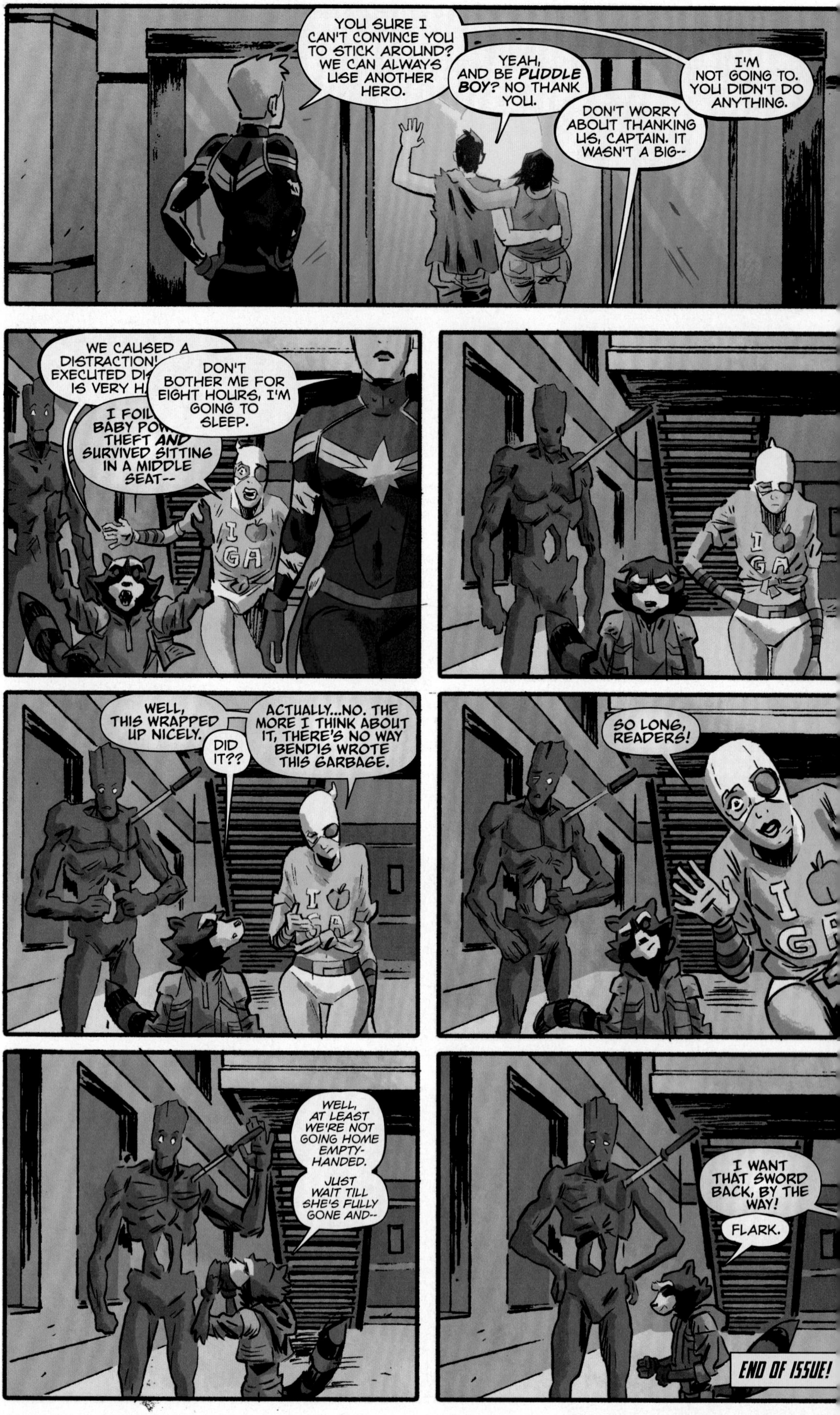
YOU SURE I CAN'T CONVINCE YOU TO STICK AROUND? WE CAN ALWAYS USE ANOTHER HERO.
YEAH, AND BE PUDDLE BOY? NO THANK YOU.
I'M NOT GOING TO. YOU DIDN'T DO ANYTHING.
DON'T WORRY ABOUT THANKING US, CAPTAIN. IT WASN'T A BIG--
WE CAUSED A DISTRACTION! EXECUTED DIS IS VERY HA
I FOIL BABY POW THEFT AND SURVIVED SITTING IN A MIDDLE SEAT--
DON'T BOTHER ME FOR EIGHT HOURS, I'M GOING TO SLEEP.
WELL, THIS WRAPPED UP NICELY.
DID IT??
ACTUALLY...NO. THE MORE I THINK ABOUT IT, THERE'S NO WAY BENDIS WROTE THIS GARBAGE.
SO LONG, READERS!
WELL, AT LEAST WE'RE NOT GOING HOME EMPTY-HANDED.
JUST WAIT TILL SHE'S FULLY GONE AND--
I WANT THAT SWORD BACK, BY THE WAY!
FLARK.
END OF ISSUE!

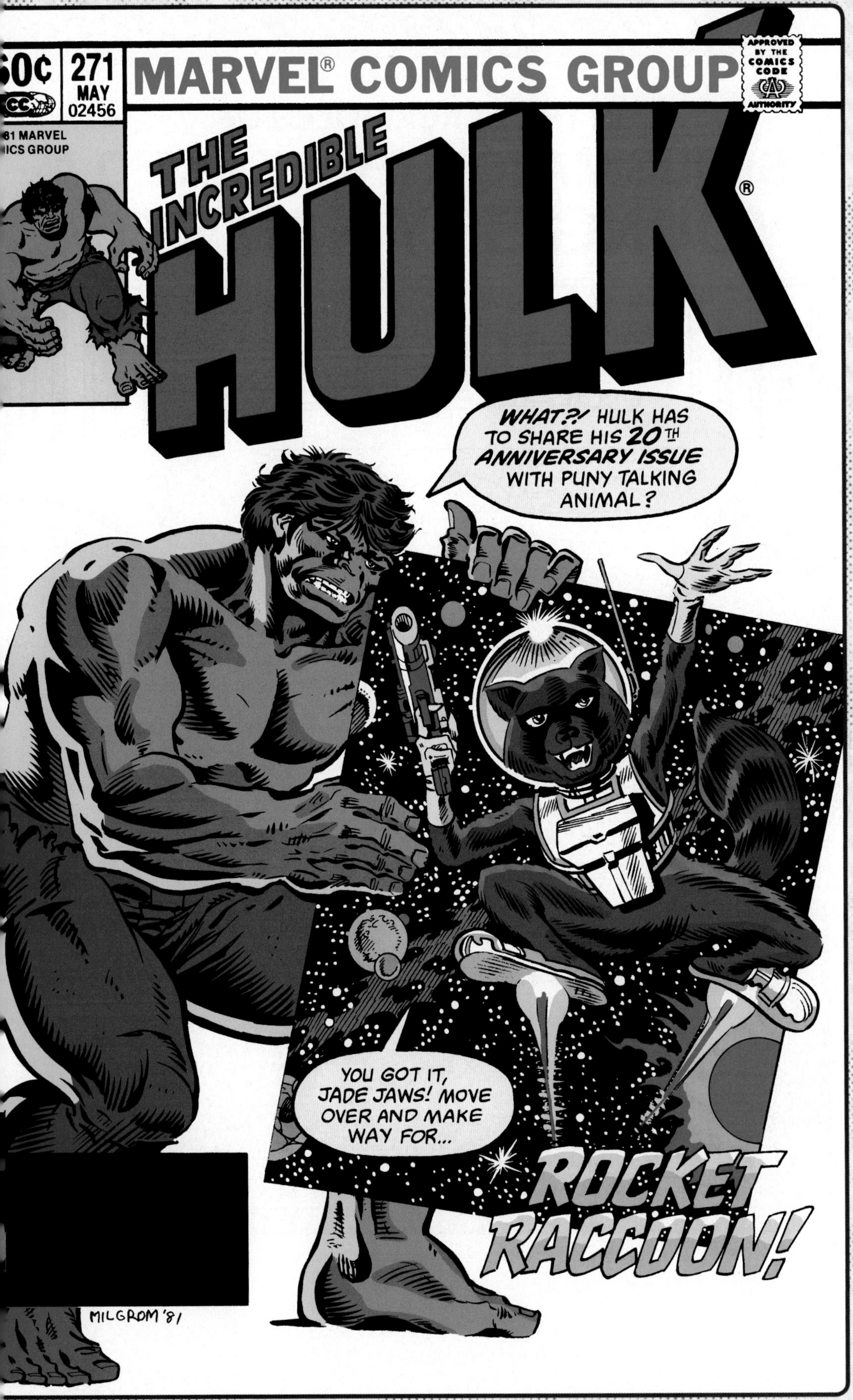
271
MAY
02456
MARVEL® COMICS GROUP
APPROVED BY THE COMICS CODE AUTHORITY
THE INCREDIBLE HULK®
WHAT?!/ HULK HAS TO SHARE HIS 20TH ANNIVERSARY ISSUE WITH PUNY TALKING ANIMAL?
YOU GOT IT, JADE JAWS! MOVE OVER AND MAKE WAY FOR...
ROCKET RACCOON!
MILGROM '81

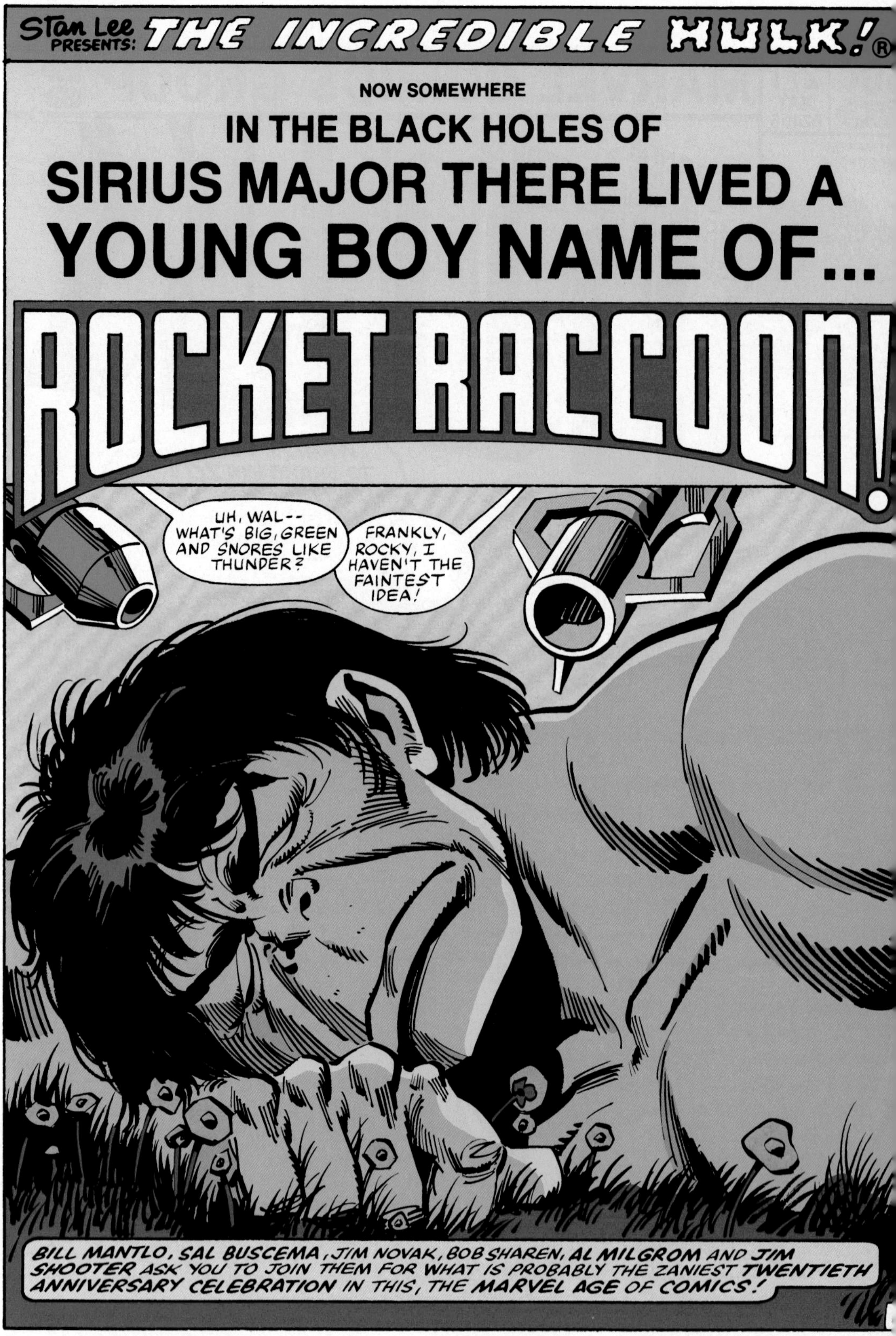
Stan Lee PRESENTS: THE INCREDIBLE HULK!®
NOW SOMEWHERE IN THE BLACK HOLES OF SIRIUS MAJOR THERE LIVED A YOUNG BOY NAME OF...
ROCKET RACCOON!
UH, WAL-- WHAT'S BIG, GREEN AND SNORES LIKE THUNDER?
FRANKLY, ROCKY, I HAVEN'T THE FAINTEST IDEA!
BILL MANTLO, SAL BUSCEMA, JIM NOVAK, BOB SHAREN, AL MILGROM AND JIM SHOOTER ASK YOU TO JOIN THEM FOR WHAT IS PROBABLY THE ZANIEST TWENTIETH ANNIVERSARY CELEBRATION IN THIS, THE MARVEL AGE OF COMICS!

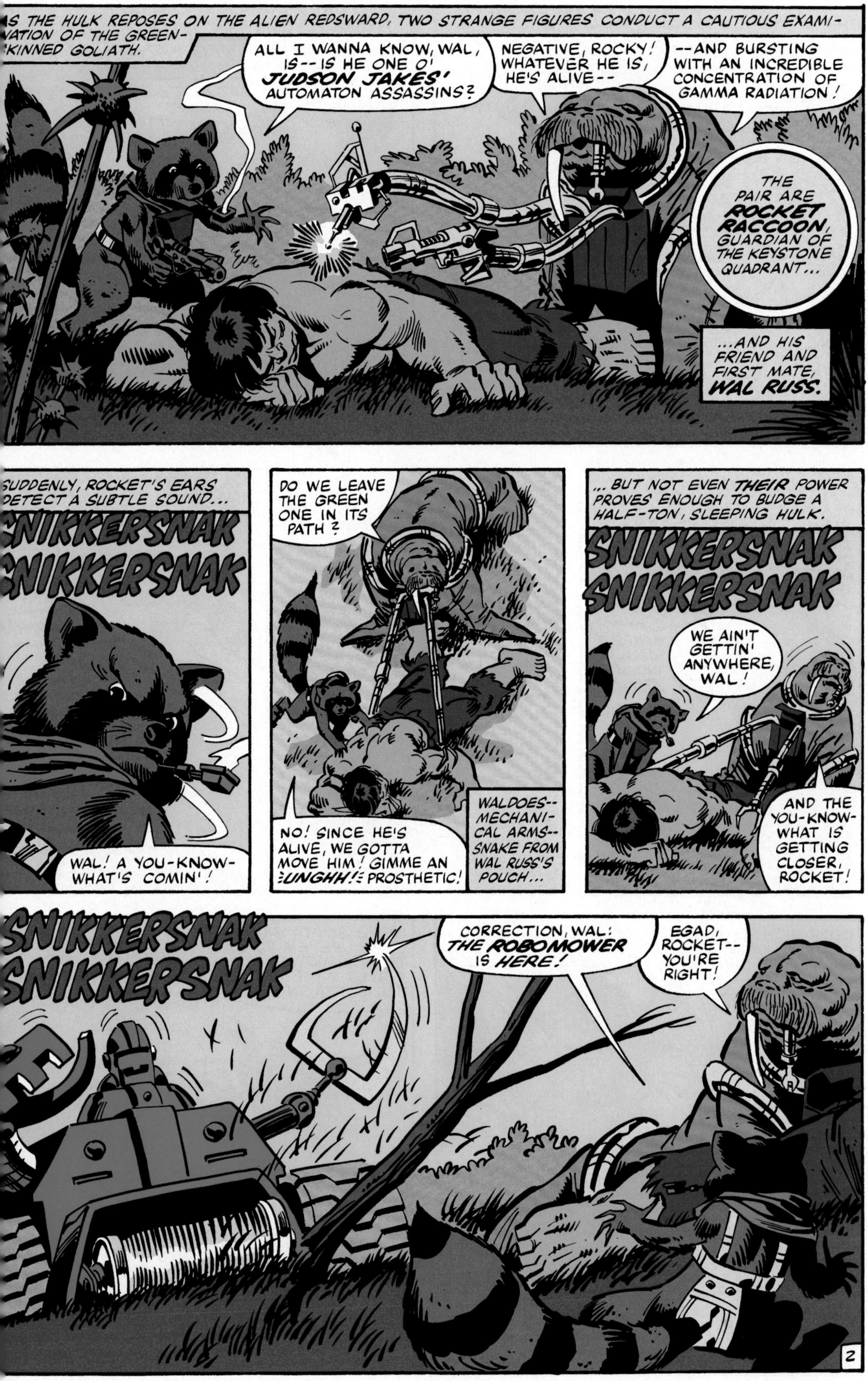
AS THE HULK REPOSES ON THE ALIEN REDSWARD, TWO STRANGE FIGURES CONDUCT A CAUTIOUS EXAMINATION OF THE GREEN-SKINNED GOLIATH.
ALL I WANNA KNOW, WAL, IS-- IS HE ONE O' JUDSON JAKES' AUTOMATON ASSASSINS?
NEGATIVE, ROCKY! WHATEVER HE IS, HE'S ALIVE--
--AND BURSTING WITH AN INCREDIBLE CONCENTRATION OF GAMMA RADIATION!
THE PAIR ARE ROCKET RACCOON, GUARDIAN OF THE KEYSTONE QUADRANT...
...AND HIS FRIEND AND FIRST MATE, WAL RUSS.
SUDDENLY, ROCKET'S EARS DETECT A SUBTLE SOUND...
SNIKKERSNAK SNIKKERSNAK
WAL! A YOU-KNOW-WHAT'S COMIN'!
DO WE LEAVE THE GREEN ONE IN ITS PATH?
NO! SINCE HE'S ALIVE, WE GOTTA MOVE HIM! GIMME AN UNGHH! PROSTHETIC!
WALDOES--MECHANICAL ARMS--SNAKE FROM WAL RUSS'S POUCH...
...BUT NOT EVEN THEIR POWER PROVES ENOUGH TO BUDGE A HALF-TON, SLEEPING HULK.
SNIKKERSNAK SNIKKERSNAK
WE AIN'T GETTIN' ANYWHERE, WAL!
AND THE YOU-KNOW-WHAT IS GETTING CLOSER, ROCKET!
SNIKKERSNAK SNIKKERSNAK
CORRECTION, WAL: THE ROBOMOWER IS HERE!
EGAD, ROCKET--YOU'RE RIGHT!
2

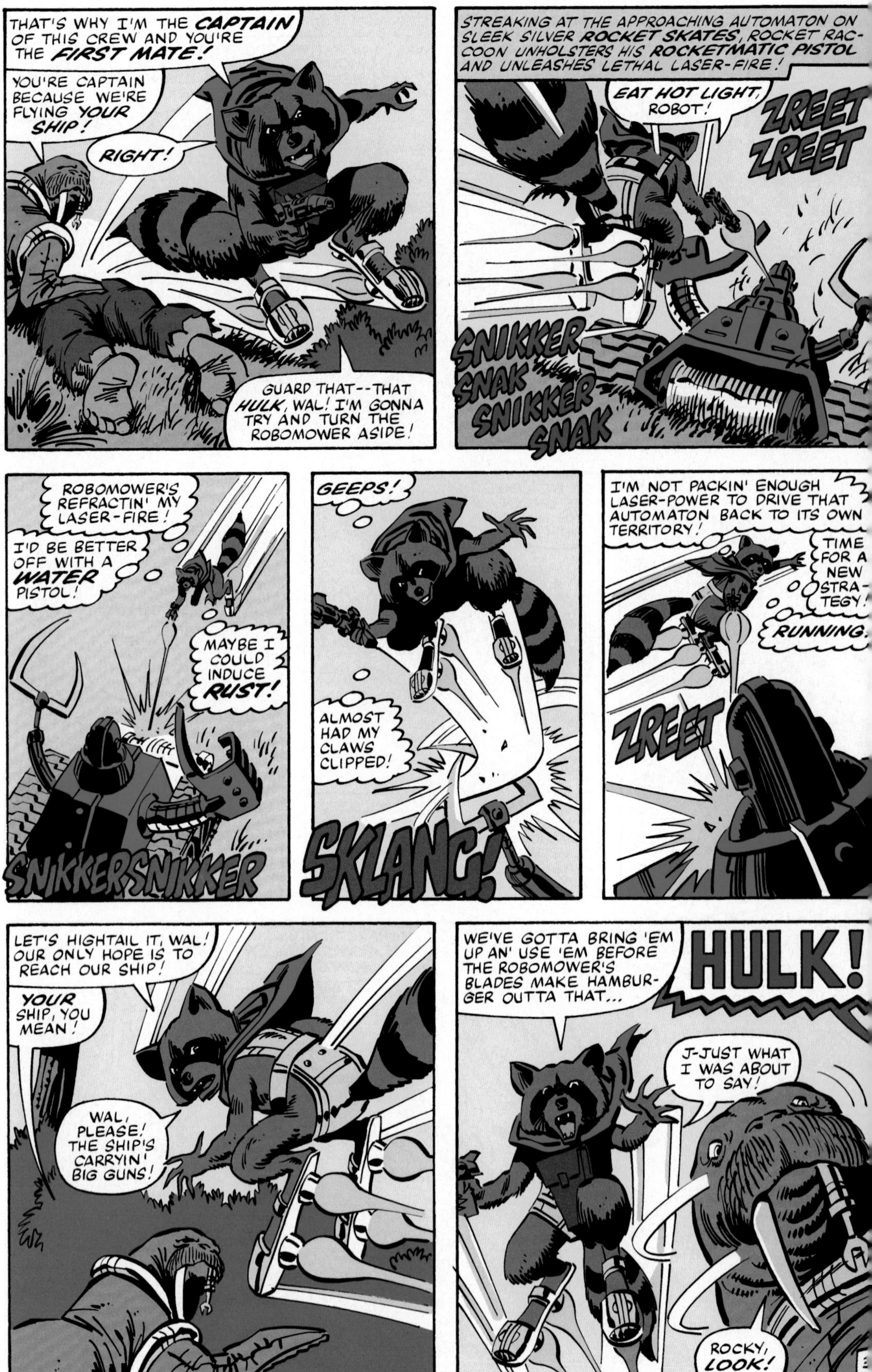
THAT'S WHY I'M THE CAPTAIN OF THIS CREW AND YOU'RE THE FIRST MATE!
YOU'RE CAPTAIN BECAUSE WE'RE FLYING YOUR SHIP!
RIGHT!
GUARD THAT--THAT HULK, WAL! I'M GONNA TRY AND TURN THE ROBOMOWER ASIDE!
STREAKING AT THE APPROACHING AUTOMATON ON SLEEK SILVER ROCKET SKATES, ROCKET RACCOON UNHOLSTERS HIS ROCKETMATIC PISTOL AND UNLEASHES LETHAL LASER-FIRE!
EAT HOT LIGHT, ROBOT!
ZREET ZREET
SNIKKER SNAK SNIKKER SNAK
ROBOMOWER'S REFRACTIN' MY LASER-FIRE!
I'D BE BETTER OFF WITH A WATER PISTOL!
MAYBE I COULD INDUCE RUST!
SNIKKERSNIKKER
GEEPS!
ALMOST HAD MY CLAWS CLIPPED!
SKLANG!
I'M NOT PACKIN' ENOUGH LASER-POWER TO DRIVE THAT AUTOMATON BACK TO ITS OWN TERRITORY!
TIME FOR A NEW STRATEGY!
RUNNING!
ZREET
LET'S HIGHTAIL IT, WAL! OUR ONLY HOPE IS TO REACH OUR SHIP!
YOUR SHIP, YOU MEAN!
WAL, PLEASE! THE SHIP'S CARRYIN' BIG GUNS!
WE'VE GOTTA BRING 'EM UP AN' USE 'EM BEFORE THE ROBOMOWER'S BLADES MAKE HAMBURGER OUTTA THAT...
HULK!
J-JUST WHAT I WAS ABOUT TO SAY!
ROCKY, LOOK!

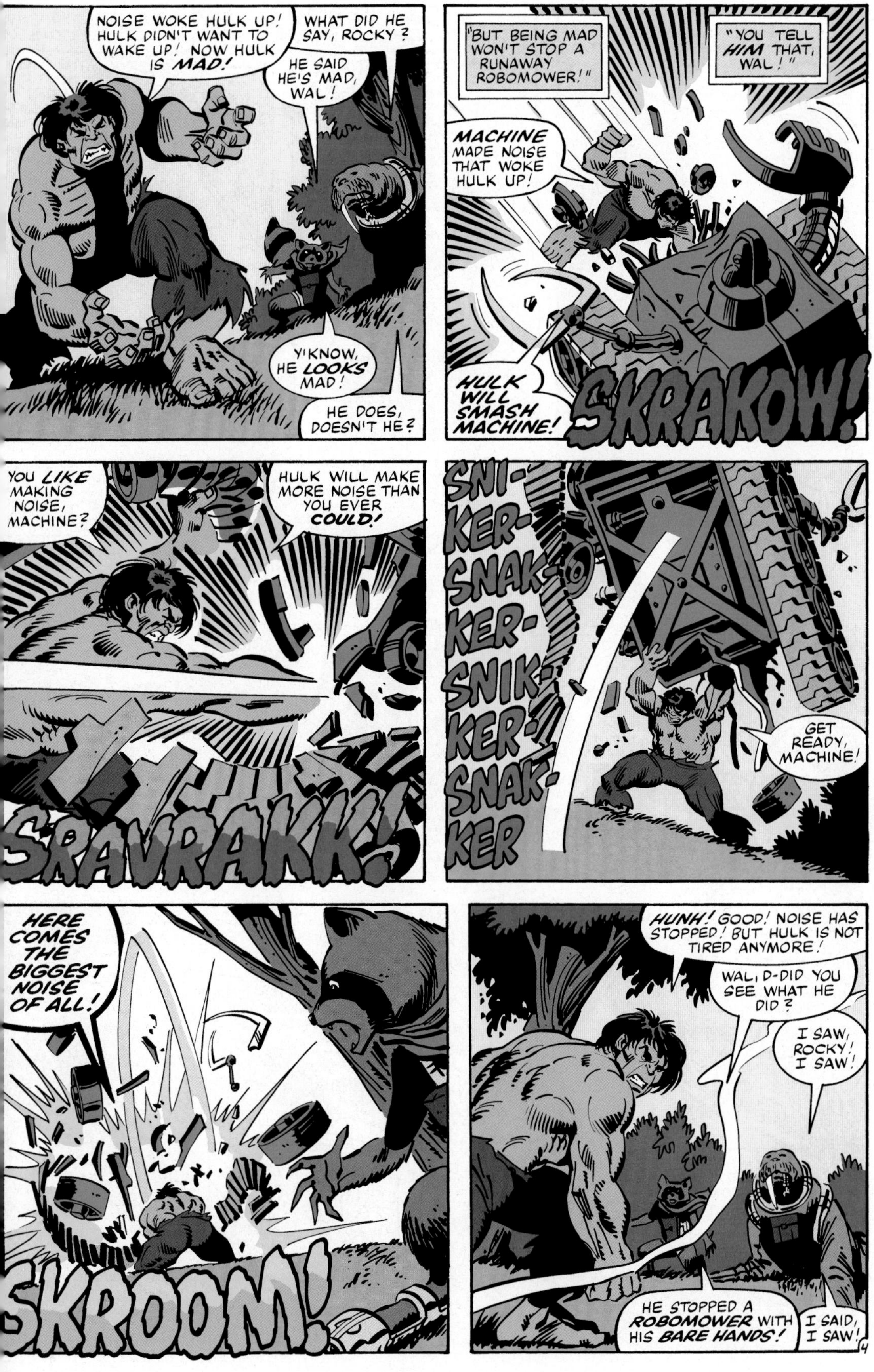
NOISE WOKE HULK UP! HULK DIDN'T WANT TO WAKE UP! NOW HULK IS MAD!
WHAT DID HE SAY, ROCKY?
HE SAID HE'S MAD, WAL!
Y'KNOW, HE LOOKS MAD!
HE DOES, DOESN'T HE?
"BUT BEING MAD WON'T STOP A RUNAWAY ROBOMOWER!"
"YOU TELL HIM THAT, WAL!"
MACHINE MADE NOISE THAT WOKE HULK UP!
HULK WILL SMASH MACHINE!
SKRAKOW!
YOU LIKE MAKING NOISE, MACHINE?
HULK WILL MAKE MORE NOISE THAN YOU EVER COULD!
SRAVRAKK!
SNI- KER- SNAK- KER- SNIK- KER- SNAK- KER
GET READY, MACHINE!
HERE COMES THE BIGGEST NOISE OF ALL!
SKROOM!
HUNH! GOOD! NOISE HAS STOPPED! BUT HULK IS NOT TIRED ANYMORE!
WAL, D-DID YOU SEE WHAT HE DID?
I SAW, ROCKY! I SAW!
HE STOPPED A ROBOMOWER WITH HIS BARE HANDS!
I SAID, I SAW!

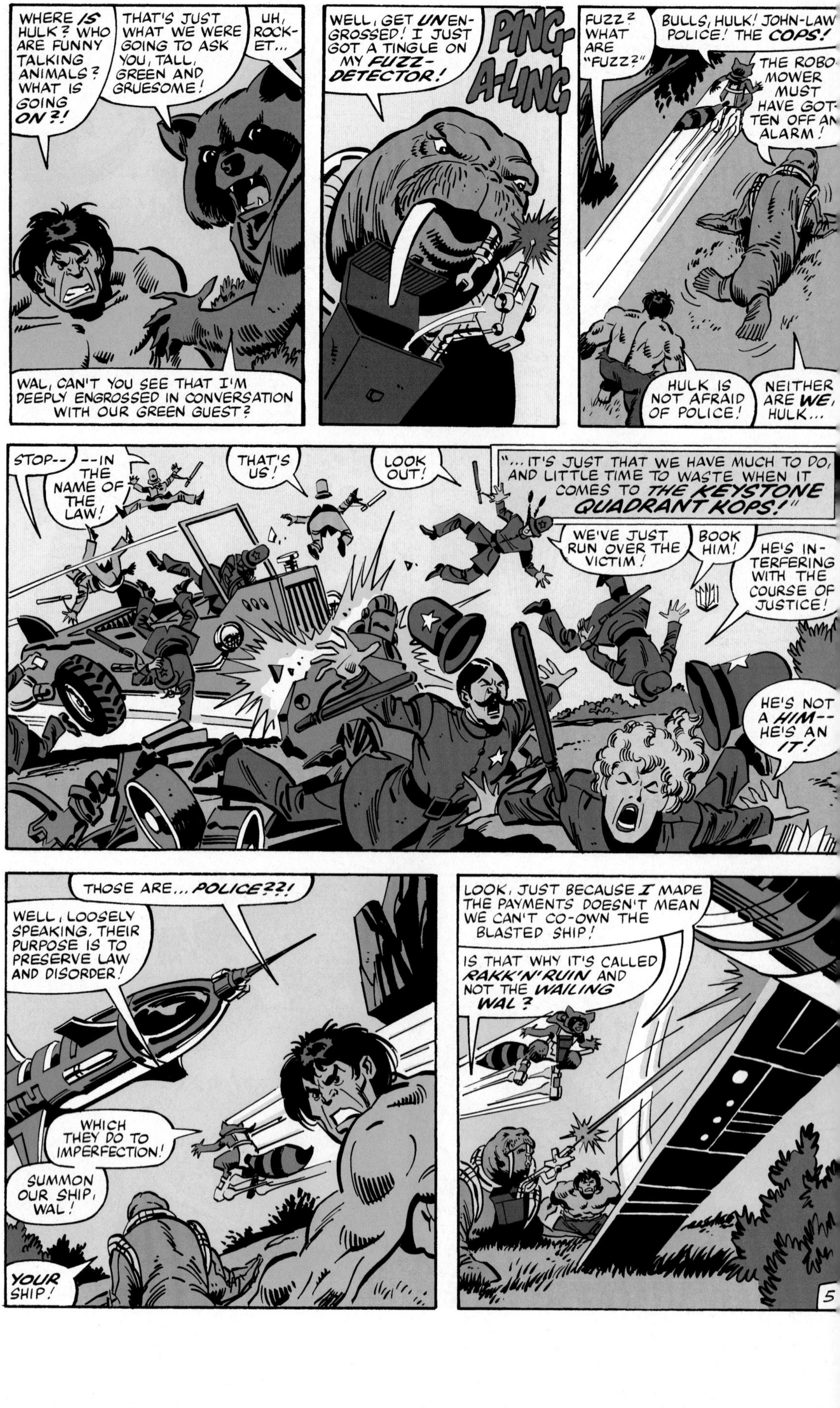
WHERE IS HULK? WHO ARE FUNNY TALKING ANIMALS? WHAT IS GOING ON?!
THAT'S JUST WHAT WE WERE GOING TO ASK YOU, TALL, GREEN AND GRUESOME!
UH, ROCKET...
WAL, CAN'T YOU SEE THAT I'M DEEPLY ENGROSSED IN CONVERSATION WITH OUR GREEN GUEST?
WELL, GET UN-ENGROSSED! I JUST GOT A TINGLE ON MY FUZZ-DETECTOR!
PING-A-LING
FUZZ? WHAT ARE "FUZZ?"
BULLS, HULK! JOHN-LAW! POLICE! THE COPS!
THE ROBO-MOWER MUST HAVE GOTTEN OFF AN ALARM!
HULK IS NOT AFRAID OF POLICE!
NEITHER ARE WE, HULK...
STOP--
--IN THE NAME OF THE LAW!
THAT'S US!
LOOK OUT!
"...IT'S JUST THAT WE HAVE MUCH TO DO, AND LITTLE TIME TO WASTE WHEN IT COMES TO THE KEYSTONE QUADRANT KOPS!"
WE'VE JUST RUN OVER THE VICTIM!
BOOK HIM!
HE'S INTERFERING WITH THE COURSE OF JUSTICE!
HE'S NOT A HIM-- HE'S AN IT!
THOSE ARE... POLICE??!
WELL, LOOSELY SPEAKING, THEIR PURPOSE IS TO PRESERVE LAW AND DISORDER!
WHICH THEY DO TO IMPERFECTION!
SUMMON OUR SHIP, WAL!
YOUR SHIP!
LOOK, JUST BECAUSE I MADE THE PAYMENTS DOESN'T MEAN WE CAN'T CO-OWN THE BLASTED SHIP!
IS THAT WHY IT'S CALLED RAKK'N'RUIN AND NOT THE WAILING WAL?

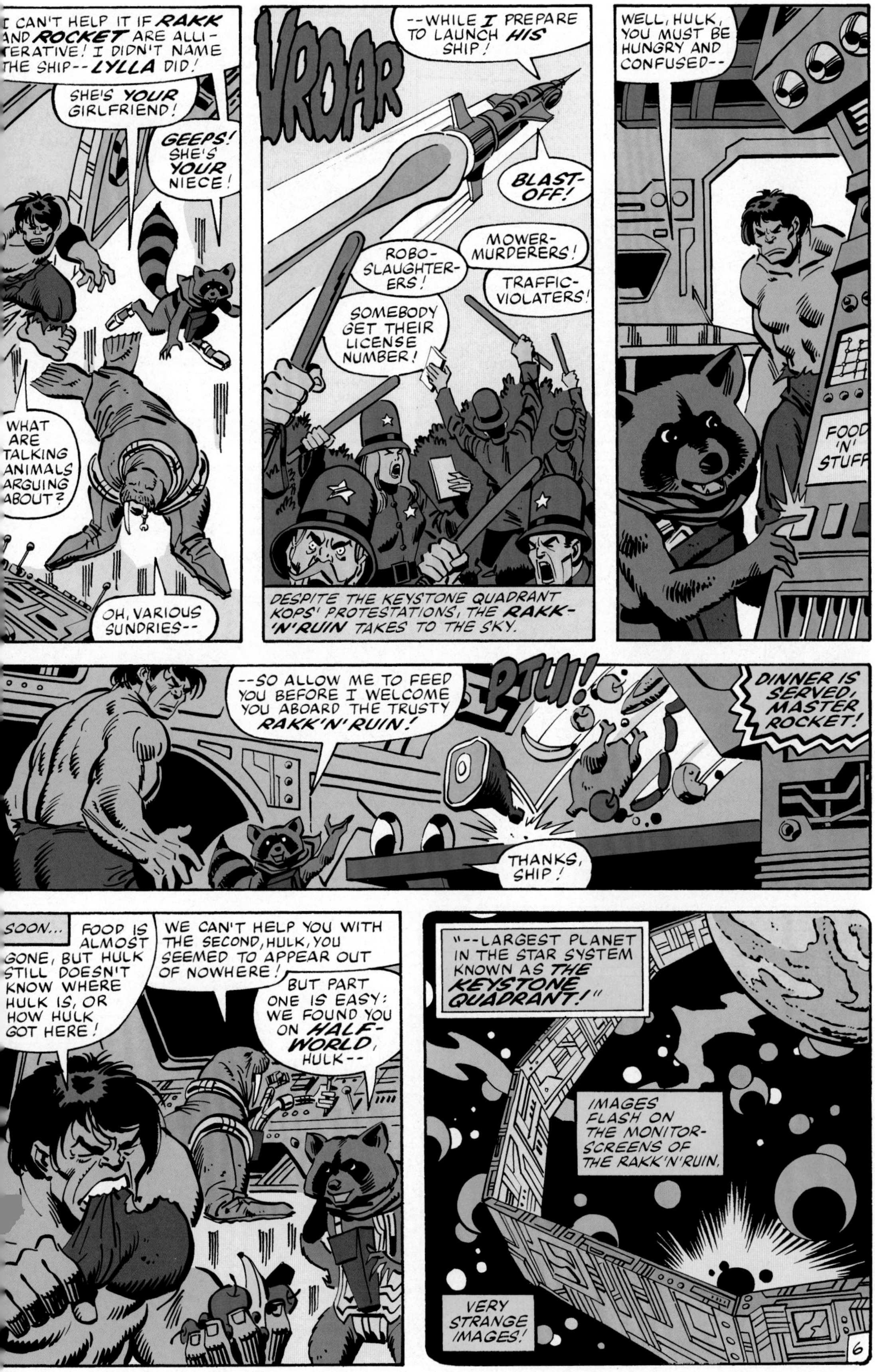
I CAN'T HELP IT IF RAKK AND ROCKET ARE ALLITERATIVE! I DIDN'T NAME THE SHIP--LYLLA DID!
SHE'S YOUR GIRLFRIEND!
GEEPS! SHE'S YOUR NIECE!
WHAT ARE TALKING ANIMALS ARGUING ABOUT?
OH, VARIOUS SUNDRIES--
VROAR
--WHILE I PREPARE TO LAUNCH HIS SHIP!
BLAST-OFF!
MOWER-MURDERERS!
ROBO-SLAUGHTERERS!
TRAFFIC-VIOLATERS!
SOMEBODY GET THEIR LICENSE NUMBER!
DESPITE THE KEYSTONE QUADRANT KOPS' PROTESTATIONS, THE RAKK-'N'RUIN TAKES TO THE SKY.
WELL, HULK, YOU MUST BE HUNGRY AND CONFUSED--
FOOD 'N' STUFF
--SO ALLOW ME TO FEED YOU BEFORE I WELCOME YOU ABOARD THE TRUSTY RAKK'N'RUIN!
PTUI!
DINNER IS SERVED, MASTER ROCKET!
THANKS, SHIP!
SOON... FOOD IS ALMOST GONE, BUT HULK STILL DOESN'T KNOW WHERE HULK IS, OR HOW HULK GOT HERE!
WE CAN'T HELP YOU WITH THE SECOND, HULK, YOU SEEMED TO APPEAR OUT OF NOWHERE!
BUT PART ONE IS EASY: WE FOUND YOU ON HALF-WORLD, HULK--
"--LARGEST PLANET IN THE STAR SYSTEM KNOWN AS THE KEYSTONE QUADRANT!"
IMAGES FLASH ON THE MONITOR-SCREENS OF THE RAKK'N'RUIN.
VERY STRANGE IMAGES!

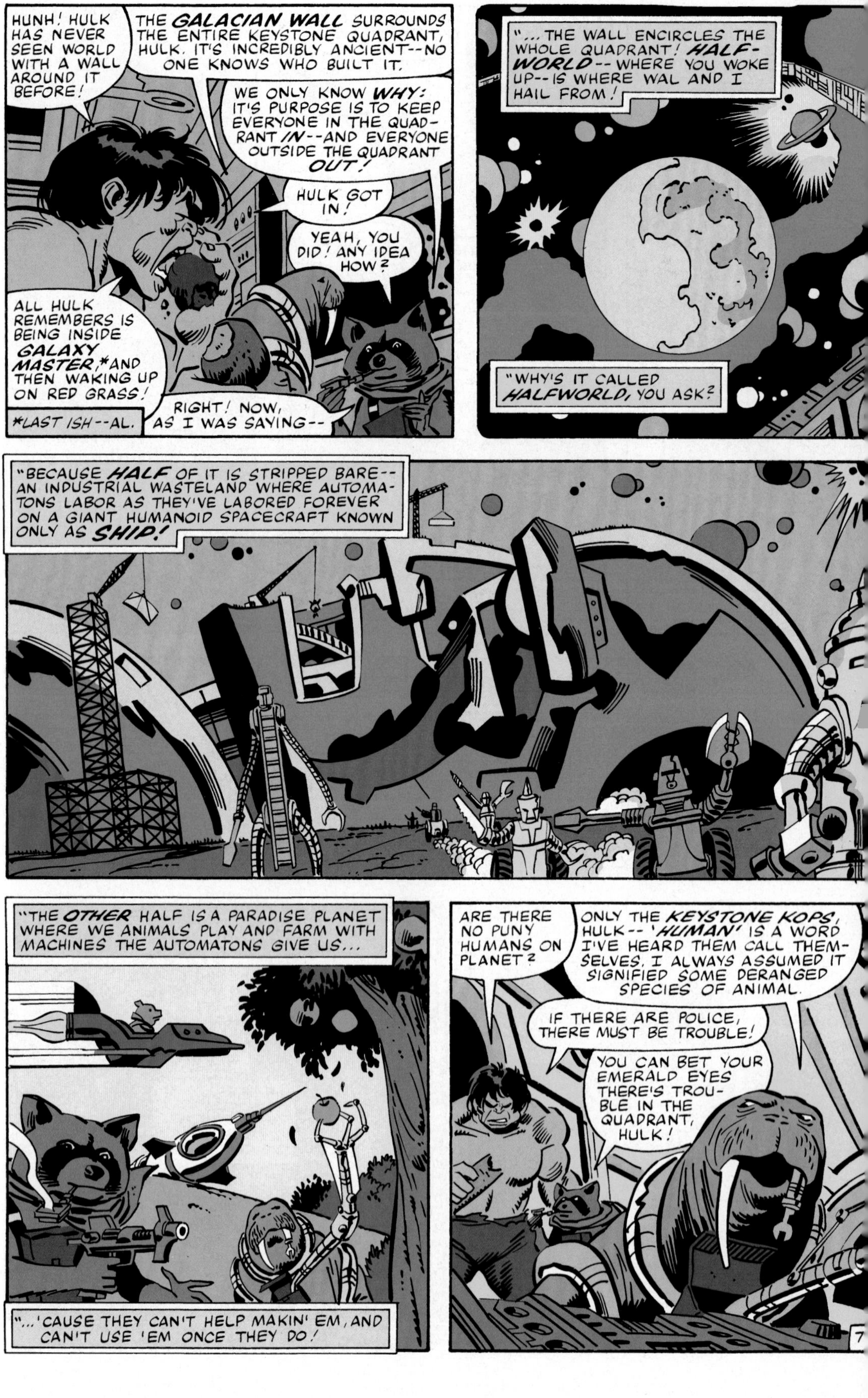
HUNH! HULK HAS NEVER SEEN WORLD WITH A WALL AROUND IT BEFORE!
THE GALACIAN WALL SURROUNDS THE ENTIRE KEYSTONE QUADRANT, HULK. IT'S INCREDIBLY ANCIENT--NO ONE KNOWS WHO BUILT IT.
WE ONLY KNOW WHY: IT'S PURPOSE IS TO KEEP EVERYONE IN THE QUADRANT IN--AND EVERYONE OUTSIDE THE QUADRANT OUT!
HULK GOT IN!
YEAH, YOU DID! ANY IDEA HOW?
ALL HULK REMEMBERS IS BEING INSIDE GALAXY MASTER,* AND THEN WAKING UP ON RED GRASS!
*LAST ISH--AL.
RIGHT! NOW, AS I WAS SAYING--
"...THE WALL ENCIRCLES THE WHOLE QUADRANT! HALF-WORLD--WHERE YOU WOKE UP--IS WHERE WAL AND I HAIL FROM!
"WHY'S IT CALLED HALFWORLD, YOU ASK?
"BECAUSE HALF OF IT IS STRIPPED BARE--AN INDUSTRIAL WASTELAND WHERE AUTOMATONS LABOR AS THEY'VE LABORED FOREVER ON A GIANT HUMANOID SPACECRAFT KNOWN ONLY AS SHIP!
"THE OTHER HALF IS A PARADISE PLANET WHERE WE ANIMALS PLAY AND FARM WITH MACHINES THE AUTOMATONS GIVE US...
"...'CAUSE THEY CAN'T HELP MAKIN' EM, AND CAN'T USE 'EM ONCE THEY DO!
ARE THERE NO PUNY HUMANS ON PLANET?
ONLY THE KEYSTONE KOPS, HULK--'HUMAN' IS A WORD I'VE HEARD THEM CALL THEMSELVES. I ALWAYS ASSUMED IT SIGNIFIED SOME DERANGED SPECIES OF ANIMAL.
IF THERE ARE POLICE, THERE MUST BE TROUBLE!
YOU CAN BET YOUR EMERALD EYES THERE'S TROUBLE IN THE QUADRANT, HULK!

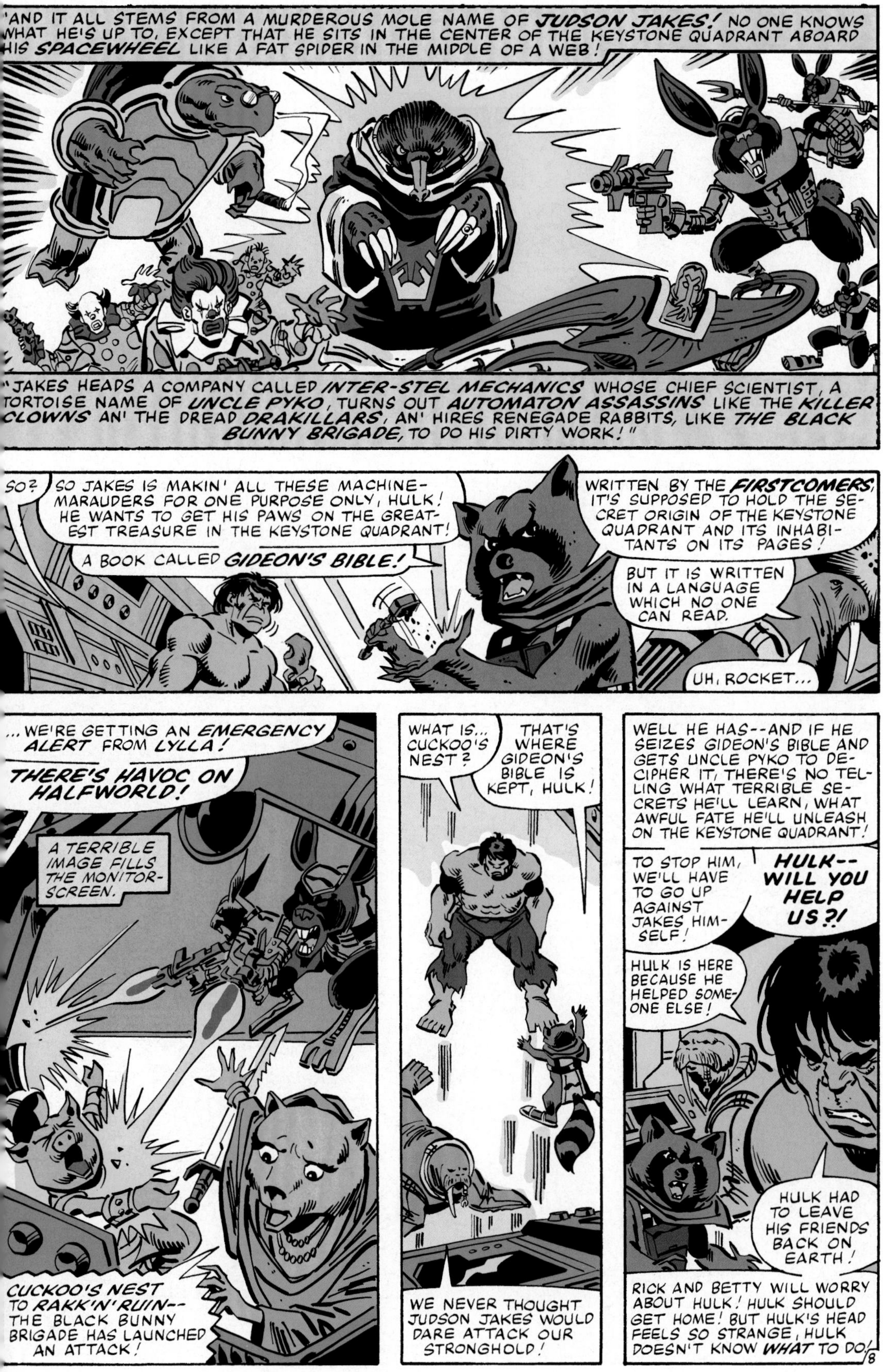
"AND IT ALL STEMS FROM A MURDEROUS MOLE NAME OF JUDSON JAKES! NO ONE KNOWS WHAT HE'S UP TO, EXCEPT THAT HE SITS IN THE CENTER OF THE KEYSTONE QUADRANT ABOARD HIS SPACEWHEEL LIKE A FAT SPIDER IN THE MIDDLE OF A WEB!
"JAKES HEADS A COMPANY CALLED INTER-STEL MECHANICS WHOSE CHIEF SCIENTIST, A TORTOISE NAME OF UNCLE PYKO, TURNS OUT AUTOMATON ASSASSINS LIKE THE KILLER CLOWNS AN' THE DREAD DRAKILLARS, AN' HIRES RENEGADE RABBITS, LIKE THE BLACK BUNNY BRIGADE, TO DO HIS DIRTY WORK!"
SO?
SO JAKES IS MAKIN' ALL THESE MACHINE-MARAUDERS FOR ONE PURPOSE ONLY, HULK! HE WANTS TO GET HIS PAWS ON THE GREATEST TREASURE IN THE KEYSTONE QUADRANT!
A BOOK CALLED GIDEON'S BIBLE!
WRITTEN BY THE FIRSTCOMERS, IT'S SUPPOSED TO HOLD THE SECRET ORIGIN OF THE KEYSTONE QUADRANT AND ITS INHABITANTS ON ITS PAGES!
BUT IT IS WRITTEN IN A LANGUAGE WHICH NO ONE CAN READ.
UH, ROCKET...
...WE'RE GETTING AN EMERGENCY ALERT FROM LYLLA!
THERE'S HAVOC ON HALFWORLD!
A TERRIBLE IMAGE FILLS THE MONITOR-SCREEN.
CUCKOO'S NEST TO RAKK'N'RUIN-- THE BLACK BUNNY BRIGADE HAS LAUNCHED AN ATTACK!
WHAT IS... CUCKOO'S NEST?
THAT'S WHERE GIDEON'S BIBLE IS KEPT, HULK!
WE NEVER THOUGHT JUDSON JAKES WOULD DARE ATTACK OUR STRONGHOLD!
WELL HE HAS--AND IF HE SEIZES GIDEON'S BIBLE AND GETS UNCLE PYKO TO DECIPHER IT, THERE'S NO TELLING WHAT TERRIBLE SECRETS HE'LL LEARN, WHAT AWFUL FATE HE'LL UNLEASH ON THE KEYSTONE QUADRANT!
TO STOP HIM, WE'LL HAVE TO GO UP AGAINST JAKES HIMSELF!
HULK-- WILL YOU HELP US?!
HULK IS HERE BECAUSE HE HELPED SOMEONE ELSE!
HULK HAD TO LEAVE HIS FRIENDS BACK ON EARTH!
RICK AND BETTY WILL WORRY ABOUT HULK! HULK SHOULD GET HOME! BUT HULK'S HEAD FEELS SO STRANGE, HULK DOESN'T KNOW WHAT TO DO!

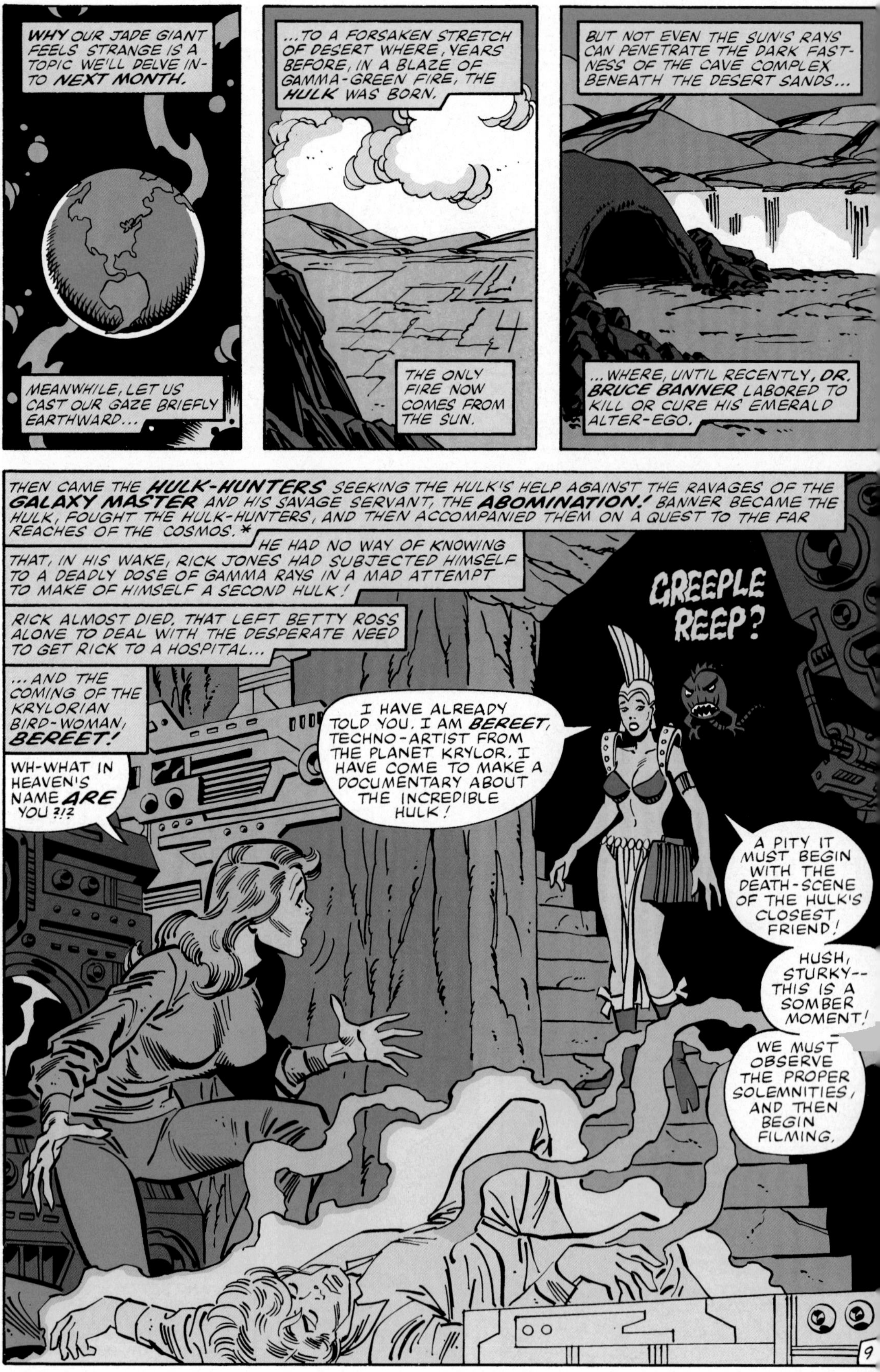
WHY OUR JADE GIANT FEELS STRANGE IS A TOPIC WE'LL DELVE INTO NEXT MONTH.
MEANWHILE, LET US CAST OUR GAZE BRIEFLY EARTHWARD...
...TO A FORSAKEN STRETCH OF DESERT WHERE, YEARS BEFORE, IN A BLAZE OF GAMMA-GREEN FIRE, THE HULK WAS BORN.
THE ONLY FIRE NOW COMES FROM THE SUN.
BUT NOT EVEN THE SUN'S RAYS CAN PENETRATE THE DARK FASTNESS OF THE CAVE COMPLEX BENEATH THE DESERT SANDS...
...WHERE, UNTIL RECENTLY, DR. BRUCE BANNER LABORED TO KILL OR CURE HIS EMERALD ALTER-EGO.
THEN CAME THE HULK-HUNTERS SEEKING THE HULK'S HELP AGAINST THE RAVAGES OF THE GALAXY MASTER AND HIS SAVAGE SERVANT, THE ABOMINATION! BANNER BECAME THE HULK, FOUGHT THE HULK-HUNTERS, AND THEN ACCOMPANIED THEM ON A QUEST TO THE FAR REACHES OF THE COSMOS.*
HE HAD NO WAY OF KNOWING THAT, IN HIS WAKE, RICK JONES HAD SUBJECTED HIMSELF TO A DEADLY DOSE OF GAMMA RAYS IN A MAD ATTEMPT TO MAKE OF HIMSELF A SECOND HULK!
RICK ALMOST DIED. THAT LEFT BETTY ROSS ALONE TO DEAL WITH THE DESPERATE NEED TO GET RICK TO A HOSPITAL...
...AND THE COMING OF THE KRYLORIAN BIRD-WOMAN, BEREET!
GREEPLE REEP?
WH-WHAT IN HEAVEN'S NAME ARE YOU?!?
I HAVE ALREADY TOLD YOU. I AM BEREET, TECHNO-ARTIST FROM THE PLANET KRYLOR. I HAVE COME TO MAKE A DOCUMENTARY ABOUT THE INCREDIBLE HULK!
A PITY IT MUST BEGIN WITH THE DEATH-SCENE OF THE HULK'S CLOSEST FRIEND!
HUSH, STURKY-- THIS IS A SOMBER MOMENT!
WE MUST OBSERVE THE PROPER SOLEMNITIES, AND THEN BEGIN FILMING.
9

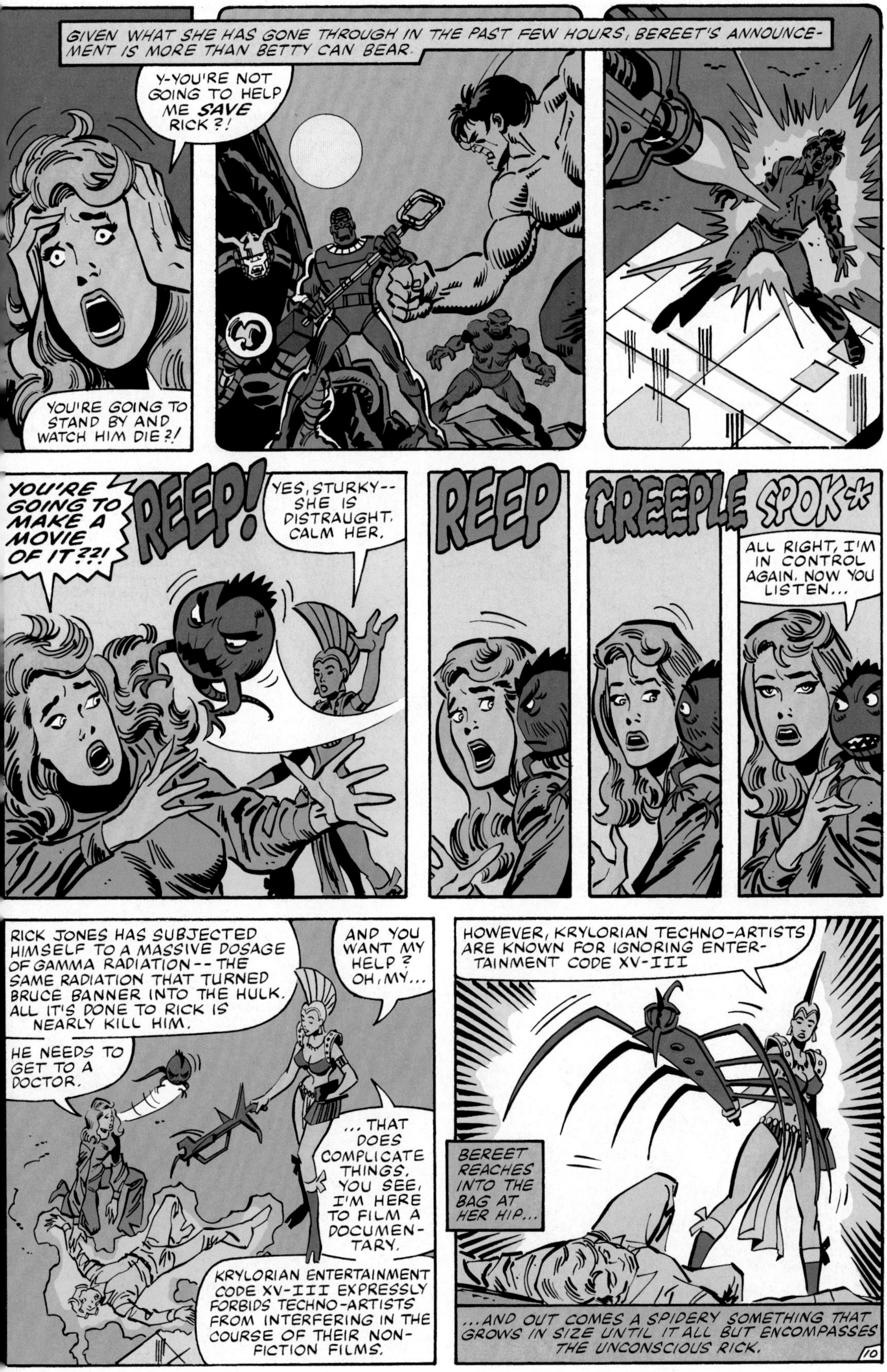
GIVEN WHAT SHE HAS GONE THROUGH IN THE PAST FEW HOURS, BEREET'S ANNOUNCEMENT IS MORE THAN BETTY CAN BEAR.
Y-YOU'RE NOT GOING TO HELP ME SAVE RICK?!
YOU'RE GOING TO STAND BY AND WATCH HIM DIE?!
YOU'RE GOING TO MAKE A MOVIE OF IT???!
REEP!
YES, STURKY-- SHE IS DISTRAUGHT. CALM HER.
REEP
GREEPLE
SPOK*
ALL RIGHT, I'M IN CONTROL AGAIN. NOW YOU LISTEN...
RICK JONES HAS SUBJECTED HIMSELF TO A MASSIVE DOSAGE OF GAMMA RADIATION -- THE SAME RADIATION THAT TURNED BRUCE BANNER INTO THE HULK. ALL IT'S DONE TO RICK IS NEARLY KILL HIM.
HE NEEDS TO GET TO A DOCTOR.
AND YOU WANT MY HELP? OH, MY...
...THAT DOES COMPLICATE THINGS. YOU SEE, I'M HERE TO FILM A DOCUMENTARY.
KRYLORIAN ENTERTAINMENT CODE XV-III EXPRESSLY FORBIDS TECHNO-ARTISTS FROM INTERFERING IN THE COURSE OF THEIR NON-FICTION FILMS.
HOWEVER, KRYLORIAN TECHNO-ARTISTS ARE KNOWN FOR IGNORING ENTERTAINMENT CODE XV-III
BEREET REACHES INTO THE BAG AT HER HIP...
...AND OUT COMES A SPIDERY SOMETHING THAT GROWS IN SIZE UNTIL IT ALL BUT ENCOMPASSES THE UNCONSCIOUS RICK.
10

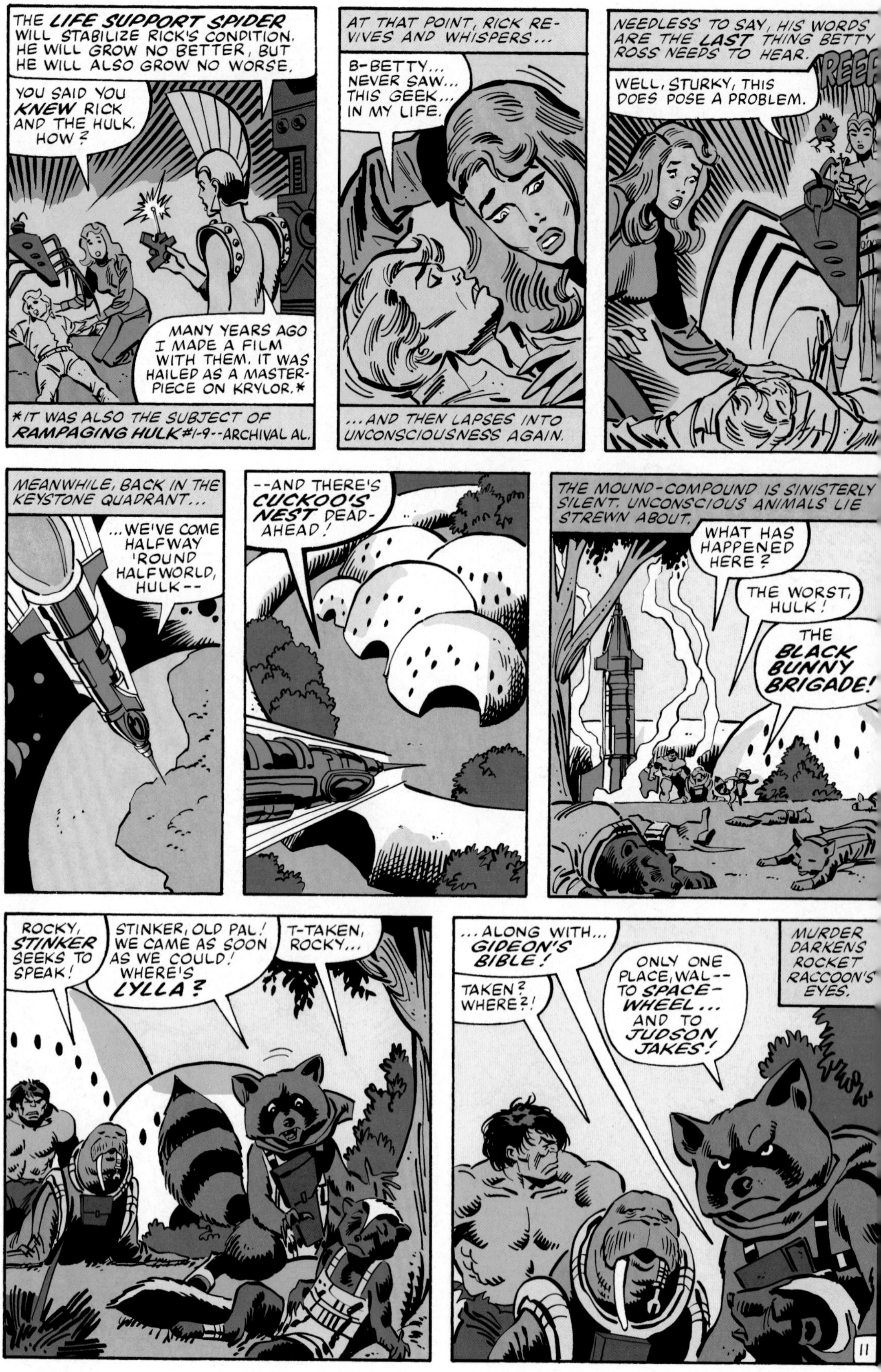
THE LIFE SUPPORT SPIDER WILL STABILIZE RICK'S CONDITION. HE WILL GROW NO BETTER, BUT HE WILL ALSO GROW NO WORSE.
YOU SAID YOU KNEW RICK AND THE HULK. HOW?
MANY YEARS AGO I MADE A FILM WITH THEM. IT WAS HAILED AS A MASTERPIECE ON KRYLOR.*
*IT WAS ALSO THE SUBJECT OF RAMPAGING HULK #1-9--ARCHIVAL AL.
AT THAT POINT, RICK REVIVES AND WHISPERS...
B-BETTY... NEVER SAW... THIS GEEK... IN MY LIFE.
...AND THEN LAPSES INTO UNCONSCIOUSNESS AGAIN.
NEEDLESS TO SAY, HIS WORDS ARE THE LAST THING BETTY ROSS NEEDS TO HEAR.
WELL, STURKY, THIS DOES POSE A PROBLEM.
MEANWHILE, BACK IN THE KEYSTONE QUADRANT...
...WE'VE COME HALFWAY 'ROUND HALFWORLD, HULK--
--AND THERE'S CUCKOO'S NEST DEAD-AHEAD!
THE MOUND-COMPOUND IS SINISTERLY SILENT. UNCONSCIOUS ANIMALS LIE STREWN ABOUT.
WHAT HAS HAPPENED HERE?
THE WORST, HULK!
THE BLACK BUNNY BRIGADE!
ROCKY, STINKER SEEKS TO SPEAK!
STINKER, OLD PAL! WE CAME AS SOON AS WE COULD! WHERE'S LYLLA?
T-TAKEN, ROCKY...
...ALONG WITH... GIDEON'S BIBLE!
TAKEN? WHERE?!
ONLY ONE PLACE, WAL--TO SPACEWHEEL... AND TO JUDSON JAKES!
MURDER DARKENS ROCKET RACCOON'S EYES.

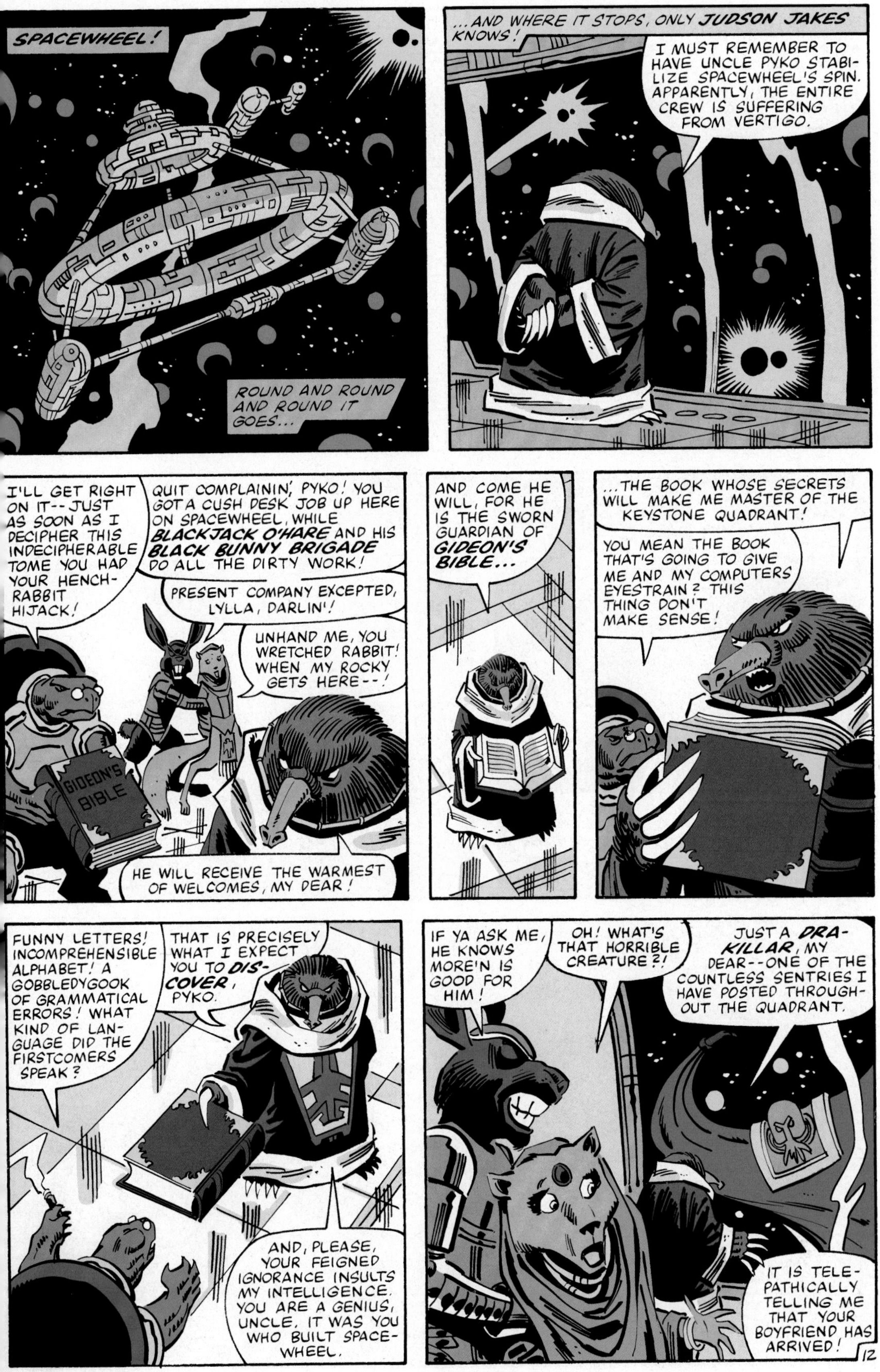
SPACEWHEEL!
ROUND AND ROUND AND ROUND IT GOES...
...AND WHERE IT STOPS, ONLY JUDSON JAKES KNOWS!
I MUST REMEMBER TO HAVE UNCLE PYKO STABILIZE SPACEWHEEL'S SPIN. APPARENTLY, THE ENTIRE CREW IS SUFFERING FROM VERTIGO.
I'LL GET RIGHT ON IT--JUST AS SOON AS I DECIPHER THIS INDECIPHERABLE TOME YOU HAD YOUR HENCH-RABBIT HIJACK!
QUIT COMPLAININ', PYKO! YOU GOT A CUSH DESK JOB UP HERE ON SPACEWHEEL, WHILE BLACKJACK O'HARE AND HIS BLACK BUNNY BRIGADE DO ALL THE DIRTY WORK!
PRESENT COMPANY EXCEPTED, LYLLA, DARLIN'!
UNHAND ME, YOU WRETCHED RABBIT! WHEN MY ROCKY GETS HERE--!
GIDEON'S BIBLE
HE WILL RECEIVE THE WARMEST OF WELCOMES, MY DEAR!
AND COME HE WILL, FOR HE IS THE SWORN GUARDIAN OF GIDEON'S BIBLE...
...THE BOOK WHOSE SECRETS WILL MAKE ME MASTER OF THE KEYSTONE QUADRANT!
YOU MEAN THE BOOK THAT'S GOING TO GIVE ME AND MY COMPUTERS EYESTRAIN? THIS THING DON'T MAKE SENSE!
FUNNY LETTERS! INCOMPREHENSIBLE ALPHABET! A GOBBLEDYGOOK OF GRAMMATICAL ERRORS! WHAT KIND OF LANGUAGE DID THE FIRSTCOMERS SPEAK?
THAT IS PRECISELY WHAT I EXPECT YOU TO DISCOVER, PYKO.
AND, PLEASE, YOUR FEIGNED IGNORANCE INSULTS MY INTELLIGENCE. YOU ARE A GENIUS, UNCLE. IT WAS YOU WHO BUILT SPACEWHEEL.
IF YA ASK ME, HE KNOWS MORE'N IS GOOD FOR HIM!
OH! WHAT'S THAT HORRIBLE CREATURE?!
JUST A DRAKILLAR, MY DEAR--ONE OF THE COUNTLESS SENTRIES I HAVE POSTED THROUGHOUT THE QUADRANT.
IT IS TELEPATHICALLY TELLING ME THAT YOUR BOYFRIEND HAS ARRIVED!
12

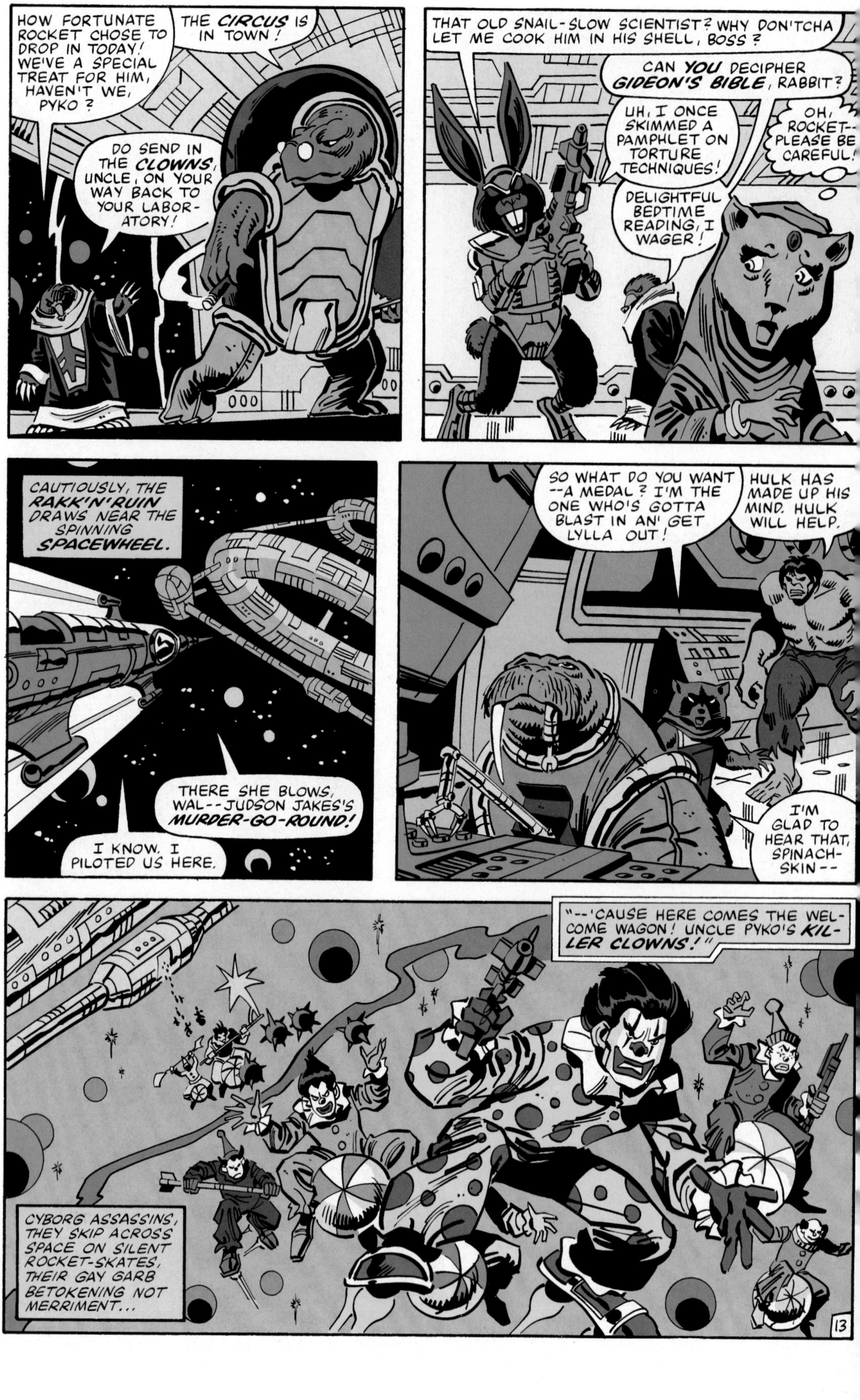
HOW FORTUNATE ROCKET CHOSE TO DROP IN TODAY! WE'VE A SPECIAL TREAT FOR HIM, HAVEN'T WE, PYKO?
THE CIRCUS IS IN TOWN!
DO SEND IN THE CLOWNS, UNCLE, ON YOUR WAY BACK TO YOUR LABORATORY!
THAT OLD SNAIL-SLOW SCIENTIST? WHY DON'TCHA LET ME COOK HIM IN HIS SHELL, BOSS?
CAN YOU DECIPHER GIDEON'S BIBLE, RABBIT?
UH, I ONCE SKIMMED A PAMPHLET ON TORTURE TECHNIQUES!
OH, ROCKET-- PLEASE BE CAREFUL!
DELIGHTFUL BEDTIME READING, I WAGER!
CAUTIOUSLY, THE RAKK'N'RUIN DRAWS NEAR THE SPINNING SPACEWHEEL.
THERE SHE BLOWS, WAL--JUDSON JAKES'S MURDER-GO-ROUND!
I KNOW. I PILOTED US HERE.
SO WHAT DO YOU WANT --A MEDAL? I'M THE ONE WHO'S GOTTA BLAST IN AN' GET LYLLA OUT!
HULK HAS MADE UP HIS MIND. HULK WILL HELP.
I'M GLAD TO HEAR THAT, SPINACH-SKIN--
"--'CAUSE HERE COMES THE WELCOME WAGON! UNCLE PYKO'S KILLER CLOWNS!"
CYBORG ASSASSINS, THEY SKIP ACROSS SPACE ON SILENT ROCKET-SKATES, THEIR GAY GARB BETOKENING NOT MERRIMENT...

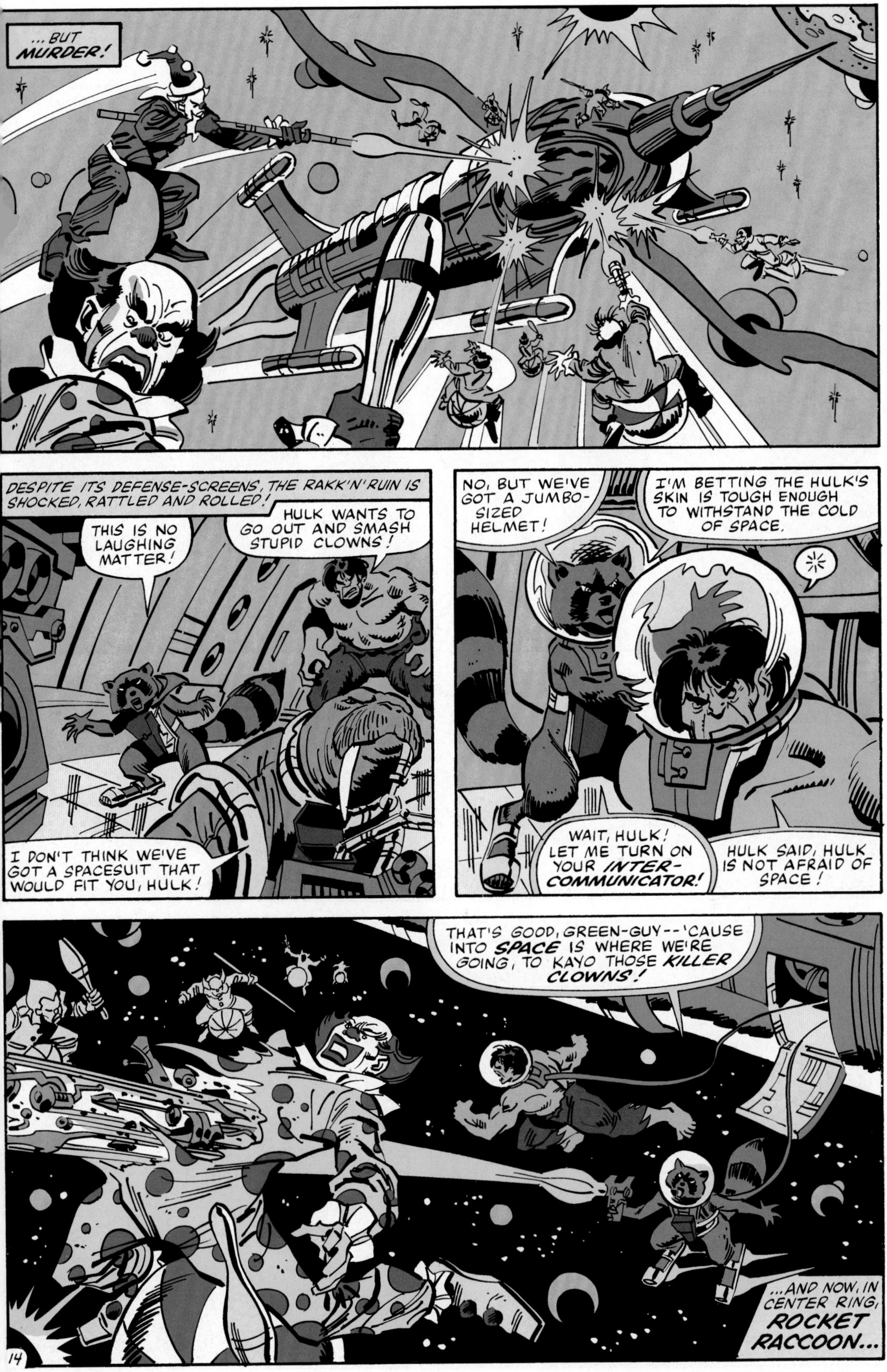
...BUT MURDER!
DESPITE ITS DEFENSE-SCREENS, THE RAKK'N'RUIN IS SHOCKED, RATTLED AND ROLLED!
THIS IS NO LAUGHING MATTER!
HULK WANTS TO GO OUT AND SMASH STUPID CLOWNS!
I DON'T THINK WE'VE GOT A SPACESUIT THAT WOULD FIT YOU, HULK!
NO, BUT WE'VE GOT A JUMBO-SIZED HELMET!
I'M BETTING THE HULK'S SKIN IS TOUGH ENOUGH TO WITHSTAND THE COLD OF SPACE.
WAIT, HULK! LET ME TURN ON YOUR INTER-COMMUNICATOR!
HULK SAID, HULK IS NOT AFRAID OF SPACE!
THAT'S GOOD, GREEN-GUY--'CAUSE INTO SPACE IS WHERE WE'RE GOING, TO KAYO THOSE KILLER CLOWNS!
...AND NOW, IN CENTER RING, ROCKET RACCOON...
14

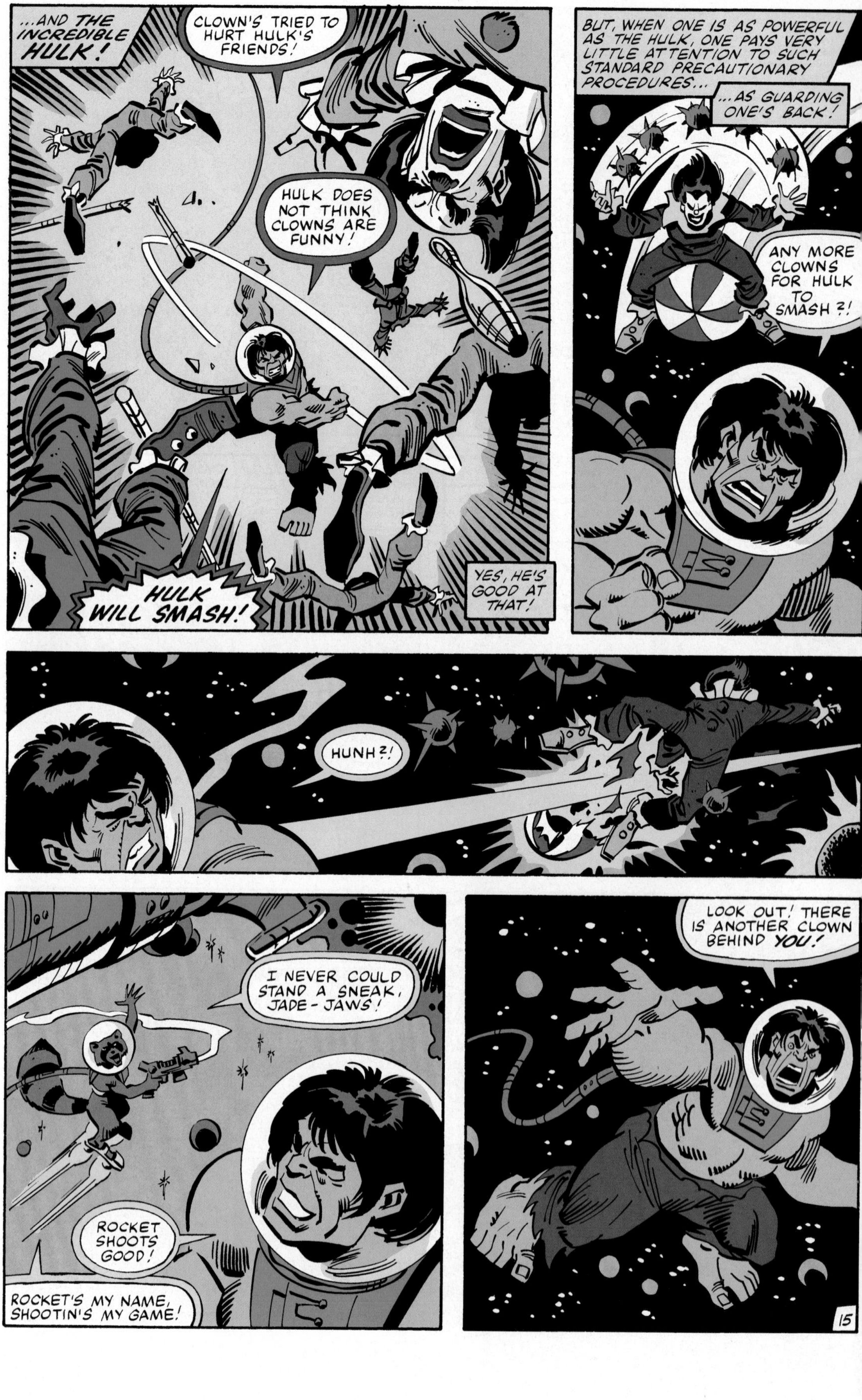
...AND THE INCREDIBLE HULK!
CLOWN'S TRIED TO HURT HULK'S FRIENDS!
HULK DOES NOT THINK CLOWNS ARE FUNNY!
HULK WILL SMASH!
YES, HE'S GOOD AT THAT!
BUT, WHEN ONE IS AS POWERFUL AS THE HULK, ONE PAYS VERY LITTLE ATTENTION TO SUCH STANDARD PRECAUTIONARY PROCEDURES...
...AS GUARDING ONE'S BACK!
ANY MORE CLOWNS FOR HULK TO SMASH ?!
HUNH?!
I NEVER COULD STAND A SNEAK, JADE-JAWS!
ROCKET SHOOTS GOOD!
ROCKET'S MY NAME, SHOOTIN'S MY GAME!
LOOK OUT! THERE IS ANOTHER CLOWN BEHIND YOU!

THE HULK'S CRY OF WARNING COMES A TAD TOO LATE, FOR THE *LEADER* OF THE *KILLER CLOWNS* IS ALREADY UPON OUR RIGHTEOUS RACCOON!

A GREAT PRIZE AWAITS THE ONE WHO SLAYS YOU, RODENT!

THE PRIZE OF *LIFE* -- TO CEASE BEING A COLD CYBORG KILLING MACHINE...

...AND BECOME INSTEAD A *LIVING BEING!*

A LIFE FOR A *DEATH,* CLOWN? CUTE TRADE!

GEEPS! *LASER CONTACT-LENSES* TRYING TO OPEN MY HELMET! *HELP!!*

HELP IS AT HAND...

RAARRHH!

HULK! THANKS A LOT!

DID ROCKET THINK THAT HULK WOULD LET CLOWN KILL HIM?

TO TELL YOU THE TRUTH, GREENSKIN, RATIONAL THOUGHT GAVE WAY TO PANIC AS THOSE LASERS STARTED TO SIZZLE MY HELMET! THIS IS ONE RACCOON WHO LIKES *BREATHING!*

CLOWNS ARE ALL GONE! NOW WHAT DO HULK AND ROCKET DO?

THE JOB WE CAME FOR, SPINACH-SKIN!

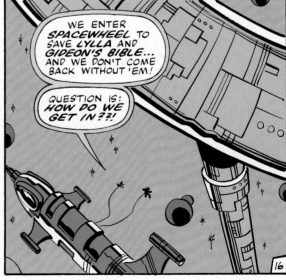

WE ENTER *SPACEWHEEL* TO SAVE *LYLLA* AND *GIDEON'S BIBLE*... AND WE DON'T COME BACK WITHOUT 'EM!

QUESTION IS: *HOW DO WE GET IN??!*

16

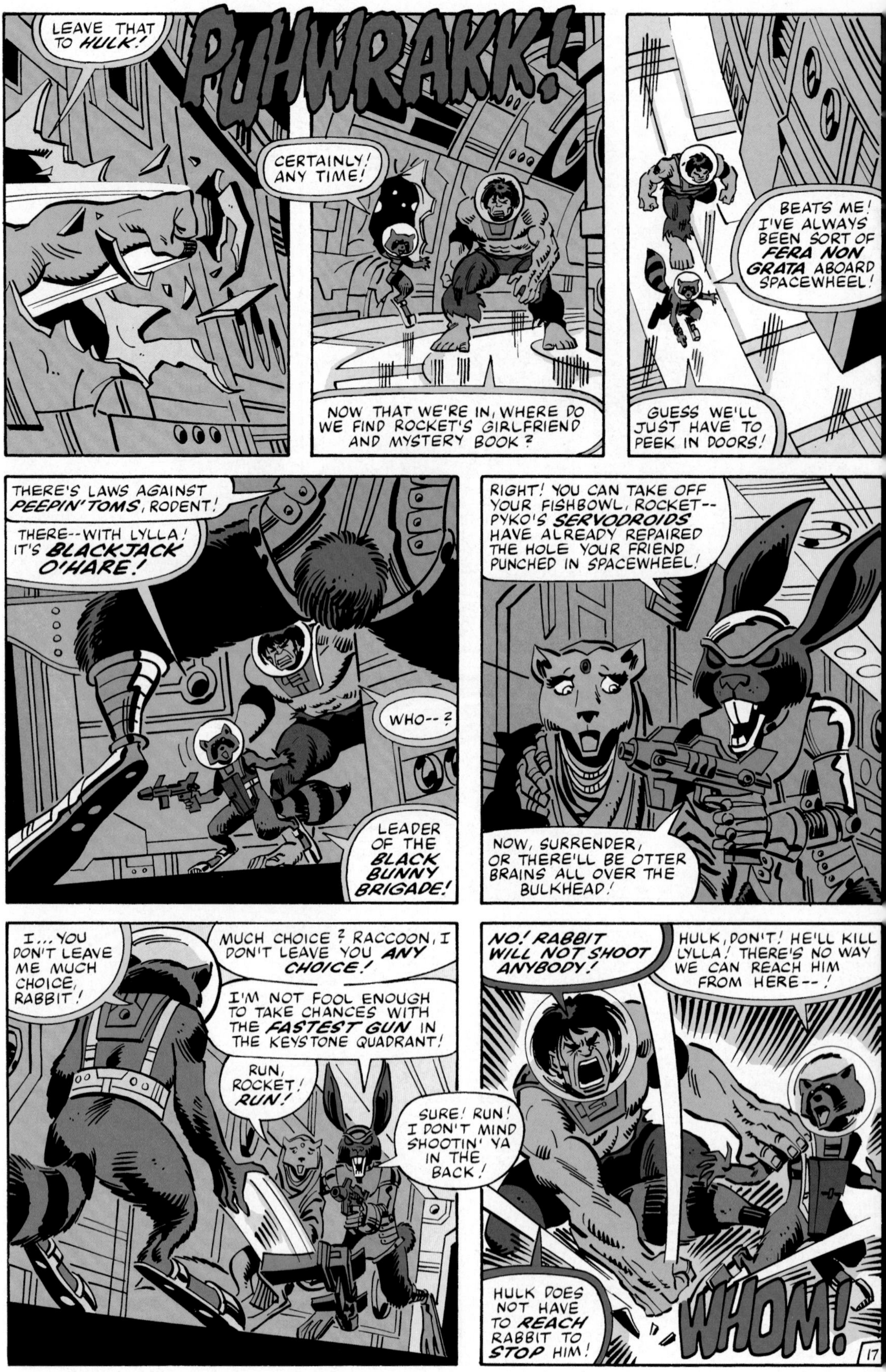
LEAVE THAT TO HULK!
PUHWRAKK!
CERTAINLY! ANY TIME!
NOW THAT WE'RE IN, WHERE DO WE FIND ROCKET'S GIRLFRIEND AND MYSTERY BOOK?
BEATS ME! I'VE ALWAYS BEEN SORT OF FERA NON GRATA ABOARD SPACEWHEEL!
GUESS WE'LL JUST HAVE TO PEEK IN DOORS!
THERE'S LAWS AGAINST PEEPIN' TOMS, RODENT!
THERE--WITH LYLLA! IT'S BLACKJACK O'HARE!
WHO--?
LEADER OF THE BLACK BUNNY BRIGADE!
RIGHT! YOU CAN TAKE OFF YOUR FISHBOWL, ROCKET-- PYKO'S SERVODROIDS HAVE ALREADY REPAIRED THE HOLE YOUR FRIEND PUNCHED IN SPACEWHEEL!
NOW, SURRENDER, OR THERE'LL BE OTTER BRAINS ALL OVER THE BULKHEAD!
I... YOU DON'T LEAVE ME MUCH CHOICE, RABBIT!
MUCH CHOICE? RACCOON, I DON'T LEAVE YOU ANY CHOICE!
I'M NOT FOOL ENOUGH TO TAKE CHANCES WITH THE FASTEST GUN IN THE KEYSTONE QUADRANT!
RUN, ROCKET! RUN!
SURE! RUN! I DON'T MIND SHOOTIN' YA IN THE BACK!
NO! RABBIT WILL NOT SHOOT ANYBODY!
HULK, DON'T! HE'LL KILL LYLLA! THERE'S NO WAY WE CAN REACH HIM FROM HERE--!
HULK DOES NOT HAVE TO REACH RABBIT TO STOP HIM!
WHOM!
17

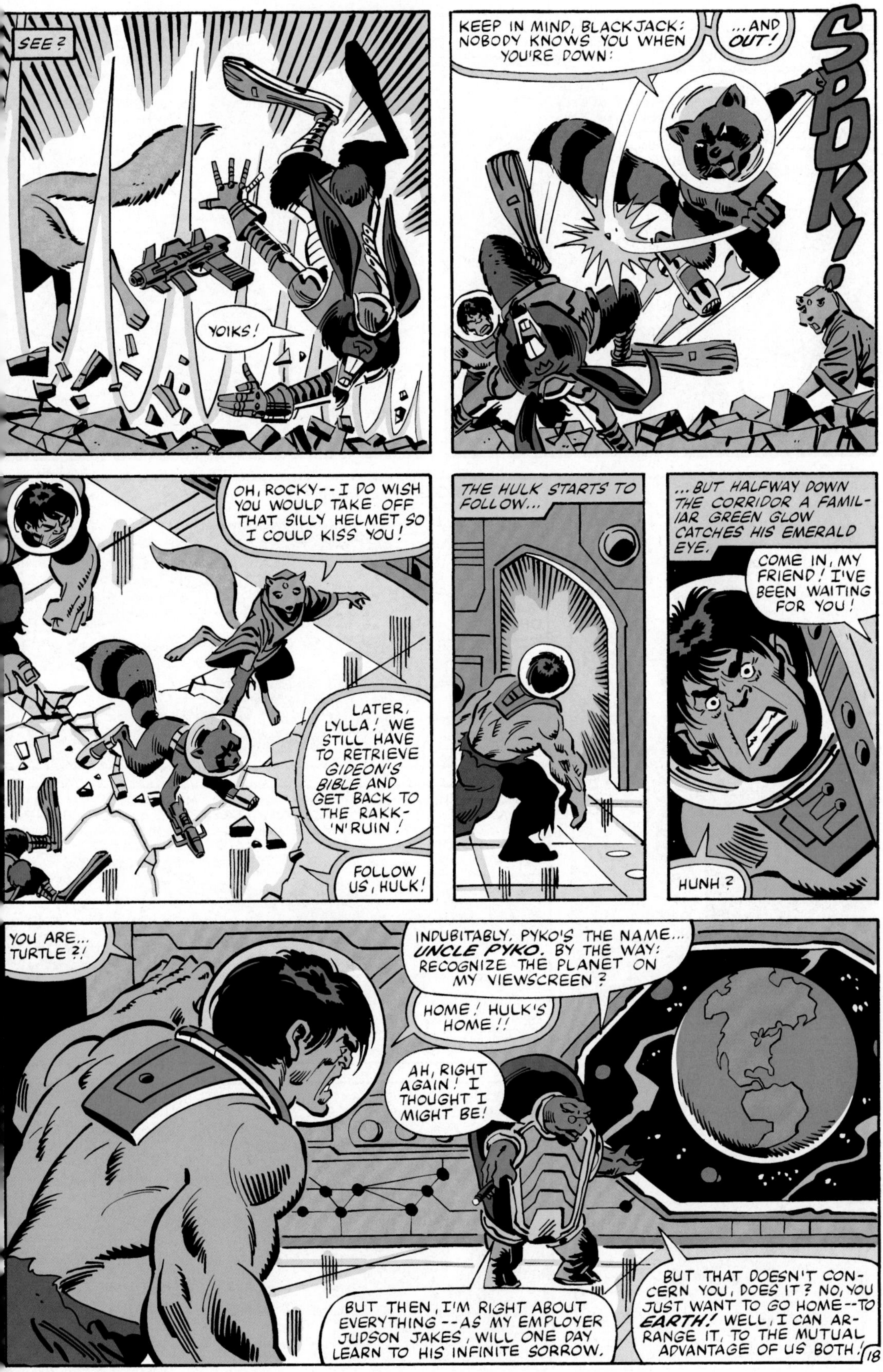

SEE?
YOIKS!
KEEP IN MIND, BLACKJACK: NOBODY KNOWS YOU WHEN YOU'RE DOWN:
...AND OUT!
SPOK!
OH, ROCKY--I DO WISH YOU WOULD TAKE OFF THAT SILLY HELMET SO I COULD KISS YOU!
LATER, LYLLA! WE STILL HAVE TO RETRIEVE GIDEON'S BIBLE AND GET BACK TO THE RAKK-'N'RUIN!
FOLLOW US, HULK!
THE HULK STARTS TO FOLLOW...
...BUT HALFWAY DOWN THE CORRIDOR A FAMILIAR GREEN GLOW CATCHES HIS EMERALD EYE.
COME IN, MY FRIEND! I'VE BEEN WAITING FOR YOU!
HUNH?
YOU ARE... TURTLE?!
INDUBITABLY. PYKO'S THE NAME... UNCLE PYKO. BY THE WAY: RECOGNIZE THE PLANET ON MY VIEWSCREEN?
HOME! HULK'S HOME!!
AH, RIGHT AGAIN! I THOUGHT I MIGHT BE!
BUT THEN, I'M RIGHT ABOUT EVERYTHING--AS MY EMPLOYER JUDSON JAKES, WILL ONE DAY LEARN TO HIS INFINITE SORROW.
BUT THAT DOESN'T CONCERN YOU, DOES IT? NO, YOU JUST WANT TO GO HOME--TO EARTH! WELL, I CAN ARRANGE IT, TO THE MUTUAL ADVANTAGE OF US BOTH!

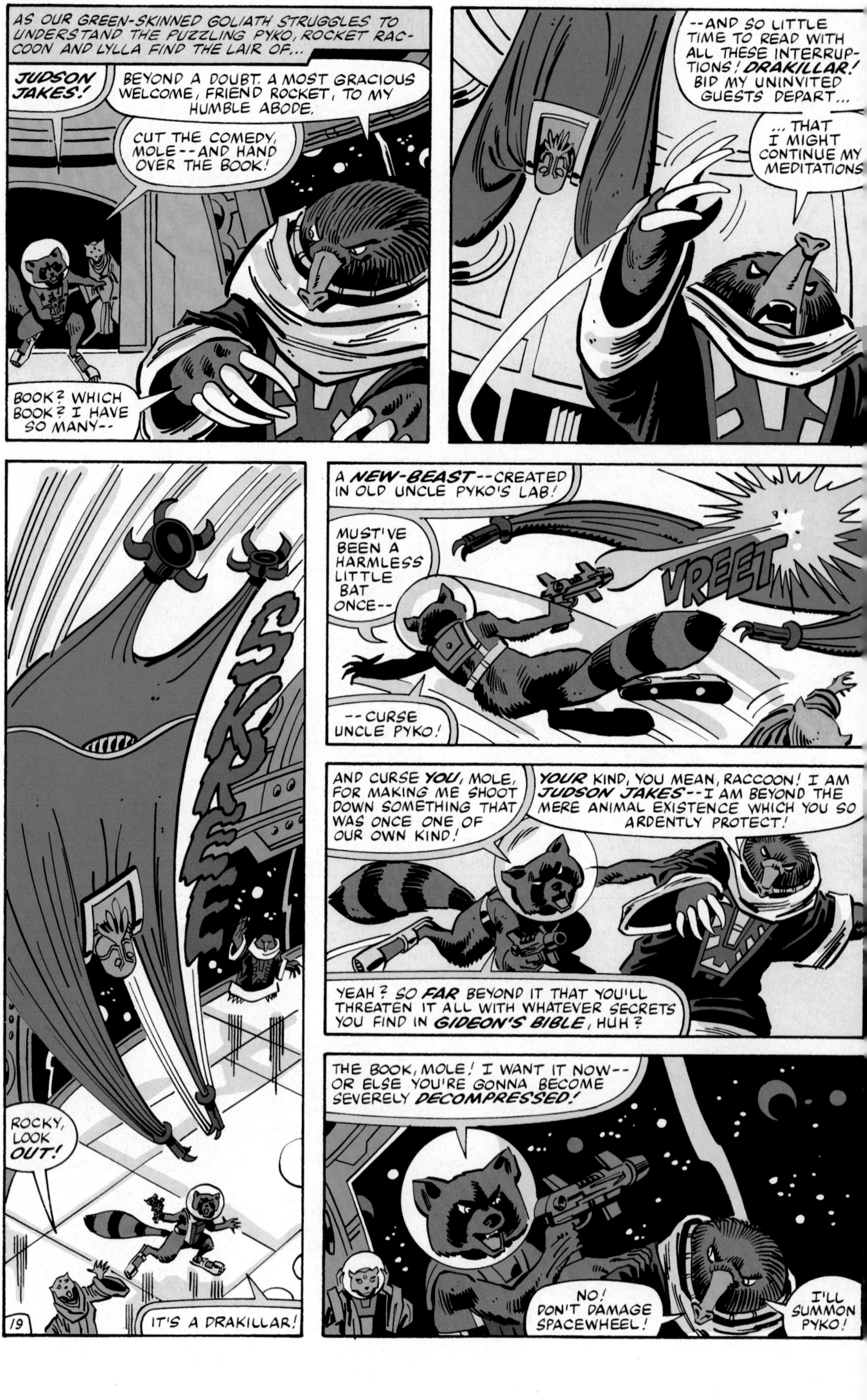
AS OUR GREEN-SKINNED GOLIATH STRUGGLES TO UNDERSTAND THE PUZZLING PYKO, ROCKET RACCOON AND LYLLA FIND THE LAIR OF...
JUDSON JAKES!
BEYOND A DOUBT. A MOST GRACIOUS WELCOME, FRIEND ROCKET, TO MY HUMBLE ABODE.
CUT THE COMEDY, MOLE--AND HAND OVER THE BOOK!
BOOK? WHICH BOOK? I HAVE SO MANY--
--AND SO LITTLE TIME TO READ WITH ALL THESE INTERRUPTIONS! DRAKILLAR! BID MY UNINVITED GUESTS DEPART...
...THAT I MIGHT CONTINUE MY MEDITATIONS
SKREE
ROCKY, LOOK OUT!
IT'S A DRAKILLAR!
A NEW-BEAST--CREATED IN OLD UNCLE PYKO'S LAB!
MUST'VE BEEN A HARMLESS LITTLE BAT ONCE--
VREET
--CURSE UNCLE PYKO!
AND CURSE YOU, MOLE, FOR MAKING ME SHOOT DOWN SOMETHING THAT WAS ONCE ONE OF OUR OWN KIND!
YOUR KIND, YOU MEAN, RACCOON! I AM JUDSON JAKES--I AM BEYOND THE MERE ANIMAL EXISTENCE WHICH YOU SO ARDENTLY PROTECT!
YEAH? SO FAR BEYOND IT THAT YOU'LL THREATEN IT ALL WITH WHATEVER SECRETS YOU FIND IN GIDEON'S BIBLE, HUH?
THE BOOK, MOLE! I WANT IT NOW--OR ELSE YOU'RE GONNA BECOME SEVERELY DECOMPRESSED!
NO! DON'T DAMAGE SPACEWHEEL!
I'LL SUMMON PYKO!

AND, IN UNCLE PYKO'S LABORATORY...

BRRZZZT

AH, THE MASTER OF SPACEWHEEL SUMMONS! HE MUST HAVE AC-KNOWLEDGED DEFEAT, AS I KNEW HE WOULD!

I KNOW SO MANY THINGS I SHOULDN'T KNOW, HULK-- SUCH AS WHO YOU ARE, WHERE YOU CAME FROM, ETCETERA.

PLANET ON SCREEN IS *EARTH*, HULK'S HOME.

THAT IS WHERE HULK'S FRIENDS-- *RICK* AND *BETTY*-- WAIT FOR HULK!

CAN TALKING TURTLE SEND HULK HOME?

OF COURSE! THE *GALACIAN WALL* SURROUNDING THE *KEY-STONE QUADRANT* PREVENTS ITS INHABITANTS FROM EVER LEAVING THIS MADHOUSE UNIVERSE --

-- BUT NO BARRIER IS INSUPERABLE TO ONE WHO HAS FATHOMED THE SECRETS OF THE *FIRST-COMERS*, TO ONE WHO COMPREHENDS THE MYSTERIES OF *GIDEON'S BIBLE!*

HULK THOUGHT THAT NO ONE COULD READ MYSTERY BOOK.

NO ONE BUT ME, HULK, AND EVEN *I* DISCOVERED HOW QUITE BY ACCIDENT...

...FROM DEEPLY-SUBMERGED MEMORIES WHICH I DREDGED FORTH ONE DAY WHEN I WAS PROBING THE ADDLED BRAIN OF A *KEYSTONE COP!* POOR CREATURE! HE DIDN'T SURVIVE THE PROBE!

IT SEEMS THAT THOSE LOONY-TUNE COPS ARE DIRECTLY DESCENDED FROM THE *FIRST-COMERS*--

-- AS ARE *YOU*, HULK! THAT'S HOW I DEDUCED WHERE YOU CAME FROM AND HOW TO SEND YOU BACK!

20

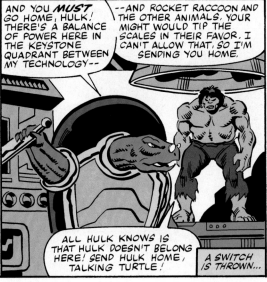

AND YOU *MUST* GO HOME, HULK! THERE'S A BALANCE OF POWER HERE IN THE KEYSTONE QUADRANT BETWEEN MY TECHNOLOGY--

-- AND ROCKET RACCOON AND THE OTHER ANIMALS, YOUR MIGHT WOULD TIP THE SCALES IN THEIR FAVOR. I CAN'T ALLOW THAT, SO I'M SENDING YOU HOME.

ALL HULK KNOWS IS THAT HULK DOESN'T BELONG HERE! SEND HULK HOME, TALKING TURTLE!

A SWITCH IS THROWN...

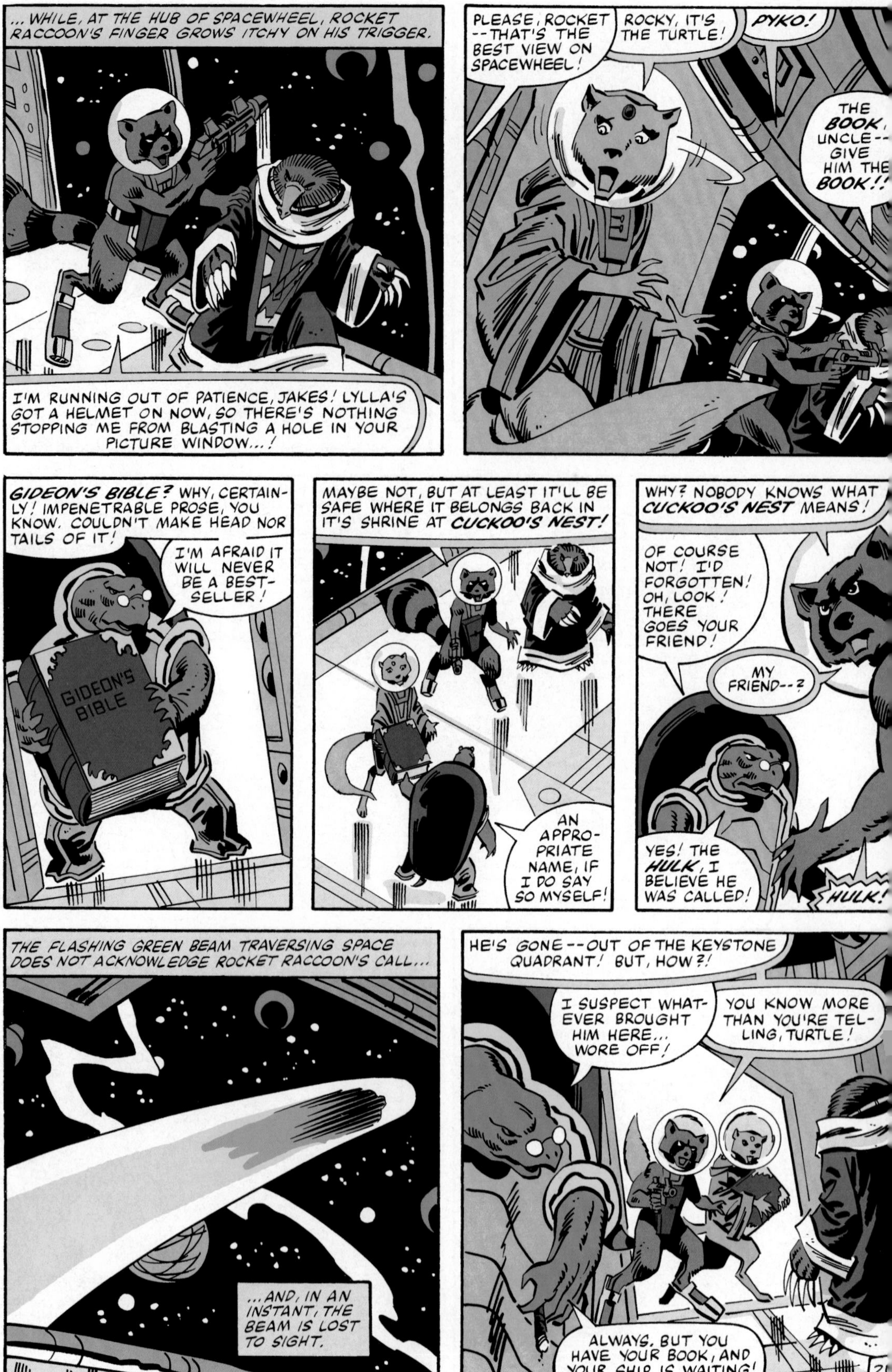
...WHILE, AT THE HUB OF SPACEWHEEL, ROCKET RACCOON'S FINGER GROWS ITCHY ON HIS TRIGGER.
I'M RUNNING OUT OF PATIENCE, JAKES! LYLLA'S GOT A HELMET ON NOW, SO THERE'S NOTHING STOPPING ME FROM BLASTING A HOLE IN YOUR PICTURE WINDOW...!
PLEASE, ROCKET --THAT'S THE BEST VIEW ON SPACEWHEEL!
ROCKY, IT'S THE TURTLE!
PYKO!
THE BOOK, UNCLE-- GIVE HIM THE BOOK!!
GIDEON'S BIBLE? WHY, CERTAINLY! IMPENETRABLE PROSE, YOU KNOW. COULDN'T MAKE HEAD NOR TAILS OF IT!
I'M AFRAID IT WILL NEVER BE A BEST-SELLER!
GIDEON'S BIBLE
MAYBE NOT, BUT AT LEAST IT'LL BE SAFE WHERE IT BELONGS BACK IN IT'S SHRINE AT CUCKOO'S NEST!
AN APPROPRIATE NAME, IF I DO SAY SO MYSELF!
WHY? NOBODY KNOWS WHAT CUCKOO'S NEST MEANS!
OF COURSE NOT! I'D FORGOTTEN! OH, LOOK! THERE GOES YOUR FRIEND!
MY FRIEND--?
YES! THE HULK, I BELIEVE HE WAS CALLED!
HULK!
THE FLASHING GREEN BEAM TRAVERSING SPACE DOES NOT ACKNOWLEDGE ROCKET RACCOON'S CALL...
...AND, IN AN INSTANT, THE BEAM IS LOST TO SIGHT.
HE'S GONE--OUT OF THE KEYSTONE QUADRANT! BUT, HOW?!
I SUSPECT WHATEVER BROUGHT HIM HERE... WORE OFF!
YOU KNOW MORE THAN YOU'RE TELLING, TURTLE!
ALWAYS, BUT YOU HAVE YOUR BOOK, AND YOUR SHIP IS WAITING!
21

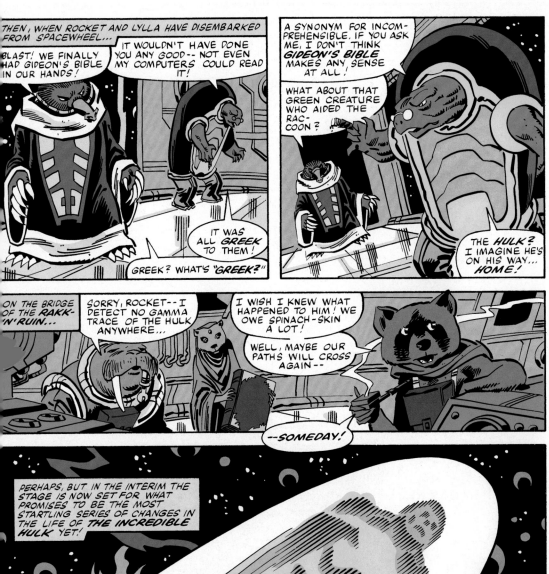

Panel 1: THEN, WHEN ROCKET AND LYLLA HAVE DISEMBARKED FROM SPACEWHEEL...

BLAST! WE FINALLY HAD GIDEON'S BIBLE IN OUR HANDS!

IT WOULDN'T HAVE DONE YOU ANY GOOD-- NOT EVEN MY COMPUTERS' COULD READ IT!

IT WAS ALL GREEK TO THEM!

"GREEK? WHAT'S 'GREEK?'"

Panel 2: A SYNONYM FOR INCOMPREHENSIBLE. IF YOU ASK ME, I DON'T THINK GIDEON'S BIBLE MAKES ANY SENSE AT ALL!

WHAT ABOUT THAT GREEN CREATURE WHO AIDED THE RACCOON?

THE HULK? I IMAGINE HE'S ON HIS WAY... HOME!

Panel 3: ON THE BRIDGE OF THE RAKK-'N'-RUIN...

SORRY, ROCKET-- I DETECT NO GAMMA TRACE OF THE HULK ANYWHERE...

I WISH I KNEW WHAT HAPPENED TO HIM! WE OWE SPINACH-SKIN A LOT!

WELL, MAYBE OUR PATHS WILL CROSS AGAIN--

--SOMEDAY!

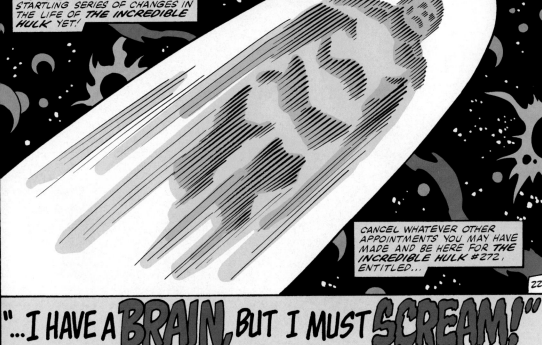

PERHAPS, BUT IN THE INTERIM THE STAGE IS NOW SET FOR WHAT PROMISES TO BE THE MOST STARTLING SERIES OF CHANGES IN THE LIFE OF *THE INCREDIBLE HULK* YET!

CANCEL WHATEVER OTHER APPOINTMENTS YOU MAY HAVE MADE AND BE HERE FOR *THE INCREDIBLE HULK* #272, ENTITLED...

22

"...I HAVE A BRAIN, BUT I MUST SCREAM!"

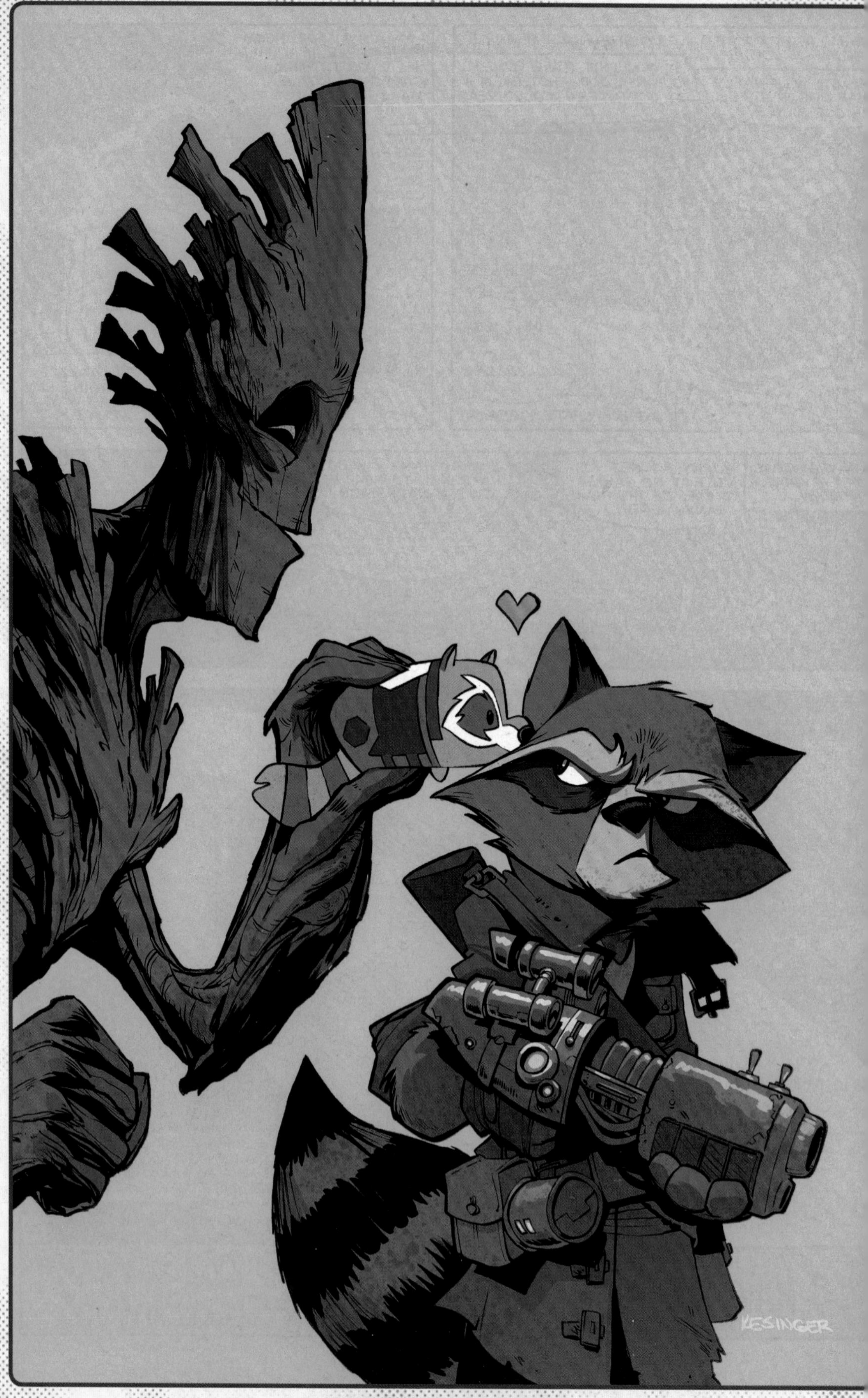
KESINGER

BRIAN KESINGER

8 MARVEL TSUM TSUM TAKEOVER VARIANT